AF581319

OBJECTS OF THE SPIRIT

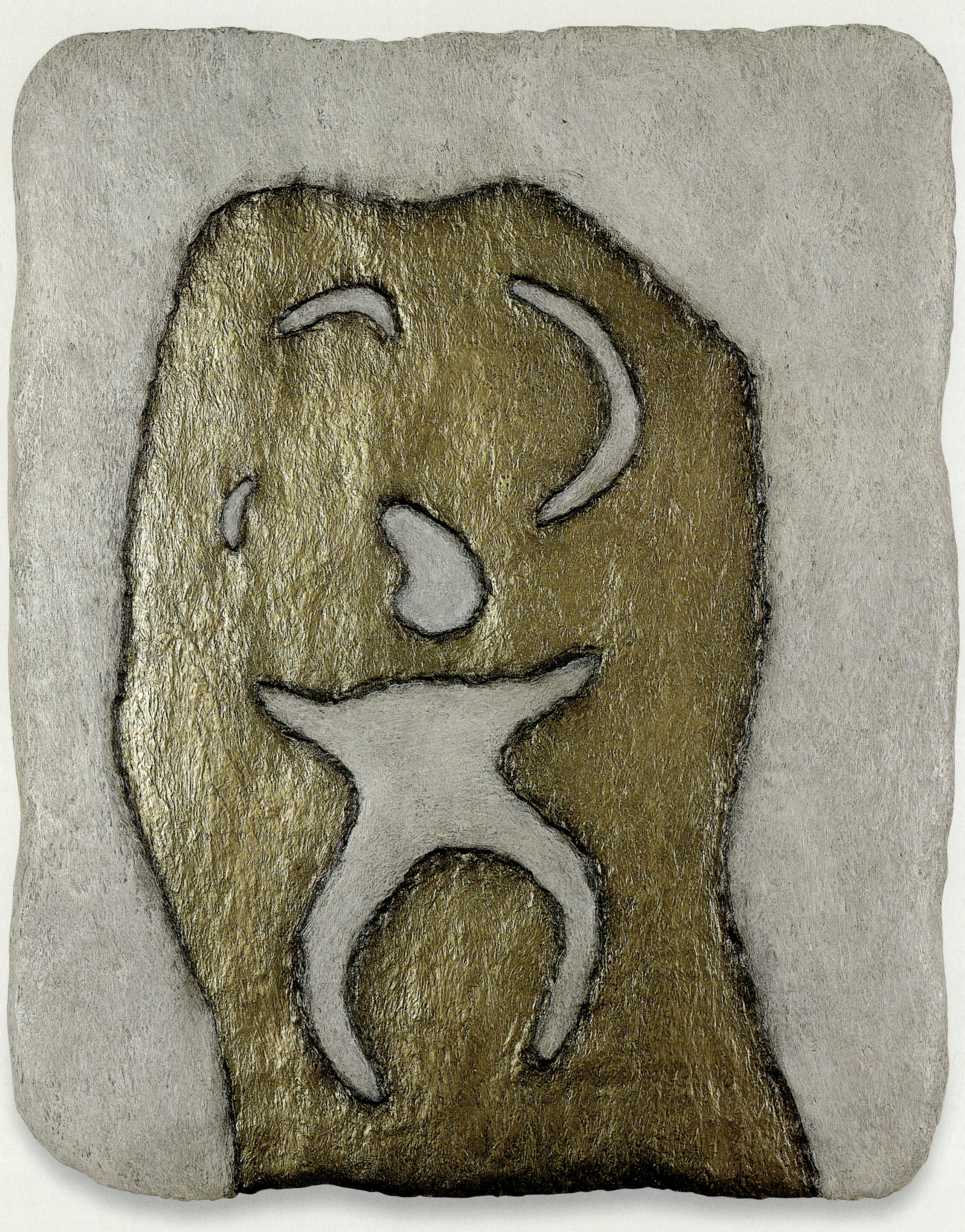

OBJECTS OF THE SPIRIT

Ritual and the Art of Tobi Kahn

EMILY D. BILSKI

Meditations by

NESSA RAPOPORT

With essays by

LEORA AUSLANDER

TERRENCE E. DEMPSEY, S.J.

TOM L. FREUDENHEIM

JONATHAN ROSEN

RUTH WEISBERG

Avoda Institute, Ltd., New York

Hudson Hills Press, New York and Manchester

The Avoda Institute—including its programming division, Avoda Arts—is a cultural and educational organization that offers participants a joyful understanding of Judaism through the arts. With innovative exhibitions, hands-on workshops, seminars for educators, and university courses, Avoda encourages people to experience for themselves the power of art, ritual, and community. Proceeds from *Objects of the Spirit* support the work of the Avoda Institute, Ltd., a 501(c)(3) organization.

This book and Avoda Arts programs have been made possible through generous grants from the Covenant Foundation, UJA–Federation of New York, the Charles H. Revson Foundation, the Carol and Arthur Spinner Charitable Fund, and the Phyllis and Jack Wertenteil Foundation.

1375 Broadway, Suite 600
New York, New York 10018
www.AvodaArts.org

Published in association with Hudson Hills Press LLC, 74-2 Union Street, Manchester, Vermont 05254
Paul Anbinder: Founding Publisher
Randall Perkins and Leslie van Breen: Co-Directors

Distributed in the United States, its territories and possessions, and Canada through National Book Network.
Distributed in the United Kingdom, Eire, and Europe through Windsor Books International.

ISBN 1-55595-247-X (cloth)

LIBRARY OF CONGRESS CATALOGING-IN-PUBLICATION DATA
Bilski, Emily D., 1956–
Objects of the spirit: ritual and the art of Tobi Kahn / Emily D. Bilski; meditations by Nessa Rapoport; with contributions by Leora Auslander ...[et al.].
p. cm.
Includes bibliographical references.
ISBN 1-55595-247-X (cloth: alk. paper)
1. Kahn, Tobi, 1952—Criticism and interpretation. 2. Judaism—Liturgical objects—United States. I. Title: Ritual and the art of Tobi Kahn. II. Kahn, Tobi, 1952– III. Rapoport, Nessa. IV. Auslander, Leora. V. Title.
NK1412.K34B55 2004
709'.2—dc22
2004041037

Front cover: *Vayti*, 1996 (Plate 19)
Back cover: *Hadahr*, 1992 (Plate 14)
Frontispiece: *Vanah*, 2000

Printed and bound in Italy

CONTENTS

FOREWORD

> *Although Judaism has emphasized words, language, and commentary, I have found the visual elements of the tradition equally illuminating. For me, the life of the spirit is integrally bound up with the beauty of the world, with the rituals and symbols that are a Jewish medium to transcendence. Like language, what we see can be a benediction.*
>
> TOBI KAHN

I first observed Tobi Kahn as an artist and a teacher when I watched him work with high school students in a summer program at The Jewish Museum in New York. Tobi was able to bring to life the power and passion of the ceremonial art in the museum's collection. He then invited the students to make their own objects—and to imbue the art with their stories. For many, the act of fashioning a ritual object was transformative, a way of understanding and "owning" their cultural inheritance, often for the first time.

In 1999, Tobi and I launched a museum exhibition and educational program called "Avoda: Objects of the Spirit." *Avodah* is a Hebrew word that can mean work, prayer, or service. The term encompasses the idea of doing, making, and creating as acts of devotion. We were convinced that the retrieval and discovery of a visual vocabulary from within Judaism, one sanctioned by Jewish thought and practice but not yet sufficiently revealed, could open an ancient interpretive tradition to today's students and seekers.

"Avoda" has grown into an institution that offers people of every age and background a way to claim their rich cultural history, to explore issues of identity, and to fashion new expressions of their tradition through the arts. Tobi Kahn has been a champion of this work, not only through his own ceremonial art but as an inspired teacher.

The original program consisted of a traveling museum exhibition of Kahn's ritual objects, a workshop where participants could make their own ritual objects, and a series of public dialogues with artists and celebrants of other religions. Since its founding, the project has engaged thousands of people. We have witnessed with exhilaration those moments when participants suddenly see the relationship between venerable rituals and their own unique history, an experience not bound by race, ethnicity, class, or religion.

In the words of Joanne Northrop, curator of the de Saisset Museum at Santa Clara University, a Catholic institution and one of the program's venues: "The 'Avoda' exhibition enabled us to illustrate visually the spiritual diversity promulgated by the university. Regardless of our faith, we all have a tremendous need to integrate ritual into our daily lives."

It has been a remarkable five years. On behalf of Tobi Kahn and the Avoda Institute, I would like to thank: Eli Evans and Lisa Goldberg of the Charles H. Revson Foundation, for their initial faith in us and the grant that made this book and the entire project possible; Dr. Judith Ginsberg and the board and staff of the Covenant Foundation, whose generous grant allowed us to teach so many people and to create our learning tools; and Rabbi Deborah Joselow and the Commission on Jewish Identity and Renewal of UJA–Federation of New York. Special thanks to our partners at New York University—the Edgar M. Bronfman Center for Jewish Student Life and Rabbi Andrew Bachman—for enabling us to create a living laboratory and to test arts-based learning as a way of exploring cultural identity.

Our remarkable working group includes Margaret Mathews Berenson, Hyim Brandes, Adam Courtney, Sharon Florin, Dan Gold, Mirele Goldsmith, Ben Hesse, Christian Kent, Debbie Krivoy,

Laura Kruger, Nicole Opper, Shirah Rubin, Judith Siegel, Jane Silverman, Shira Stein, and Jill Vexler. Together, we have created memorable learning sessions for students and have established a new field in Jewish education.

A book is a major undertaking. Thank you to Mary DelMonico and Sheila Schwartz at Offsite: Publications, Planning, Projects; Neil Rosini, our lawyer; and Katy Homans, our graphic designer. To our authors, Leora Auslander, Terrence Dempsey, Tom Freudenheim, Jonathan Rosen, and Ruth Weisberg: your contributions remind us why ritual matters.

To Emily Bilski, our editor and major contributor, thank you for your unique ability to weave together all the threads of Tobi's work, placing it within the Jewish, artistic, and human experience of the twenty-first century. To Carolyn Hessel, of the Jewish Book Council, a special thank you for your guidance and encouragement. To Judith Siegel and Shira Stein, congratulations on a job well done. To Leslie van Breen and Randall Perkins, codirectors of Hudson Hills Press, thank you for your belief in this project; your support has ensured that *Objects of the Spirit* will reach a wide audience.

Ruth Weisberg and the University of Southern California School of Fine Arts, the fiscal sponsor of this work, have been excellent partners.

This foreword would not be complete without thanking Nessa Rapoport for her gorgeous meditations, which were written especially for the "Avoda" project. Nessa has been an active contributor to the "Avoda" program, and her counsel and care have been truly from the heart.

Thank you to all the owners of Kahn's works presented in these pages for sharing your collections with us; we hope that you will pass down these wonderful objects for many generations.

Last, to my family, Art and Rebecca Spinner, thank you. This project really started when Rebecca looked at Michelangelo's frescoes in Florence and asked me why Jews didn't teach in the same way. Your support, in all its forms, means so much to me.

CAROL BRENNGLASS SPINNER
Executive Director, Avoda Arts

ACKNOWLEDGMENTS

In the spring of 1998, over a hurried breakfast looking out onto 57th Street, Tobi Kahn told me of his idea to create a book combining the ritual objects he had made with the poetic meditations written by his wife, Nessa Rapoport. When he tactfully asked if I might be interested in contributing a discussion of the relationship of his works to a broader tradition of Jewish ceremonial art for this proposed publication, I was delighted. As someone who had long admired his paintings and sculptures, I felt there was another story to tell as well—namely, the interface between Kahn's ceremonial objects and the legacy of modernism and abstraction.

The realization of this book has taken several years and was ultimately linked to a much larger project: the exhibition and educational programs that constitute "Avoda: Objects of the Spirit." Carol Brennglass Spinner, executive director of the Avoda Arts organization, has been tireless in her promotion of the project. I thank her for her dedication, enthusiasm, and talent for always finding ways to make things happen. Judith Siegel, associate executive director, has graced Avoda Arts with her keen intelligence and unmatched educational and interpretive expertise, both in art and Jewish issues. I am deeply grateful for her wise advice and her unstinting support of every facet of this book. Laura Kruger organized the exhibition of Kahn's ceremonial objects that became "Avoda: Objects of the Spirit" and convinced Kahn that these initially private works should be shown to a wider public; without her, this project would not have taken the form it did. Debbie Krivoy, managing director, has been the heart and soul of Avoda Arts, coordinating between the project's various elements and Kahn's studio. Thanks to Nancy Chandross and Shira Stein for their work on securing the book's illustrations and permissions; and to Jill Vexler and Margaret Mathews Berenson, traveling exhibition managers, who have been responsible for ensuring that diverse audiences will see the "Avoda: Objects of the Spirit" exhibition.

I am grateful to Sharon Florin and to studio assistants Ray Abary, Joel Haffner, Nils Karsten, Christian Kent, Noah Landfield, and Mark Stack; and to Dana Stewart, who was responsible for the casting of Kahn's works into bronze. Thanks as well are due to Nicholas Walster for his expert photography.

My gratitude to Avigdor Shinan and Sharon Assaf for directing me to sources in midrash and Venetian art, respectively, which enriched my essay.

All aspects of preparing *Objects of the Spirit: Ritual and the Art of Tobi Kahn* for publication were managed by Mary DelMonico and Sheila Schwartz of Offsite: Publications, Planning, Projects. I want to thank Sheila Schwartz for her expert and perceptive editing of all the manuscripts. Mary DelMonico has shepherded the book from initial idea to the bookshelf and has been involved in each facet of its editorial content, design, and production. I thank her for her superb handling of every detail, her consummate professionalism, and her unflappable good humor. Janice Meyerson's knowledge and sensitivity, coupled with her extraordinary eye, make her the copy editor par excellence.

Though *Objects of the Spirit: Ritual and the Art of Tobi Kahn* presents the work of a single artist, it raises many questions pertaining to spirituality and ritual in contemporary life, the relationship of objects to their owners and makers, and the role of the artist in these phenomena. We are fortunate to have secured the talents of a distinguished group of authors to delve into these issues from the vantage points of a variety of disciplines and perspectives. My deep appreciation to Leora Auslander, Terrence Dempsey, Tom Freudenheim, Nessa Rapoport, Jonathan Rosen, and Ruth Weisberg for sharing their insights, and to Jennifer Sylvor for creating the snappy and informative glossary. I also drew on Nessa Rapoport's editorial experience to help resolve questions of style and transliteration. All of us are indebted to Katy Homans, whose inspired design of the book has made our words and Tobi Kahn's art come alive on these pages.

I have enjoyed the encouragement (and often the warm hospitality, as well) of Judith and Jeffrey Siegel; Berthold and Vicki Bilski; and Mark, Tracey, Amanda, Meredith, and Charlotte Bilski. I am blessed every day with the intellectual stimulation and loving support of my husband, Gabriel, and my sons, Theo and Alex Motzkin; without them nothing would be possible.

Following the Hebrew saying *aharon, aharon, haviv* ("the last and most pleasant"), my heartfelt thanks to Tobi Kahn. It has been a privilege to engage with his art in this intense fashion. I thank him for opening up every nook and cranny of his studio to my inquisitive eye, for the many frank and illuminating conversations we have had over the years, and for his patience in entertaining numerous requests and inquiries. Kahn's inherent generosity as an artist and human being comes across, I think, in his art. It has been a great pleasure for me to experience this personally in the course of our creating this book together.

E.D.B.

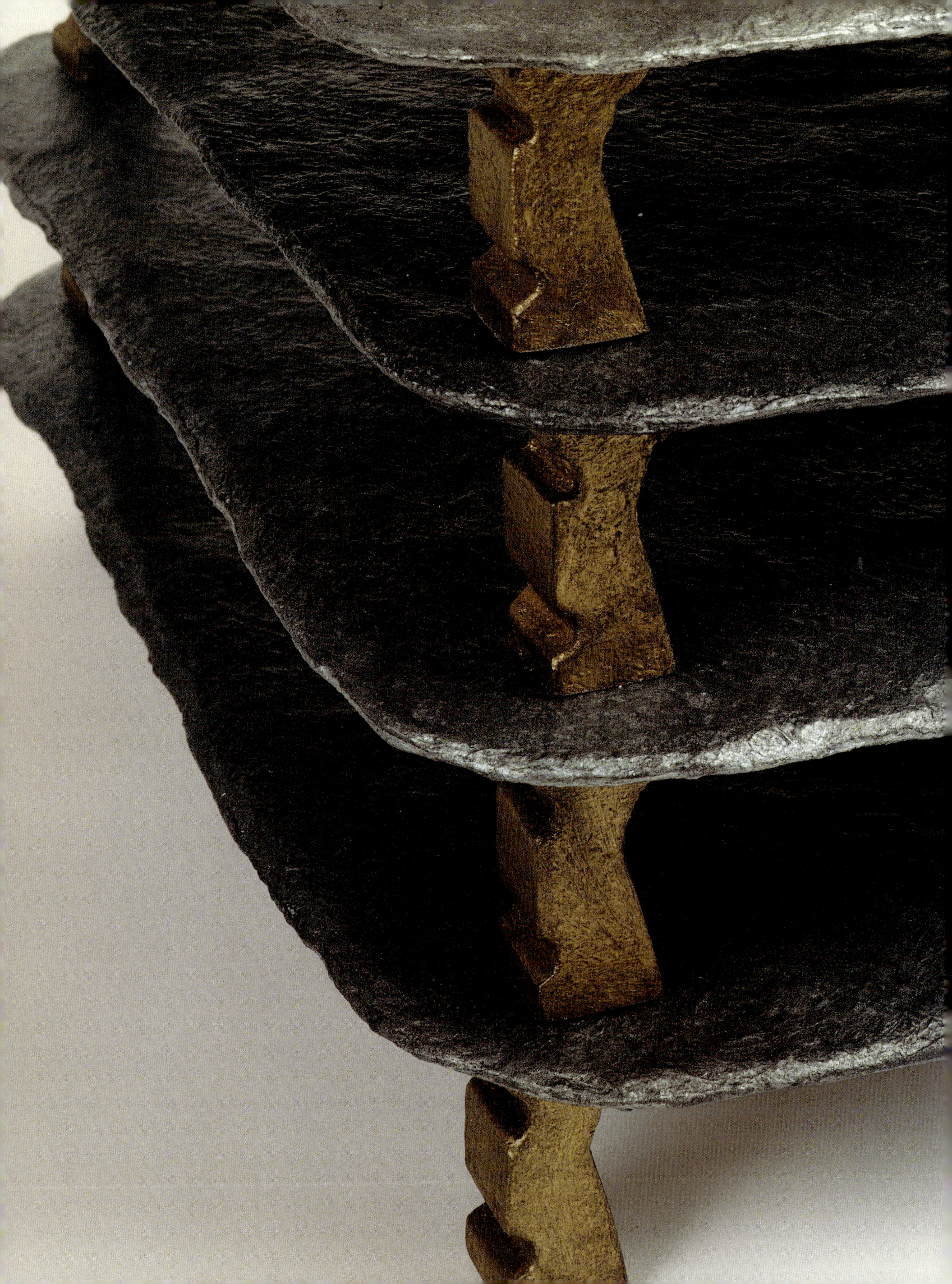

INTRODUCTION

TOM L. FREUDENHEIM

Aspersions have long been cast on the traditional divides between so-called art and so-called craft, even when we recognize that these categories are relatively recent constructs. Rather than suggesting useful measures for approaching the world of "things"—accommodating and increasing our visual and intellectual access—the art/craft divide is better understood as a political paradigm, reflecting the world of creators and curators, sellers and collectors. There are, alas, few signs that these synthetic categorizations are likely to end soon, least of all in the world of Jewish artifacts.

But an occasional shift in the paradigm gives cause for hope. The recent impressive series of invitational exhibitions at Jewish museums in San Francisco and Chicago has encouraged a range of artists to engage with the challenges of Jewish ceremonial objects.[1] By focusing on the object (not on the self-definition of its creator), these museums were able to engage a range of artists, from so-called craftspeople, to designers, architects, and even the occasional sculptor or painter. The focus was the Jewish object (Hanukkah lamp, kiddush cup, sukkah, seder plate, and so on), with the (not necessarily Jewish) artist often moving into an entirely new field of endeavor in the process of engaging with Jewish life and ceremonies. These extensions are positive aspects of the creative process precisely because our pigeonholing tendencies are thereby confounded. We need all the confusion we can get!

Tobi Kahn's appearance in this context is all the more remarkable, since he conforms to none of the matrices that function in the field of Judaica. This is not Chagall working with biblical themes or creating stained-glass synagogue windows. This is not a Lipchitz sculpture finding its way into some ritual space resulting from the confluence of Jewish theme and Jewish artist. Kahn's Jewish ceremonial objects—his "Avoda" works—are singular for their focus on the complex relationship between the mitzvah—that is, the performance goals—and the spiritual engagement of their creator. Appropriate descriptive terminology comes only with great difficulty, given a traditional vocabulary of Jewish ceremonial art that seems inadequate here. Yet there is no dilemma at all in this, since the answer lies in a single simple (and complex) word: Jew.

There is no perceptible gap at the intersection where Kahn works as an artist and as a Jew. Indeed, his mobilization of the concept of *avodah* explains everything, because it encompasses worship and service and labor. Similarly, its related nominal form includes servant, slave, worshiper, laborer. Understanding this doesn't require the leap of faith we need to grasp the Trinity. Nor do we need the linguistic skill to follow semitic word roots into their several conceptual directions. If we have adequately engaged in using our observational skills, the artist has already given us a singular and unified *avodah* as concept and object.

Nevertheless, one is tempted to address Kahn's work in more conventional ways. Material is often a good starting point for trying to understand works such as these—but the material seems inconsequential and is seldom clearly expressed. It is puzzling and even amusing to wonder what materials lie at the core of these seductive artifacts. Colors also do not usefully inform us, and indeed, as with the materials, we are often not certain of the appropriate words to describe the colors we see. At best, they are referential to the artist's paintings, but it is precisely the elusive quality of those paintings and their evocative forms that give Kahn's work its power; so cross-references to objects of use seem of no avail here. Therein lie both the appeal and the puzzle of Kahn's "Avoda" objects.

Erhu, 1996
(detail, Fig. 70; Plate 18)

Fig. 1
Aviya II, 1998

Fig. 2
Zedek III, 1989–99

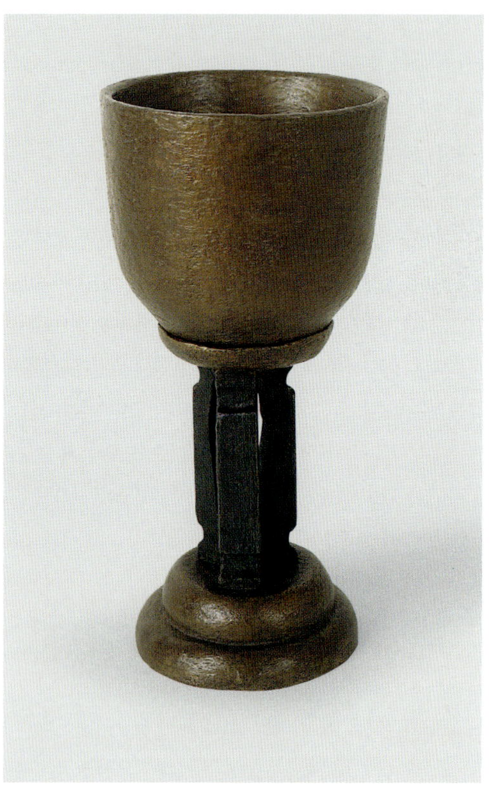

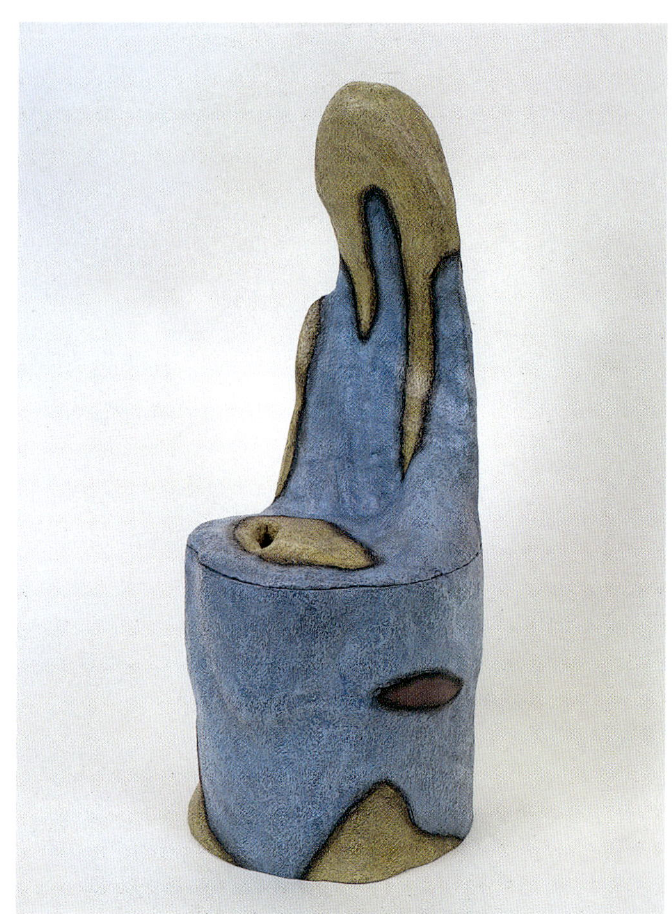

There are further puzzles. We know that the artist conceives of these objects for ceremonial use. We know about such objects. We have used them ourselves. We have seen them in museums. Yet Kahn's objects seldom look anything like what we have seen or used. Is there the vague suggestion of a ruse? Or is Kahn actually trying to refocus us? Perhaps he is asking us to think about the mitzvah—the act of worship or service—rather than about the object itself. Or does such nonconformity force us in precisely the opposite direction, confusing us as to the object's use? On the other hand, it might be that Kahn is tampering with our understanding of the mitzvah itself—asking us to consider what it means to drink a ceremonial cup of wine (Fig. 1) or to place money in an alms container (Fig. 2). Gradually, it may dawn on us that we had better reconsider our relationship to the observance of the mitzvah itself.

It is the combination of these qualities and these questions that gives such a tantalizing edge to Kahn's "Avoda" objects. We know the outlines of Jewish observance, and we know the implements involved, but find ourselves somewhat lost in the world of "Avoda." We cannot locate the work in conventional visual chronologies: the forms suggest some indefinable ancient objects. Are we in the ancient Near East—or is it the Far East? Are we lost in a world of archaeology, and, if so, which culture have we unearthed? Yet the biomorphic forms are also suggestive of a visual syntax that we recognize from twentieth-century modernists. Is this more Dalí than Miró, more Matisse than Calder? Have these objects escaped from a Max Ernst painting? Sometimes we know we have seen these forms elsewhere, but we can never quite locate them in our mental data bank.

In this puzzlement we come to realize that Tobi Kahn bridges various important gaps that our eyes have become accustomed to avoiding. The emergence of significant numbers of Jews as artists over the past two centuries remains the subject of study and generally has involved a concern with how the gradual availability of full participation in the mainstream acts or counteracts on the artist's identity as a Jew. Hamlet's desperate question seems always to haunt the artist—from the warm shtetl evocations of Ilya Schor to the numinous spaces of Mark Rothko. The world usually seems either too much or too little with us—and the artist feels compelled to enunciate the dilemma, which explains the many exhibitions and books devoted to exploring a predicament in which the artist acts as our surrogate, expressing in creative form what most of us only feel.

Perhaps we ought to see Kahn outside of this traditional Jewish/artistic context. He may, in fact, be the forerunner of a new set of paradigms. Kahn sees no conflict between his life as a New York artist and his life as a Jew—between his life as a husband/father and his life as a teacher/creator. It is all quite seamless: the man and his life and his work, the Jewish observance and the life observance. Everything is reflected in everything else, like some infinitely projected house of mirrors. But unlike the realm of mirrors, here there are no distortions. "Avoda" objects are works of art and of utility and of devotion. They are very personal in ways that are still strange to most of us, because we live our lives in segments—at worst surrounded by various walls, at best enclosed by fences we can jump over. Seldom are we invited to engage in the kind of wholeness with which Kahn asks us to look, to use, to pray, to be. It's not a cute moniker for him to call these works "Avoda." It is a description of his working and living mode, and it is an invitation for us to participate—and perhaps to find ways of unifying our own varied forms of living.

1. The Spertus Museum, Chicago, awards the Phillip and Sylvia Spertus Judaica Prize biennially, accompanied by exhibitions: "The Seder Plate," 1996; "The Havdalah Spice Container," 1998; "Judging the Book by its Cover" (Torah coverings), 2000; and "Mezuzah," 2002. The Jewish Museum of San Francisco has presented: "The Sukkah Competition," 1984; "Purim Mask Invitational," 1989 and 1990; "Light Interpretations: A Hanukah Menorah Invitational," 1995; and "L'Chaim: A Kiddush Cup Invitational," 1997.

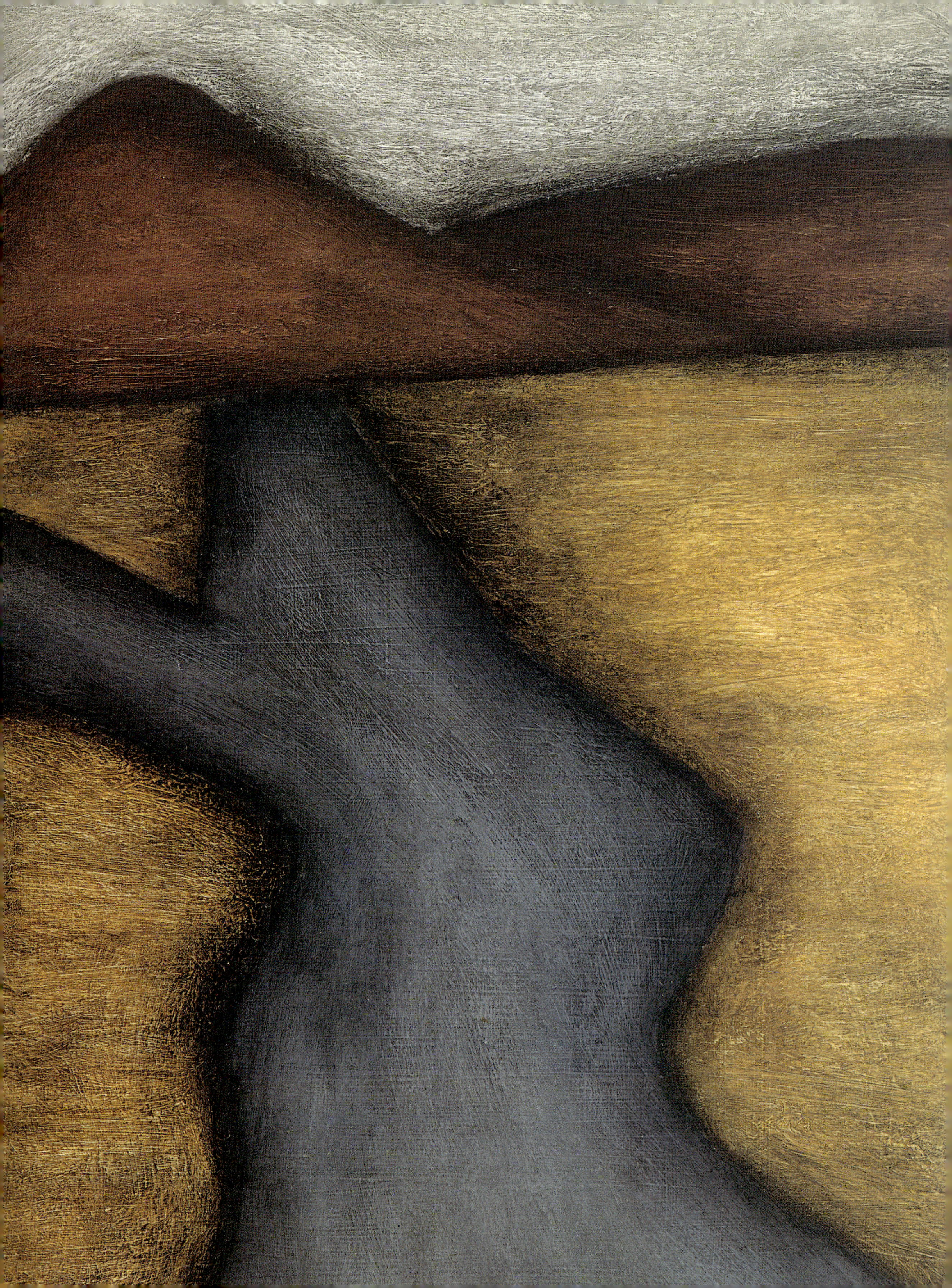

EMILY D. BILSKI

Tobi Kahn's Objects of the Spirit

Art is an abstraction; derive this abstraction from nature while dreaming before it, but think more of creating than of the actual result. The only way to rise towards God is by doing as our divine Master does, create.
PAUL GAUGUIN, 1888[1]

The true fully Jewish artist would not be Jewish in subject matter, but rather Jewish in modality; he would scarcely paint something biblical, educational, or episodes from the past, but rather he would paint something contemporary with a Jewish spirit (by which I mean: with spirit).
KURT HILLER, 1912[2]

Tobi Kahn's ceremonial objects are an artistic "perfect storm," the embodiment of more than twenty years of creative passions and practices filtered through family history and a powerful personal, spiritual, and religious commitment. In these works, a host of artistic influences—German Romanticism, the American abstract landscape tradition, New York School artists such as Mark Rothko and Clyfford Still, the Arts and Crafts Movement, and the Wiener Werkstätte—meet up with the aesthetic sensibilities of German-Jewish Orthodoxy and the freedom found on Manhattan's Upper West Side for Jewish self-expression and reinvention.

To those familiar with Tobi Kahn's paintings and sculpture, his ceremonial objects seem like such natural outgrowths of the artist's oeuvre and personal history that their groundbreaking nature may initially escape attention. Jewish ceremonial art has traditionally been a fairly conservative art form whose style evolved in conjunction with local decorative arts, yet held fast to established iconography and time-honored symbols. Kahn's objects, however, though they give priority to ritual function and *halakhic* requirements, bear none of the symbols that we have come to associate with Judaica: there are no rampant lions, no depictions of the implements of the ancient Temple such as the menorah, incense table, or shofar, and no Stars of David. Indeed, there are no Hebrew inscriptions to "mark" these works, to identify them as Jewish objects and to elucidate their ceremonial function.[3] Instead, both the imperative to create ceremonial objects and their formal and aesthetic qualities derive from Kahn's own life needs and artistic personality.

Like many artists, Kahn is keenly sensitive to the visual attributes of his environment. The spaces in which he lives and works bear the mark of his formal concerns. Inspired by a visit to Charleston, the Sussex farmhouse that became the home of Bloomsbury artists Vanessa Bell and Duncan Grant (Fig. 3), Kahn began creating his own painted furniture—first closets and cupboards (Fig. 4), and eventually baby cradles, rocking horses, and other domestic objects. In the same spirit, he embarked on another creative journey, making the ritual objects he needed to celebrate the rituals and rites of passage in his own life.

The technique that Kahn had developed for his paintings lent itself to the creation of ritual objects. For years, the supports of his paintings have included wood panels fashioned and primed in his studio, with the frames an integral part of each work. The larger works are painted on canvas stretched over wood supports. Both wood and canvas supports are then prepared by adding ten

Isa, 1985 (detail, Fig. 11)

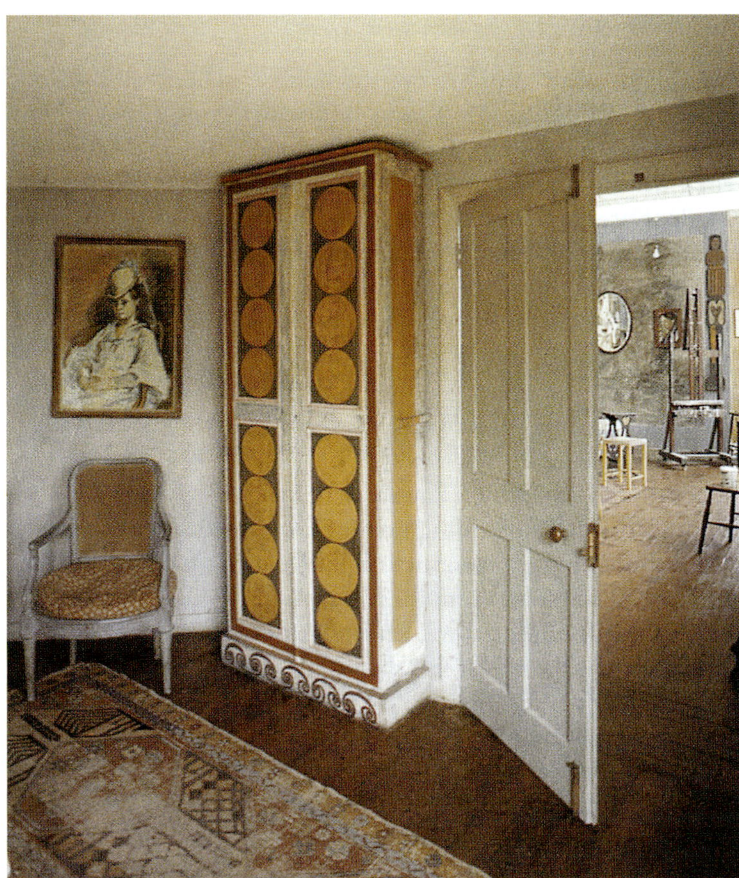

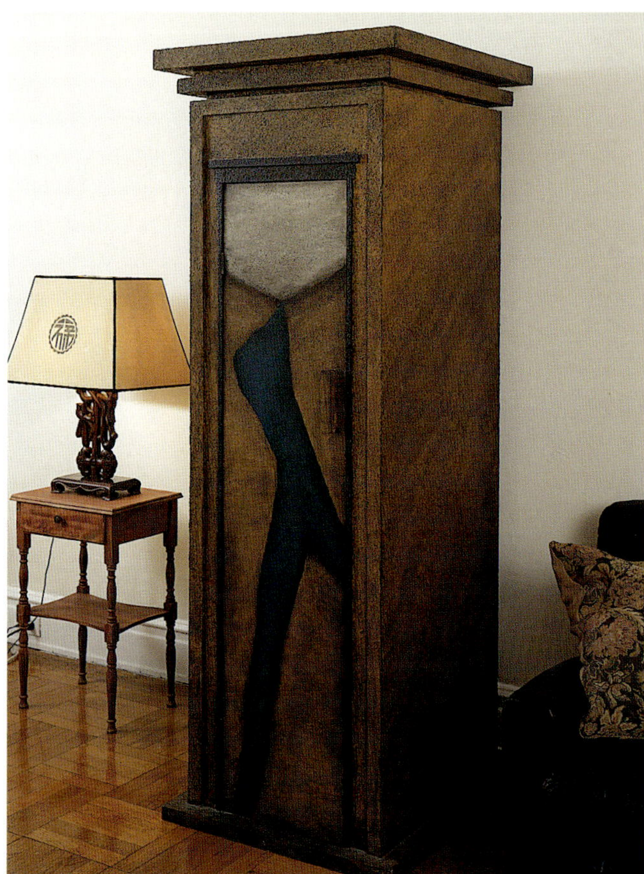

Fig. 3
Vanessa Bell, cupboard, c. 1917, in the artist's bedroom at Charleston, Sussex, England

Fig. 4
Wardrobe, 1985, in the artist's home

layers of gesso, each layer sanded before the next one is applied, to ensure an extremely smooth surface, with no trace of the texture of the material. On this prepared surface, Kahn executes a black-and-white drawing; he then starts building up the surface with a mixture of modeling paste and acrylic polymer. This is followed by eight to ten layers of opaque pigment, over which Kahn applies a final fifteen layers of transparent washes of acrylic paint that resemble glazes. Thus he achieves the richly luminous surfaces that have been a hallmark of his expressive paintings. By building up multiple layers of modeling paste and pigment, he creates tactile surfaces resonating with a rare depth of color. From early on in his career, Kahn's works have straddled the ever murkier boundary between painting and sculpture. Indeed, his paintings have the quality of "thingness," of constructed three-dimensional objects, which usually hang on the wall but, in the case of the smaller pieces, can sit just as comfortably on a shelf or surface.[4] It is this physicality that facilitated the adaptation of the technique for objects.

Kahn's "shrines"—houselike structures harboring small expressive sculptures—by their very name and form evoke religious and ritual associations (Figs. 5, 15). Begun in 1978, these works attest to Kahn's early and abiding interest in grappling with questions of sacred space:

> *When I conceived this series of sculptures in 1978, I was fascinated by the depiction in Leviticus of the Holy of Holies, a space within a space that housed a sacred object in its innermost chamber. Throughout my travels I noticed that it was the space surrounding the sacred object in various cultures that interested me. In these sculptures I try to replicate the aura of a chosen object in communion with its own constructed space.*[5]

Creating ritual objects for private use, Kahn began with carved wood structures covered with many layers of pigment. Initially, these were objects whose final form made sense in wood, and surfaces were painted with images or colors that enhanced the significance of their ritual function. As Kahn went on, however, he started making wood models for objects whose function dictated

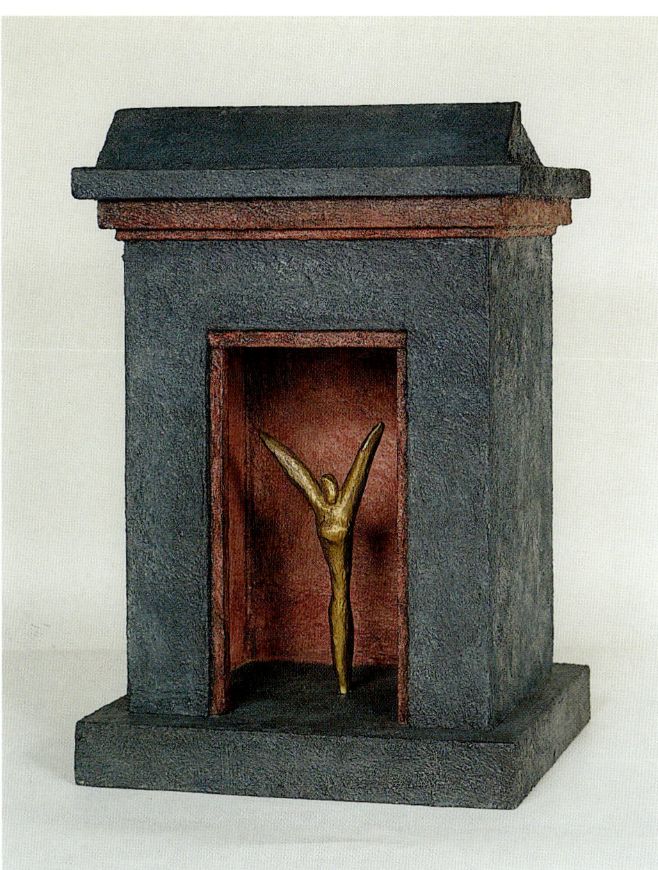

Fig. 5
Lifanah, 1985

that they eventually be cast in metal—for example, lamps, candleholders, and drinking vessels. In these cases, the painted surfaces of the wood prototypes render the desired patina for the final cast objects.

The motifs and images painted on the surfaces are also in keeping with Kahn's overall concerns: organic forms derived from the natural world and the human body. Over the years, these images have been inspired by landscapes, aerial views, celestial formations, flowers, plants, the human figure, or cell biology. What unites all this imagery is a paradox: a simultaneous embrace of the human experience and celebration of the physical world, along with a desire to transcend that world and achieve a higher spiritual state.

What gives Kahn's ceremonial objects their power is the joining of these spiritual impulses with an understanding that, in Judaism, transcendence is achieved through small actions, through a sanctification of the most mundane acts of human existence—through rituals performed in conjunction with the rhythms of the day, the week, the month, and the year, and throughout the cycles of a human life. Judaism does not revolve around grand gestures or declamations of faith, but rather around the performance of mitzvot, the 613 commandments of required actions and behavior. Behaving as a Jew is the crux of the matter. Belief is often the motivation, but it is not compulsory—only the deeds are deemed essential. The objects used by Jews in their rituals are thus both the simplest of daily tools and the means to transcendence, since the performance of mitzvot brings one closer to the divine. That these objects should be beautiful, because beauty enhances the ritual act, is a Jewish tradition called *hiddur mitzvah*. This concept is rooted in the exegesis of a verse from Exodus 15:2, from the song sung by the Israelites at the crossing of the Red Sea: "The Lord is my strength and might [song]; He is become my deliverance. This is my God and I will enshrine [glorify] Him; the God of my father, and I will exalt Him."[6] The Hebrew word *anvehu*, translated as "glorify" or "enshrine," can also be understood in its literal meaning as "make Him lovely; beautify or adorn Him." It came to be understood that God could be adorned through the use of beautiful objects in the performance of mitzvot,[7] which became the basis for the making and commissioning of objects of beauty for use in Jewish ritual. As is written in the Talmud: "Make a beautiful sukkah in His honor, acquire a beautiful lulav, a beautiful shofar, beautiful *tzitzit* [fringes on the prayer shawl], a beautiful Torah scroll written with fine ink and a fine reed by a skilled scribe and wrap it about with beautiful silks."[8]

Many of these objects of beauty were commissioned from artists and artisans; in Europe, until the early nineteenth century, their makers were almost exclusively Christian.[9] When in the course of nineteenth-century Emancipation new professions opened up to Jews, ritual objects could be commissioned from Jewish artists and artisans, a practice that continues to this day. What distinguishes Tobi Kahn's objects is that they were "commissioned" by his own need for them. Many were produced in connection with rites of passage in his own life, namely, his marriage to Nessa Rapoport in 1986 and the birth of their first child, Josh, in 1988. Kahn then began to explore the act of creating ceremonial objects and to question the ways in which this undertaking affected his relationship to ritual, tradition, and spirituality. The artistic process involves a complex interweaving of elements: plumbing the Jewish tradition for texts and artistic forms for inspiration; relating to family traditions surrounding specific rites; and adapting one's own visual idiom and modes of expression to the particular object to be created. Kahn's commitment to this process motivated him to share what he had learned with a wider audience. From this evolved the workshops he created to encourage students of varying backgrounds and faiths to make their own ritual objects as a way of connecting with the power of ritual. The energy unleashed in the process has been prodigious.

BEGINNINGS

A few isolated works from before Kahn's marriage in 1986 set the stage for what would become the outpouring that constitutes "Avoda," the title Kahn has given to the body of work consisting of ceremonial objects. In 1979, he accompanied a group of students to Central and Eastern Europe to visit sites associated with the destruction of European Jewry. As a child of parents and grandparents who fled Germany in the 1930s, Kahn has an awareness of the Holocaust that is integral to his Jewish identity. He is named for an uncle who was one of the first Jews murdered by the Nazis, in April 1933.[10] This family history motivated an early example of his teaching: "I led a group through Eastern Europe because I found it disturbing that so many people knew nothing about the Holocaust."[11] As part of that 1979 trip, Kahn visited the Altneuschul in Prague. Upon his return to New York, he was inspired to create a *tzedakah* (alms) container in the form of the synagogue's distinctive architectural silhouette.

With his marriage serving as a catalyst, Kahn turned his attention to the creation of ceremonial objects in a systematic way, beginning with a *huppah*, or marriage canopy. The *huppah* is usually constructed using a piece of fabric attached to four poles, held above the heads of the bride and groom during their vows and the recitation of the "seven blessings" that constitute the Jewish marriage service. But the four poles, held up by four individuals, can prove awkward, requiring quite a bit of strength to keep them aloft for any length of time. In addition, the four pole-holders should ideally be of equal height; otherwise, the visual effect is sloppy. Kahn also objected to this system from a more symbolic point of view: "I never liked the idea of a hand-held *huppah*. How could I choose four people to be the pillars of our new home? I wanted to build an open space, freestanding and sturdy, through which anyone could walk and feel at home. . . . Marriage requires a solid foundation."[12] Kahn wanted to create a *mis-en-scène* where the bridal couple would be standing as a unit unto themselves—symbolizing the new life on which they were embarking—but that was also open to their families standing around them and to the congregation that had come to celebrate with them. Kahn's *huppah*, *Odyh* (1986; Fig. 6, Plate 24), was designed with all these needs in mind. Wide

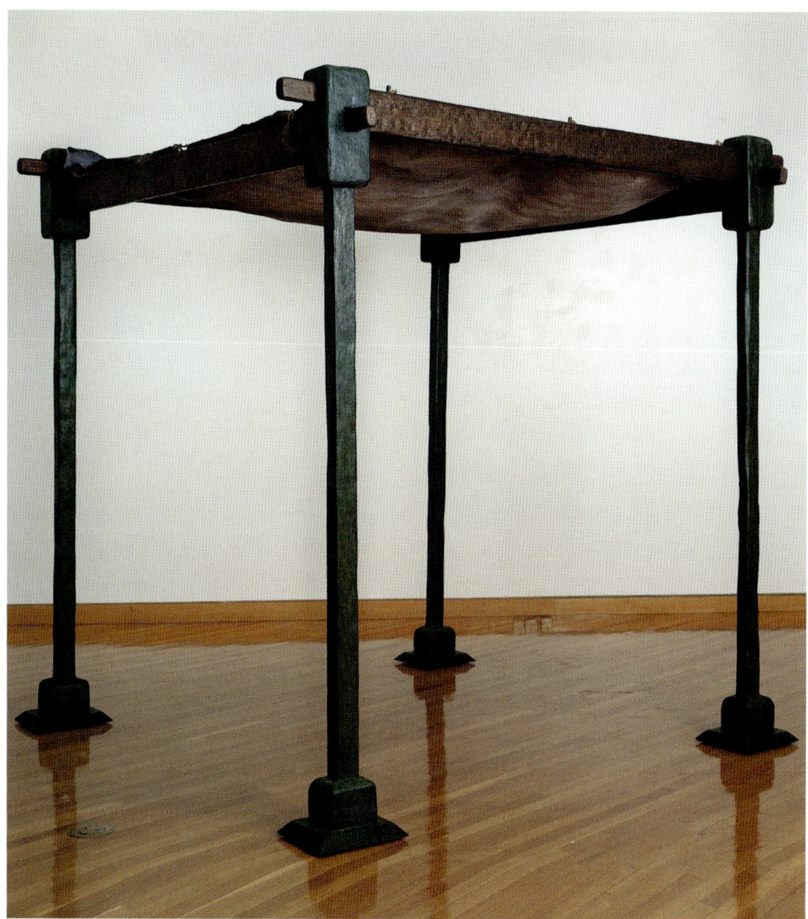

Fig. 6
Odyh, 1986

enough to accommodate only two people standing beneath it, the canopy is attached to four solid poles that rest firmly on the ground, eliminating the need for pole-holders. Thus this *huppah* is both a solid structure and one open to all four sides.

Odyh's method of construction conveys much of the work's symbolism. There are no screws: the frame for the canopy, the poles, and the bases are connected by means of grooves that fit one into the other. This system of interlocking pieces was inspired by the early works of Isamu Noguchi and by Kahn's conversations with Noguchi, an artist he much admired. Noguchi described this method of construction in connection with his works of 1928: "Joints, if possible, were never fixed (no welding) but grooved, held by gravity or tension."[13] This seems a fitting analogy to the manifold forces at work in keeping a marriage together.

In conversation, Kahn has also connected *Odyh*'s construction to that of the altar in the ancient Temple in Jerusalem, which, he relates, was built without screws or metal pieces.[14] The colors of the canopy are inspired by those of the *parokhet* (veil) that covered the entrance to the Holy of Holies in the ancient tabernacle as described in Exodus 26:31: "You shall make a curtain of blue, purple, and crimson yarns, and fine twisted linen." One side of the canopy is blue, the other a combination of crimson and purple, and the *huppah* can be assembled with either side facing up, according to the couple's preference.[15] The green poles of *Odyh* are meant to invoke nature.

In its evocative use of color, references both to biblical motifs and the history of modern art, and sensitivity to the performative aspects of ritual, *Odyh* lays out many of the themes developed in the objects that constitute "Avoda." Each object is a meditation on Jewish tradition, mediated by the artistic language of Western modernism as filtered through Kahn's specific Jewish and artistic sensibilities and his appreciation of the theatrical element of ritual. Kahn is not a linear thinker; rather, his mind bounces from association to association, and his works reflect these mental leaps.

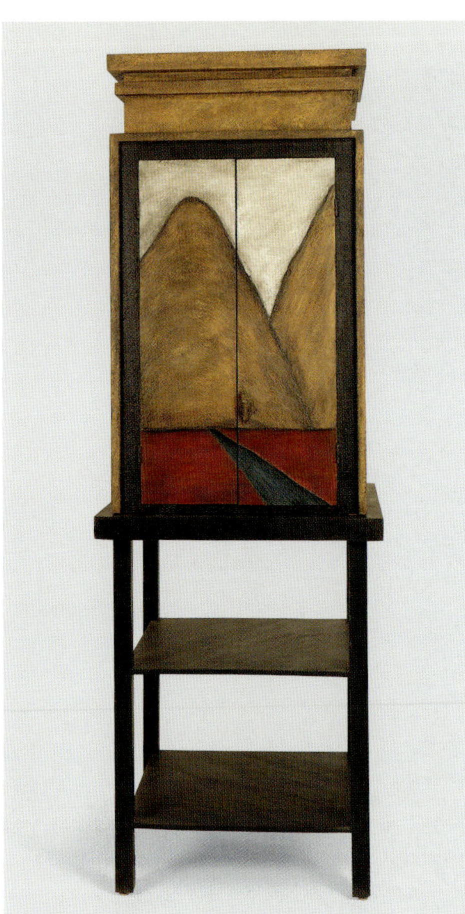

Fig. 7
Orah, 1987

ORAH

Orah (1987; Fig. 7, Plate 1) is paradigmatic for understanding Kahn's process of creating ceremonial objects. It was made to serve as a portable Torah ark, inspired by a shivah visit—a condolence call to the home of those in mourning for a deceased relative—where an "ugly pine box" had been brought into the home to serve the congregation gathering there for daily prayers. Kahn was upset that this Torah ark was dull and depressing, even allowing for the impromptu nature of the services in the mourners' home. There was no excuse for not having an attractive object that would fulfill the commandments. He thus created *Orah*, an easily transportable ark for use by a variety of congregations.

Historically, Torah scrolls have been stored either in niches carved into the walls of synagogues or in freestanding cabinets. *Orah* can be related to the latter type, particularly to painted arks from Renaissance Italy that resemble nonreligious furniture.[16] In its wood form and relatively small scale, *Orah* harks back to Torah arks such as the one dated 1472 from Modena, Italy (Fig. 8), which was designed to be easily transportable in the event that the community was forced to move. Whereas the Italian arks generally are richly adorned with a variety of carved architectural and decorative elements, Kahn's ark is radically simplified, almost stripped down. The cornice crowning the composition is a form he favors (see *Aruga I*, Fig. 23), but as in many of his works, it also has a functional *raison d'être*. The cornice in *Orah* contains a hollowed-out space to house the *rimmonim*, the finials of the Torah scrolls placed inside, so that they will be hidden from view when the ark is opened. Kahn has explained: "I don't always like the silver of the *rimmonim*; at times, they look like a woman wearing too much makeup."

This "less is more" philosophy and the disdain of gratuitous ornament reveal Kahn's place within the mainstream of those twentieth-century design movements that shunned ornament employed for its own sake and declared that beauty was to be found in the utilitarian and practical qualities of objects. Instead of decoration in *Orah*, there is a strong architectural form, a meaning-laden image painted on the doors, married to a simple base. This base, in the form of a bookshelf,

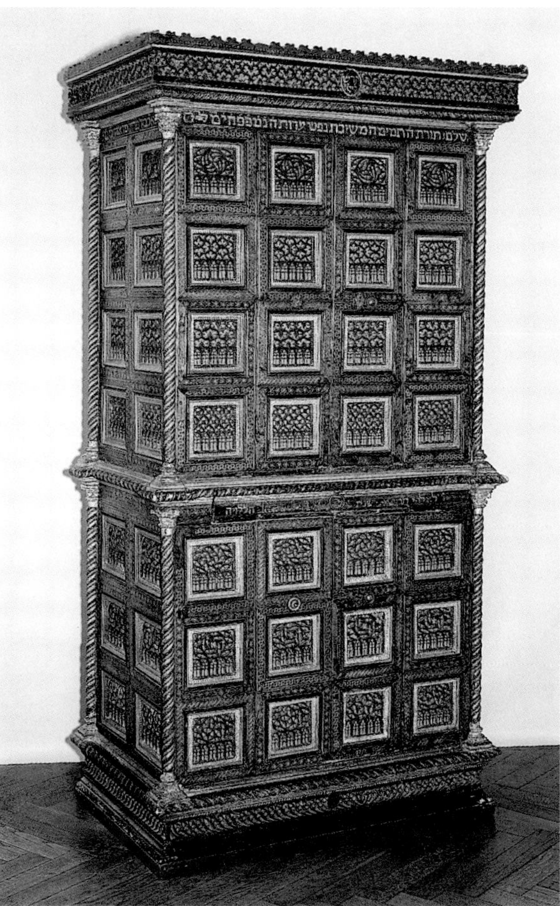

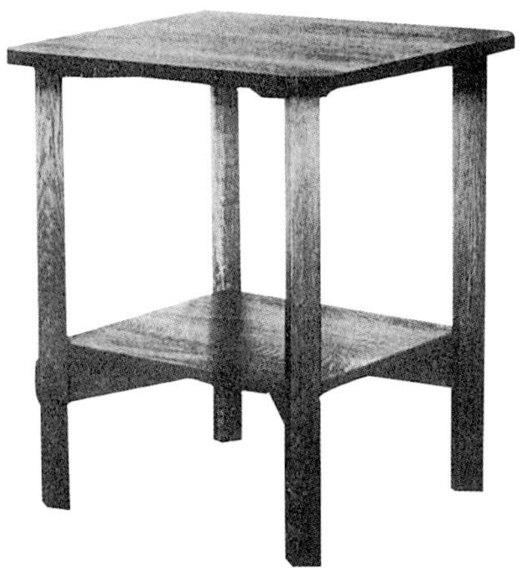

Fig. 8
Torah ark, Modena, Italy, 1472

Fig. 9
Gustav Stickley, square table, from 1909 Craftsman furniture catalogue

is meant to hold prayer shawls or books, but refers as well to the significance of the Torah as an object of continuous learning and interpretation. The ark is built as a study in contrasts between the two parts, top and bottom. The top is an enclosed space, rich in imagery rendered in sensuous hues dominated by gold; the base is an open form, with the austerity of the Shaker and Stickley furniture that inspired it (Fig. 9).

The imagery in the top portion reflects Kahn's notion that Torah arks should not "look like vaults; the cover [facade] should already encompass a narrative." In *Orah*, that "narrative" relates the giving of the Torah at Mount Sinai, evoked through the schematic landscape of a blue path cutting through a blood-red foreground, terminating at the foot of two cone-shaped golden mountains. The shape of the two mountains recalls the rounded tops of the two tablets of the Law, a form found on traditional Torah arks and Torah ark curtains (Fig. 10).[17] The choice of gold for the mountains is consistent with its use in depictions of the tablets of the Law, where it signifies a source of light and revelation. The use of gold is laden with other associations as well: the false gold of the golden calf versus the true value of the laws contained in the Ten Commandments and the Torah.[18] As the Psalmist declares: "Rightly do I love your commandments more than gold, even fine gold. Truly by all your precepts I walk straight. . . . Your decrees are wondrous; rightly do I observe them. The words you inscribed give light and grant understanding to the simple" (Psalms 119:127–30). This concept is expressed in *Orah* by the straight blue path leading to the mountains of gold, which emanate light.

The landscape of *Orah* is a variation on a work that Kahn had painted two years earlier, *Isa* (1985; Fig. 11), which also depicts a road leading to two mountains and shares the palette of gold, red, blue, and grayish white. The relationship between *Isa* and *Orah* provides an illuminating instance of Kahn's reworking and adaptation of motifs drawn from his pictorial repertoire. In *Isa*, the blue of the road and its undulating form suggest a flowing river as much as a path through a landscape; and

Fig. 10
Leah, wife of Hananiah Ottolenghi, curtain for Torah ark, Italy, 1698/99

Fig. 11
Isa, 1985

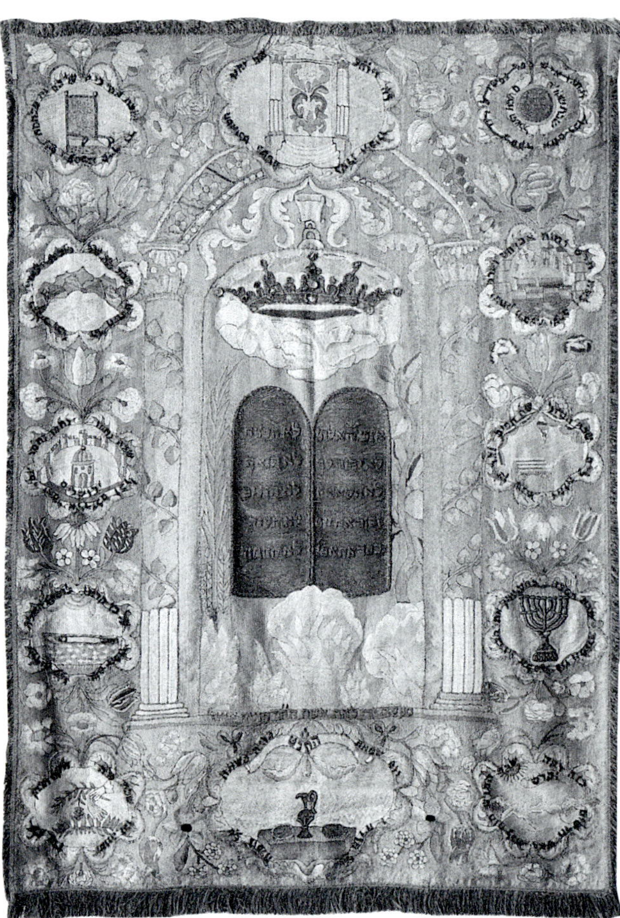

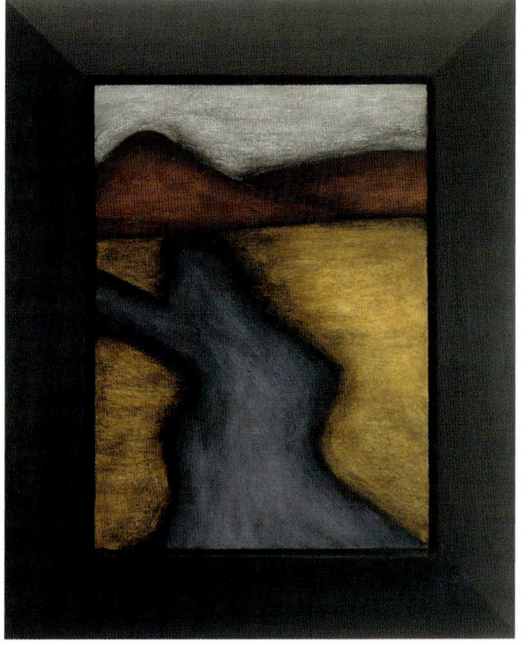

its large scale relative to the small mountains and narrow strip of sky makes it the dominant element in the composition. The path or water bifurcates as it reaches the middle ground, with an "arm" veering off to the left. Together with the overall shape of the blue form, this imparts a strong anthropomorphic element. The split path influences the way we read the painting's content as well, evoking associations of the diverging path, of the crossroads of life, of the choices that human beings make as they negotiate through the landscape. Indeed, the "arm" seems to be pointing to an alternative direction, away from the mountains and off to the left, out of the picture plane.

By contrast, in *Orah*, the mountains dwarf all other elements in the composition. Instead of the tilted picture plane of *Isa*, which provided the ground for the animation of the blue path/figure, the foreground in *Orah* is a much narrower strip, receding into the depth of the pictorial space, with the two mountains towering over all. The meandering and ambiguous blue form in *Isa* has been reconfigured into a straight and definitive path or river,[19] leading as if inexorably toward a predetermined fate embodied in the twin golden peaks. The viewer's vantage point is that of someone standing on the plain beneath the mountains, so that we feel ourselves situated within the landscape—in keeping with the idea that all Jews, past, present, and future, stood at Mount Sinai to receive the Law. The congregation praying before this ark and reading from the Torah scrolls housed within it are actors in the epic historical drama of the Jewish people. This is the narrative related by *Orah*: devotion to the teachings and laws of the Torah given to the Israelites at Mount Sinai, expressed through the language of the landscape.

If we are meant to stand at the foot of Mount Sinai, why are there two mountains? As noted, the two mountains refer to the tablets of the Law. In Kahn's subtly nuanced imagery, however, the allusions enrich one another rather than conflict. Even as we locate ourselves on the plain of Mount Sinai, the image of the tablets received by Moses on the mountain shimmers in the mind. And the pairing of the mountains resonates with other symbolism. As in many of Kahn's works, a thinly veiled sensuality pulsates within the landscape. The organic forms suggest a woman's body, the two mountains evoking breasts, the blue path or river the birth canal, the red of the landscape human blood. Indeed, birth metaphors can be recognized in the biblical texts describing the Exodus of the Jews from Egypt and the crossing of the Red Sea: the moment of the giving of the Law at Mount Sinai represents the birth of the Jewish people as a nation defined by adherence to the laws of the Torah. The form of the ark itself, a closed container, can be understood in Freudian terms as alluding to a woman's body. And the word "Torah" in Hebrew is a feminine noun. Certainly Nessa Rapoport's meditation inspired by *Orah*—"Open to me, my sister, my bride" (p. 84)—captures the ripeness of associations inherent in the linguistic and artistic forms as well as in the painted image.

But there is one more association in *Orah*, one less obvious, which reflects the tradition of Jewish exegesis. In addition to the two painted mountains in the landscape, the hollow knob on the door of the ark was intended by Kahn to signify a third mountain. Kahn had in mind the midrash that tells of Mount Tabor, Mount Carmel, and Mount Sinai, each competing to be the one chosen by God for the site of the giving of the Torah. Ultimately, God chose the smallest mountain—Sinai: "God said: My wish is to dwell only on Sinai because Sinai is the lowliest of all of you."[20] The message conveyed by this midrash—that the seemingly least impressive objects are often selected for greatness—is found in many biblical passages, such as Psalms 118:22: "The stone that the builders rejected has become the chief cornerstone."

Though Kahn's incorporation of the midrash of the three mountains will not be evident to most users of this ark, it exemplifies his familiarity with Jewish sources and also his whimsical appreciation of the possible interchange between this tradition and his visual imagination. The reference to this particular midrash seems a fitting accompaniment to the stylistic messages contained in *Orah*. God's choice of the smallest mountain argues for modesty and simplicity—a polemic, if you will, against the gaudy, overdecorated forms that typify many Torah arks. Kahn finds an expression of beauty and sanctity in the simple pairing of a spiritually infused landscape and a functional cabinet, both joined to an elegant bookcase.

The landscape depicted in *Orah* is not an image to be decoded, but rather one that invites contemplation and interpretation. This may be why Kahn gravitated to the legend of the three mountains: it enabled him to create a more fluid, multivalent image. No element in the landscape operates as a fixed symbol. In fact, if one is tempted to "read" one of the mountains painted on the ark's front as an image of Sinai, Kahn's slightly subversive message is that we should be paying closer attention and not miss the knob, the structural element that actually opens up to the Torah scrolls themselves. The meanings retrievable in *Orah* are associative and emotional, dependent on each individual, influenced perhaps by the particular biblical texts that are read at different times in the ark's presence.

The interpretative imperative extends to Kahn's practice of creating titles for his works with words of his own invention, or by appropriating allusive Hebrew words—*Orah* instead of "Torah ark" or its Hebrew equivalent, *aron kodesh*. As Peter Selz has noted: "This is to elicit free associations, as none of his pieces are meant to be descriptive or narrative, and the title 'Untitled' became a bore some time ago."[21] Many of Kahn's titles are derived from Hebrew words. Because of the antiquity of the language, Hebrew words often have a primal impact, with many instances of onomatopoeia. For example, a pull-toy that Kahn made for his children is called *Gal-Gal* (Fig. 79), which means "wheel" in Hebrew. But the sound itself evokes the whimsy of a toy as well as the repetitive sounds of play and of the toy in use. *Orah* derives from the Hebrew word for "light," *or*, and the form *orah* appears in certain liturgical texts. (And, of course, it lacks only the initial letter *t* of the word "Torah.") But *Orah* also evokes the English word "aura," with all its concomitant associations, ranging from the aura of sanctity to the aura of the work of art.

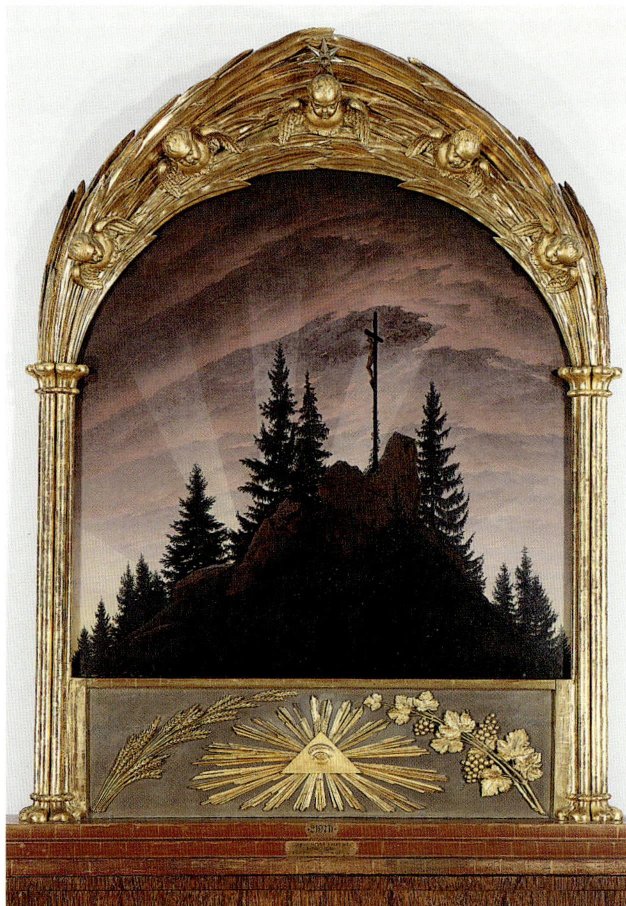

Fig. 12
Caspar David Friedrich, *Das Kreuz im Gebirge* [*The Cross in the Mountains*] (*Tetschen Altarpiece*), 1807–8

THE SPIRITUAL LANDSCAPE

How can we define a spiritually infused landscape in the context of Jewish ceremonial art? This question has to be addressed in connection with many of the works of "Avoda." What is the meaning of a mountain landscape as the focus of prayer, as in *Orah*? In shunning the traditional iconography of Jewish ceremonial art and substituting for it the pictorial language of nature, Kahn is retracing the steps of Romantic artists of the late eighteenth and early nineteenth centuries, as well as drawing on the experiences of the American painters of spiritually infused abstracted landscapes, beginning with Albert Pinkham Ryder in the late nineteenth century, and continuing, in the first half of the twentieth century, with Arthur Dove, Marsden Hartley, and Georgia O'Keeffe.[22]

For German Romantic painters, nature was a manifestation of the divine, and so its study and depiction in art was a means of communing with God, a form of religious observance. As the painter Carl Gustav Carus wrote in *Letters on Landscape Painting* (1835):

> *Stand on the peak of the mountain, contemplate the long ranges of hills, observe the courses of rivers and all the glories offered to your view, and what feeling seizes you? It is a calm prayer, you lose yourself in unbounded space, your whole being undergoes a clarification and purification, your ego disappears, you are nothing, God is everything.*[23]

Carus was a friend and disciple of Caspar David Friedrich, the first artist to make a landscape image the focus of religious devotion in the revolutionary and controversial work *The Cross in the Mountains*, known as the *Tetschen Altarpiece* (1807–8; Fig. 12). Friedrich famously declared: "The divine is everywhere, even in a grain of sand."[24] Unlike this pantheistic credo of God's presence in nature, Kahn's landscapes are witnesses to the divine rather than embodiments of divinity. In this sense, they express the relationship between the natural world and God articulated in phrases that have been incorporated into the liturgy, such as in the verse "The Heavens declare the glory of God" (Psalms 19:2).

Images of mountain, sky, and water are mobilized in Kahn's ceremonial objects to nudge us toward contemplation of a concept posited in Jewish texts, wherein the natural world bears witness to God's presence and mastery over the universe. The landscape imagery in "Avoda" encourages those who use the ritual object to celebrate divinity wherever it is manifest. In the words of the Psalmist:

> *Let the sea and all within it thunder, and the world and its inhabitants; let the rivers clap their hands, the mountains sing joyously together at the presence of the LORD.* (Psalms 98:7–9)

Randall Suffolk has noted that Kahn's landscapes are based on memory: "It is the *memory* of a place visited or a site seen which provides the impulse for a work, *not* the place or site itself. . . . As the image develops there is the continued suppression of the personal and the particular. Landscapes . . . have been stripped of individual histories, the landmarks of civilization, and any sense of defined historical moment."[25] In Kahn's landscapes, the giving of the Law is continually being reenacted, as is God's role in history and in the natural world.

RITUAL AS PERFORMANCE—PERFORMANCE AS RITUAL

Kahn's intuitive understanding of the relationship between ritual and theater—no doubt enhanced by his experiences as an actor in his late teens and early twenties—was already evident in the *huppah* he made for his marriage, which functioned as a stage set for the performance of the marriage rites. In anticipation of the birth of his first child, Kahn embarked on the creation of a group of chairs that were intended to be used in the ceremonies associated with the birth of a baby: *brit milah* (circumcision) in the case of a boy; and *simhat bat* (rejoicing in the birth of a daughter, usually referred to in English as a baby naming) in the case of a girl. As the gender of the unborn child remained unknown, Kahn created chairs for both ceremonies.

The chair used in the circumcision ceremony is called an Elijah's chair and is used by the *sandak* (godfather), who holds the baby in his lap during the ceremony. Traditional examples range from wood benches with depictions of circumcision elements to elaborately carved and sumptuously upholstered chairs.[26] *Osha* (1987; Fig. 13, Plate 22), Kahn's Elijah's chair, expresses the anxieties of impending parenthood, along with ambivalent feelings about the rite of circumcision. The somber palette of the painted images, the heaviness and archaic form of the chair—the back resembling a cenotaph and the front an altar—express the weight of tradition in the circumcision rite. Many contemporary parents approach this rite with queasiness. In the end, the importance of tradition usually carries the day, but the ambivalence often serves to heighten the commitment to the covenant between the Jewish people and God (or the Jewish tradition and past). In other words, if it were easy, if it were nothing but joy and pleasure, there would be no test of conviction.

This notion of being put to the test is inherent in the circumcision ceremony, rooted in the biblical story of the *Akedah*, the sacrifice of Isaac. Abraham was ready to obey God's command and sacrifice Isaac, having already prepared the altar, when the angel of the Lord stayed his hand. It is this altar that suggested the form for the seat and chair back of *Osha*. Kahn acknowledged what many contemporary parents feel when he said, in connection with *Osha* and the circumcision ceremony: "I don't totally get it, but I'll do it."

Osha is the only chair Kahn has made with a closed base, which contains a niche housing a small sculpture, transforming the lower part of the chair into one of Kahn's shrines (compare Fig. 15).[27] The austerity of *Osha*'s form is matched by the phallic image on the back of the chair: a barren landscape bisected by a straight road leading to a high horizon (Fig. 14). Landscapes with these three simple elements appeared earlier in Kahn's oeuvre—for example, in *Azba II* (1984; Fig. 16); but in *Osha*, the path rises at a particularly steep angle and shoots straight up, much like

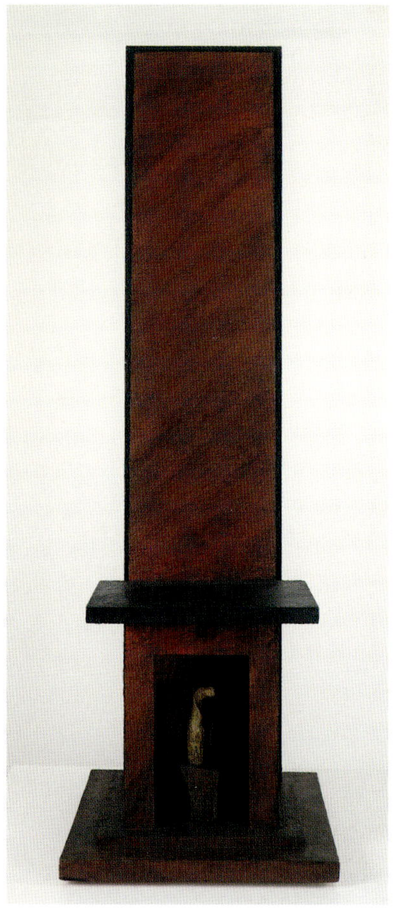

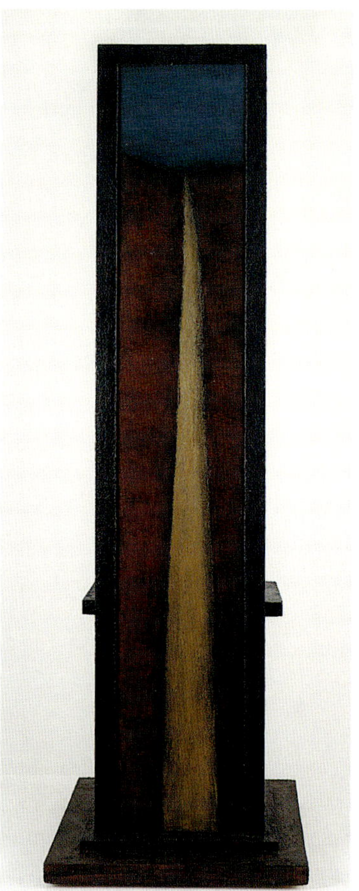

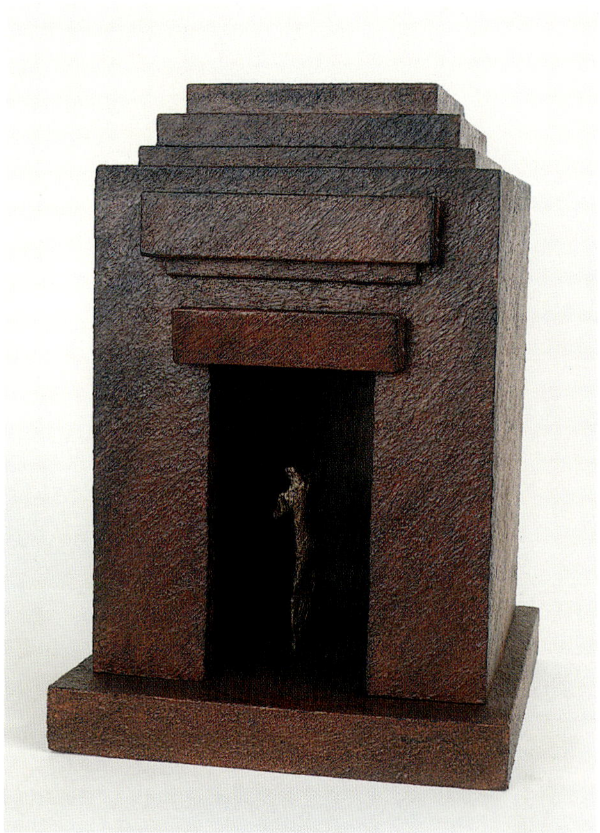

Fig. 13
Osha, 1987, front view

Fig. 14
Osha, 1987, rear view

Fig. 15
Ollu, 1985

a young plant sprouting out of the earth to convey the dynamism of new life. Although the straight, perpendicular path can be attributed to the narrow vertical frame of the chair, it also yields to symbolic associations. Kahn has related the path's form to the child's need to find its own path, and also to the birth canal.

For all its archaic quality and sense of the burden of religious obligation, *Osha*, like the much cheerier three chairs created for the *simhat bat* ritual that constitutes *Natyh* (1987; Fig. 17, Plate 23), was inspired by chairs designed by Gerrit Rietveld in the late 1910s and the 1920s (Figs. 18, 19). The seat of *Osha* is constructed of a wood shelf that extends into space, perpendicular to the back and parallel to the wide base. In the *Natyh* chairs, with the emphasis on the interplay between closed and open spaces, between the positive spaces of the chair back and the negative spaces created by the interstices between back and seat and between the slats and struts of the chair bases, one sees an even greater debt to Rietveld's designs. The overall proportions of these chairs, however, with their attenuated backs, are based on the high-back chairs designed by the influential nineteenth-century Scottish architect and designer Charles Rennie Mackintosh (Fig. 20).

The activation of the negative space is crucial to the conception of *Natyh*: the three chairs were created as a single composition, energized by the empty spaces between each one. *Natyh* must be understood within the context of a performance of a new ritual, which Kahn and Nessa Rapoport created in the event that their firstborn child would be a girl. As part of the ceremony, the newborn girl would be welcomed into the world and into the Jewish community with her mother seated in the center chair, flanked on either side by a grandmother. Members of the congregation would walk into the hall and see the backs of the chairs; the three women would only turn around and face the congregation as they played their parts in the ritual. Both the form of the chairs and their activation by means of ritual performance are reminiscent of the sculptural objects created by Robert Wilson, which appear as props and protagonists in his theatrical productions (Fig. 21).[28]

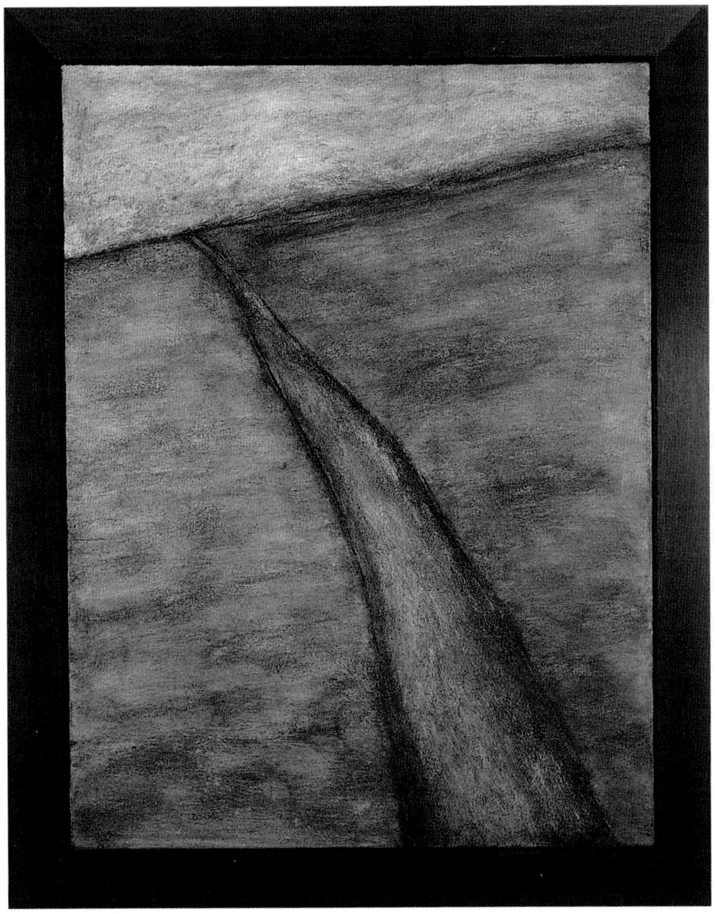

Fig. 16
Azba II, 1984

Rapoport and Kahn's first child was a boy, but *Natyh* was eventually used in the *simhat bat* ceremonies of their two daughters, born several years later. Before then, however, *Natyh* was pressed into service for the performance of composer Elizabeth Swados' contemporary oratorio *Song of Songs*, for which Kahn had been asked to create the stage sets. The biblical Song of Songs had inspired Kahn as he developed the imagery of *Natyh*. The sensuality of the natural forms, the gently rising land masses suggestive of swelling breasts and rounded bellies parallel the poetic language of the ancient verses. Moreover, when the three chairs are arranged side by side, the various land formations seem to reach out for one another, yet never quite connect. If the spaces between the chairs were closed, it would be apparent that the contours do not meet or form a continuous line—as in the Song of Songs, where the woman unsuccessfully seeks her lover and thrice repeats the verse: "I sought but found him not" (3:1, 2; 5:6). Kahn has also referred to the phallic form in the left-most chair as related to the shepherd in the Song of Songs. The palette of purplish reds and blues recalls the many references to wine in the poem, while the red floating forms allude to the lover's praise, "Your lips are like a crimson thread" (4:3).

Yet no form is a single symbol. As in many of Kahn's works, the shapes evoke multiple associations. For example, Kahn has said that the alternation of two, one, and two red floating "islands" was suggested by the geometry of the relations between two parents and one child. The images vacillate, appearing as islands in a sea surrounded by distant mountains, but also as elements of the female body, or of facial features, as in Kahn's paintings, where the "islands" acquire characteristics of a nose, eye, or mouth (Fig. 22).[29] Kahn has described this process of shifting allusions:

> *The shapes I have chosen are deliberately simplified into archetypes of mountain, island, sea and sky. Later I may find a human form in the mountain and change the mountain to disclose both images. So, the actual mountain (the fact) is remembered as an archetype and then recast into*

Fig. 17
Natyh, 1987

Fig. 18
Gerrit Rietveld, *Berlin Chair*, 1923

Fig. 19
Gerrit Rietveld, *Children's Chair*, 1919

Fig. 20
Charles Rennie Mackintosh, high-back chair for Ingram Street Teahouse, 1900

Fig. 21
Robert Wilson's production of *A Dream Play*, by August Strindberg, 2000

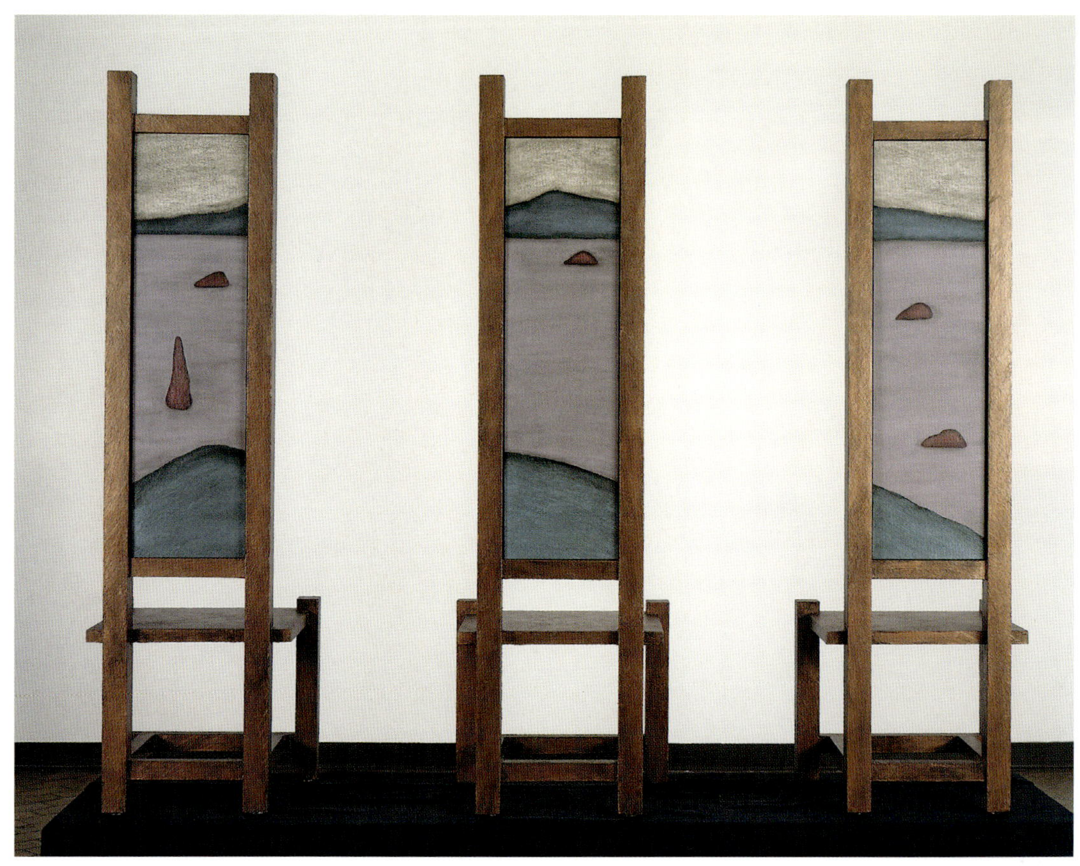

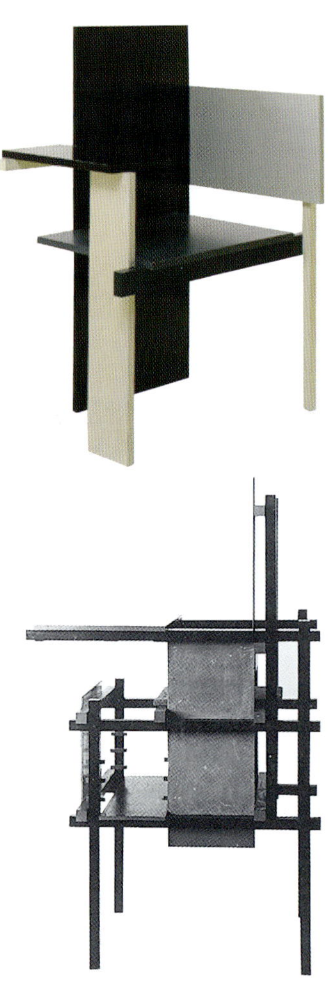

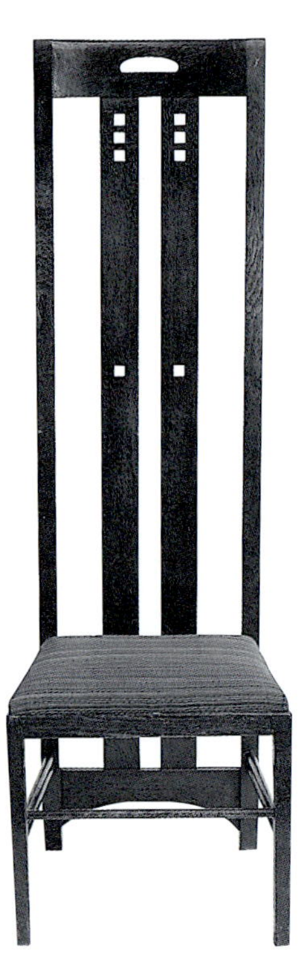

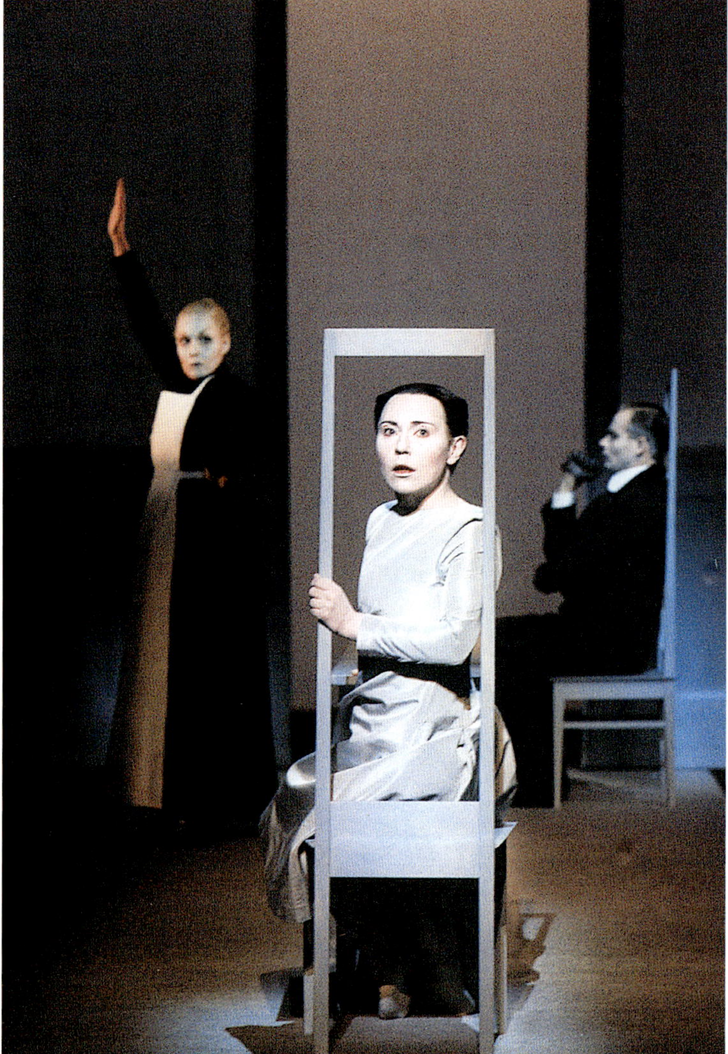

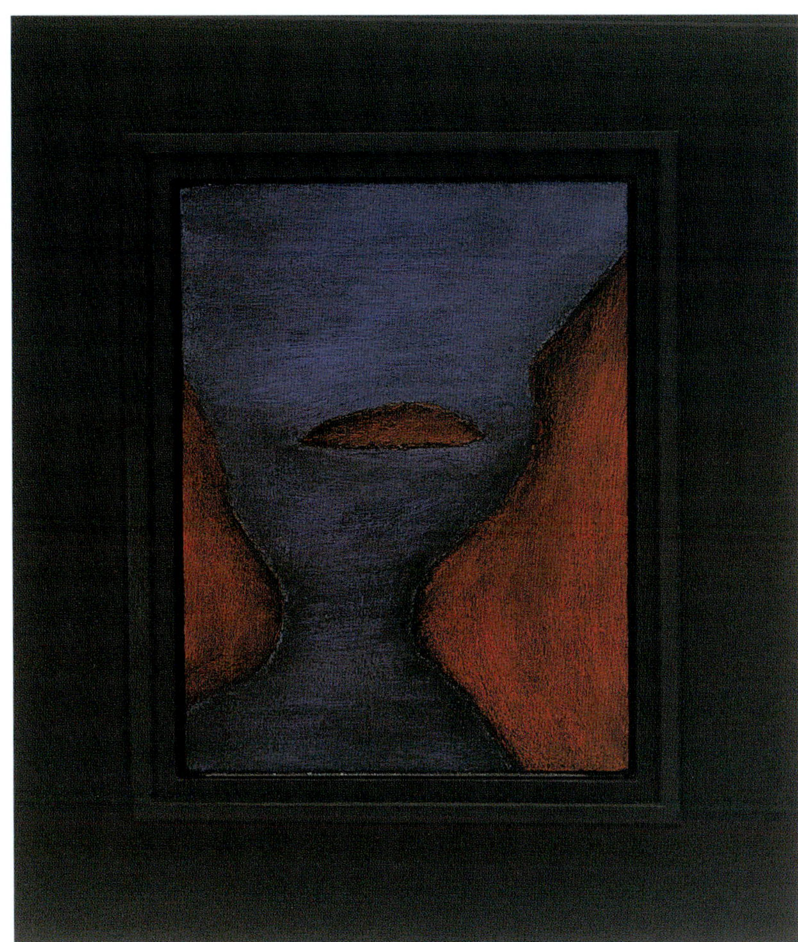

Fig. 22
Golg, 1985

another form as well. . . . The paintings are then both landscapes, referring to reality, and composites of free-floating forms, otherworldly and seductive in their allusiveness, their suggestion of something you think you know. They are meant to evoke a place you once visited but can no longer quite recall, remote as dreams.[30]

Kahn draws on images from nature to initiate his newborn children into the world, the world we all inhabit and through which the child will have to find its way.

FROM THE PUBLIC RITUAL SPACE TO OBJECTS OF PRIVATE DEVOTION

The early furniture works of "Avoda" arose from Kahn's sense of the relationship between actor and stage set, between the public performers of ritual and the objects that constitute public ceremonial space. His experience as a theatrical set designer nurtured this practice and was in turn enriched through his explorations of Jewish public ritual. Once Kahn began to make furniture for the public rituals of his life, it was a natural extension to fashion objects for the private ceremonies of the Sabbath and Jewish holidays. These works, created from the late 1980s on, demonstrate many of the qualities we noted in the furniture works: the absence of Hebrew inscriptions or traditional Jewish iconography, and the use of forms and motifs related to those being explored in Kahn's contemporaneous paintings and sculptures. Moreover, Kahn began to receive commissions for specific ceremonial objects from a variety of private individuals and public institutions, and the exigencies of the clients also played a role in the creative process. The production of several different objects of the same type also allowed Kahn to explore the variety of moods evoked by the same holiday or ritual.

Aruga I (1987; Fig. 23), a container for spices used in the havdalah (literally, "separation") ceremony to mark the end of the Sabbath, is architectural in design. The shape of the tiered top, the columns demarcating the central image, and the wood construction are elements drawn from the architecture of Polish synagogues (Figs. 24, 25) and are found in many of Kahn's shrines.[31] *Aruga I*

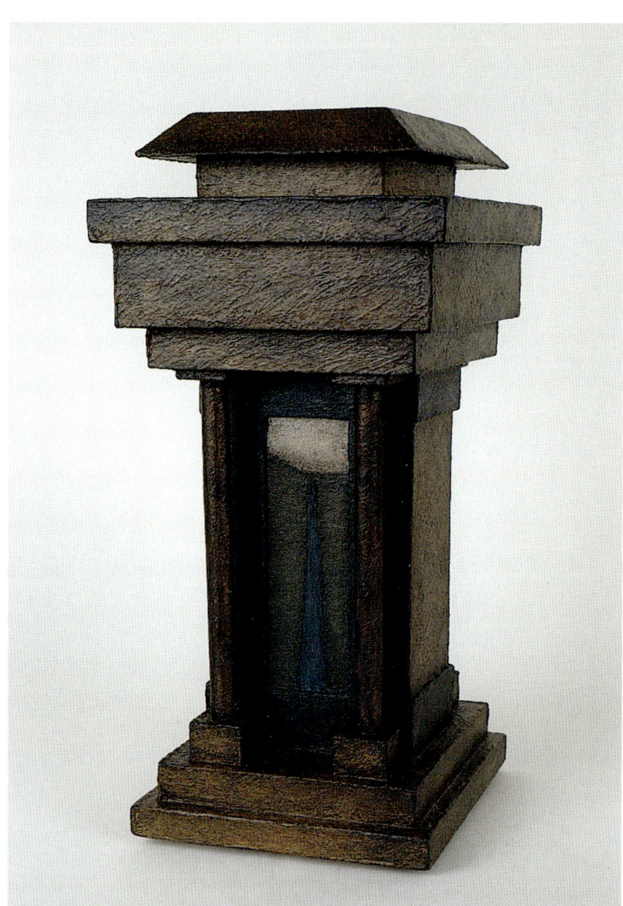

Fig. 23
Aruga I, 1987

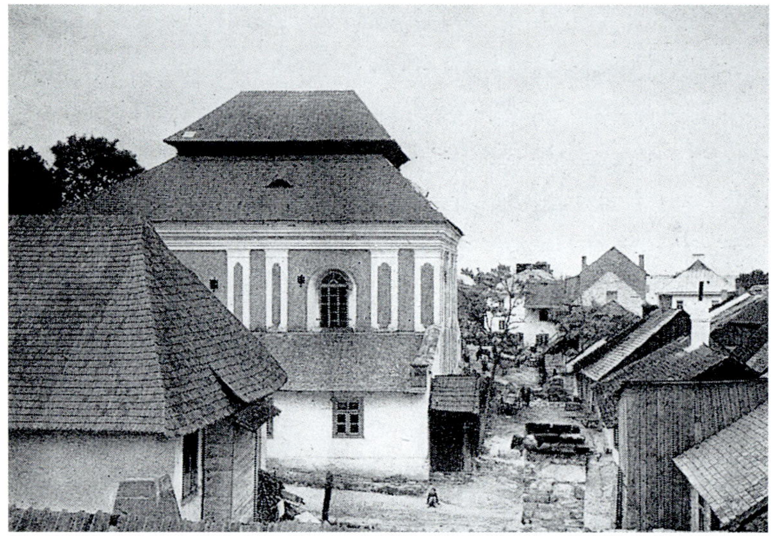

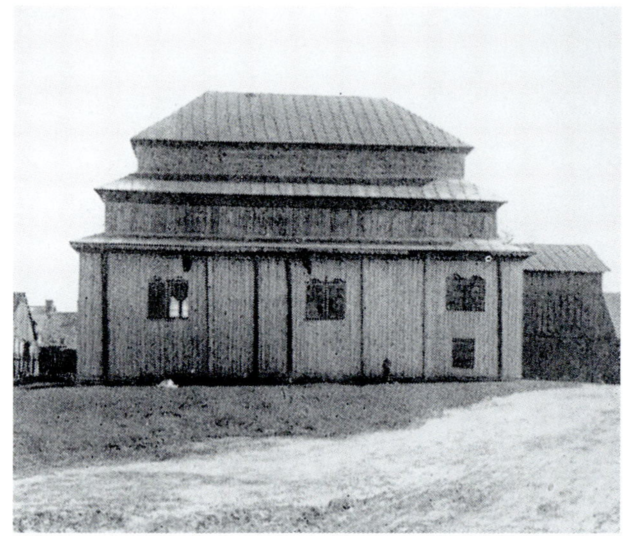

Fig. 24
Synagogue in Szczebrzeszyn, Poland; from *Jewish Art in European Synagogues (From the Middle Ages to the Eighteenth Century)*, by George Loukomski, 1947

Fig. 25
Synagogue in Nowe-Miasto, Poland, view of south front; from *Jewish Art in European Synagogues (From the Middle Ages to the Eighteenth Century)*, by George Loukomski, 1947

also relates in its form and image to other Kahn works of the same year, such as *Osha* (Fig. 14). Traditional European spice containers were often inspired by the towerlike structures of local architecture (Fig. 27).[32] In medieval Europe, spices were a precious commodity and stored in fortified towers. By basing *Aruga I*'s form on examples of traditional Jewish architecture, Kahn is engaging with the tradition of Jewish ceremonial art on two different levels.

As in all of Kahn's objects, form also follows function: the overhang of the top tier of the roof offers the user a good grip by which to pull open the container and remove the top to smell the spices; and the slender columns provide a handle for holding the container so that one never touches the painted image. This image, of a road in a landscape, relates to that on the back of the circumcision chair and to other paintings from the same period—for example, *Arekah* (1987; Fig. 26).

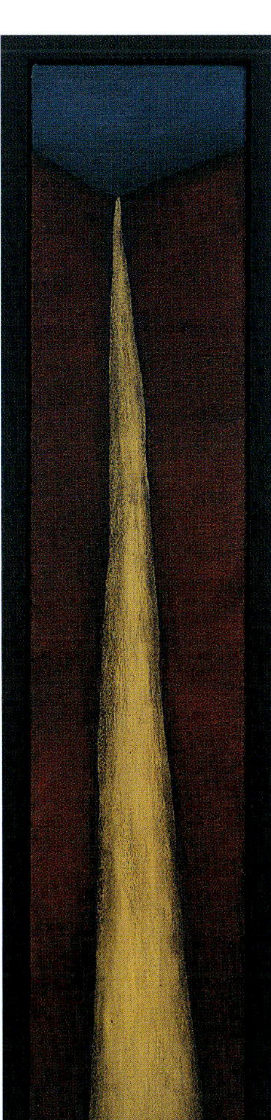

Fig. 26
Arekah, 1987

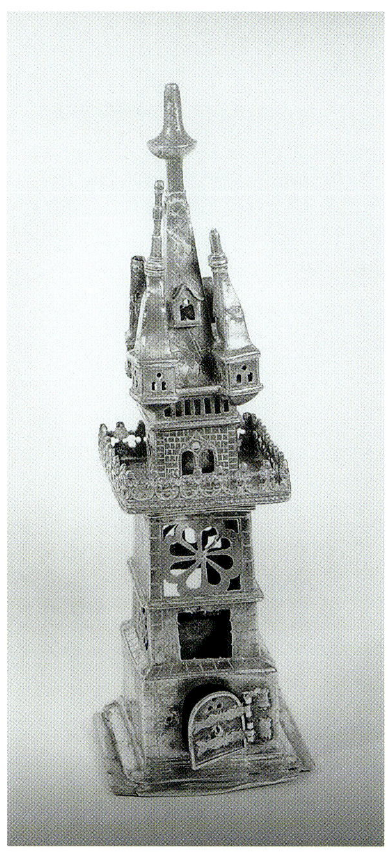

Fig. 27
Spice container,
Frankfurt, mid-fourteenth
century

Kahn's other spice containers, inspired by vegetal forms, engage with another type found in historical Judaica. In *Aruga II* (1993; Fig. 28), a pod situated on a branch is actually a hinged container for spices. Examples of nineteenth-century Polish spice containers are configured like fruits perched on leafy vines (Fig. 29). Similar pods litter the streets and balconies of Jerusalem at various times of the year. As we have seen before with Kahn's objects, the impetus for a new form derived as well from practical considerations. By 1993, Kahn's first two children were old enough to participate actively in the havdalah ceremony each Saturday evening, and they found *Aruga I* too heavy to pass around. *Aruga II* was created as a lighter alternative. In its soaring quality, reminiscent of a bird in flight, the energetic thrust of its form, and its plantlike effect, *Aruga II* owes a debt to Jugendstil, the German form of Art Nouveau (Fig. 30). The contrast between *Aruga I* and *Aruga II* can also be understood within the context of a general shift in Kahn's paintings during the intervening six years. Along with the strongly horizontal landscapes, often with monumental mountains, Kahn was also creating more close-focused imagery, including works that evoke flowers, branches, and buds. *Aruga II* is related to the branchlike forms in paintings such as *Amhi* and *Leemor* (Figs. 31, 32).

This close relationship between Kahn's ceremonial objects and his paintings is sometimes even more explicit, as in the alms container *Zedek II* and the painting *Keba* (Figs. 33, 34). *Keba* evokes a primal landscape of rock formations, sky, and water, with the floating red and blue forms suggesting islands, clouds, boulders, or strangely unmoored eyes or mouths. This anthropomorphic quality is strongest in the two brown shapes, which call to mind the heads of Easter Island or those of Cycladic figures, reproduced in a catalogue that Kahn keeps in his studio (Fig. 35).[33] Kahn recalls that *Keba* also reflects his musings about impending parenthood, the two large heads facing each other suggesting expectant parents, while the negative space between them forms an amorphous

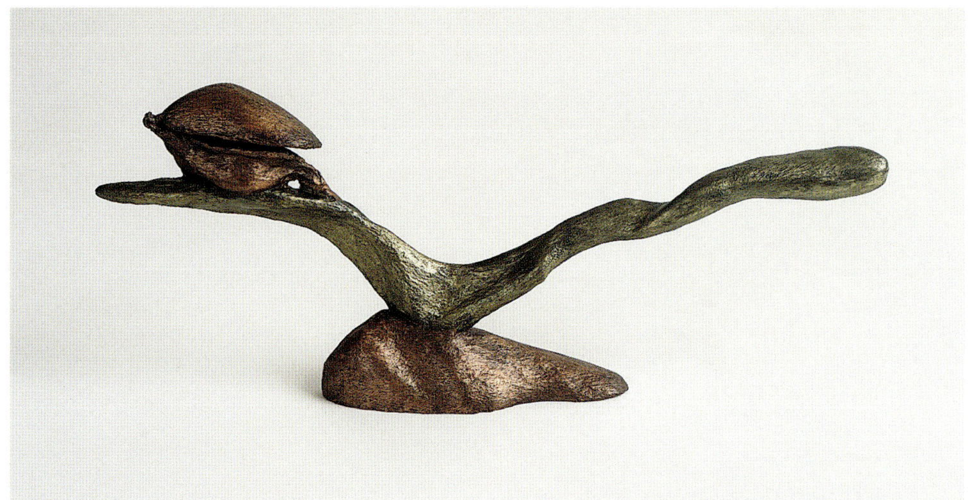

Fig. 28
Aruga II, 1993

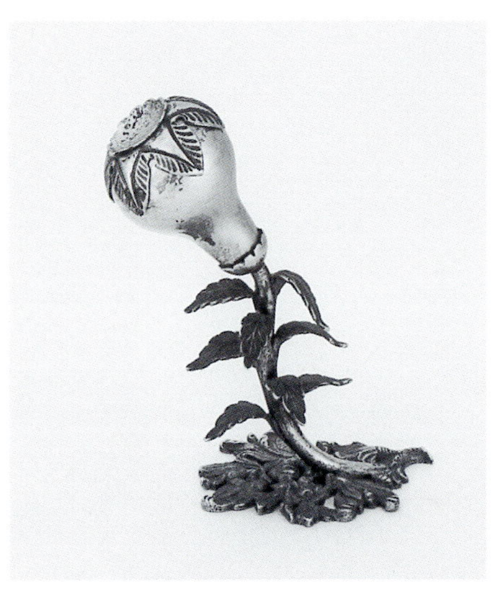

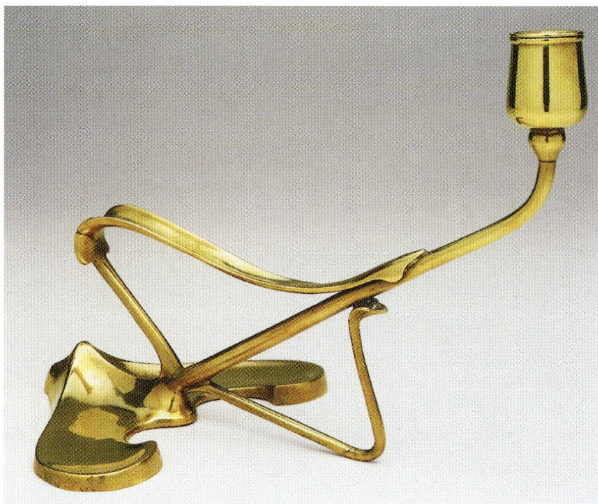

Fig. 29
Nagalski and Psyk,
spice container, Poland,
c. 1900–1921

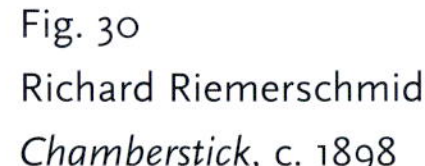

Fig. 30
Richard Riemerschmid,
Chamberstick, c. 1898

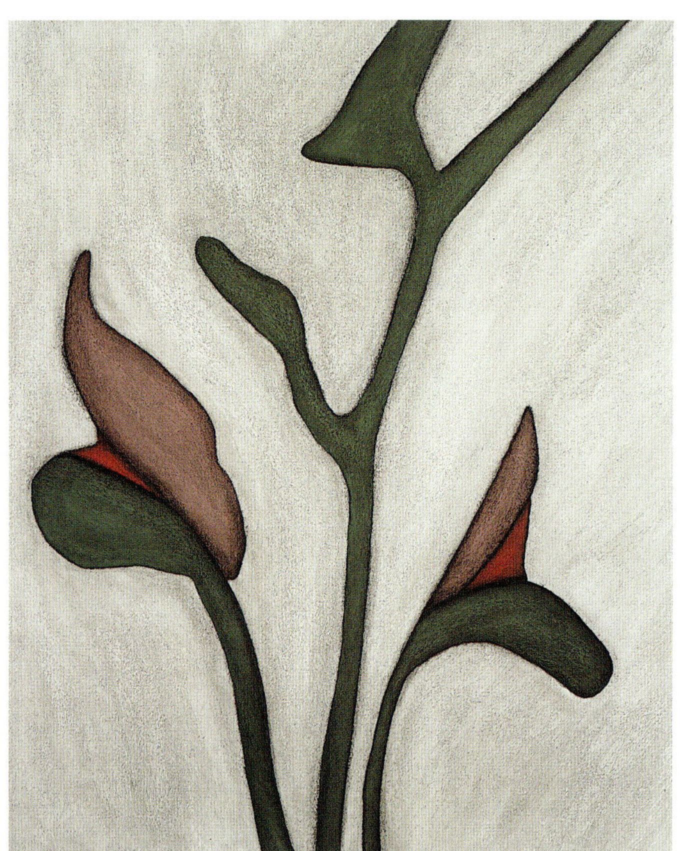

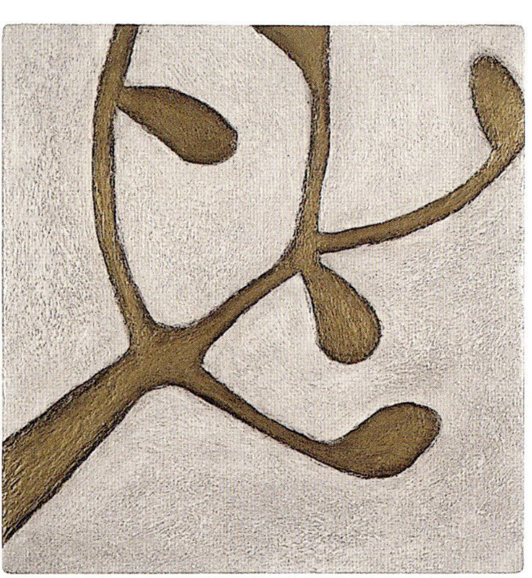

Fig. 31
Amhi, 1992

Fig. 32
Leemor, 1992

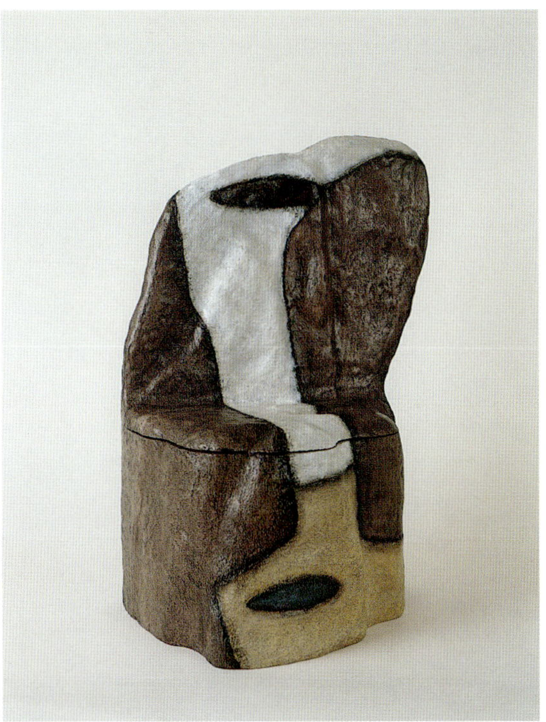

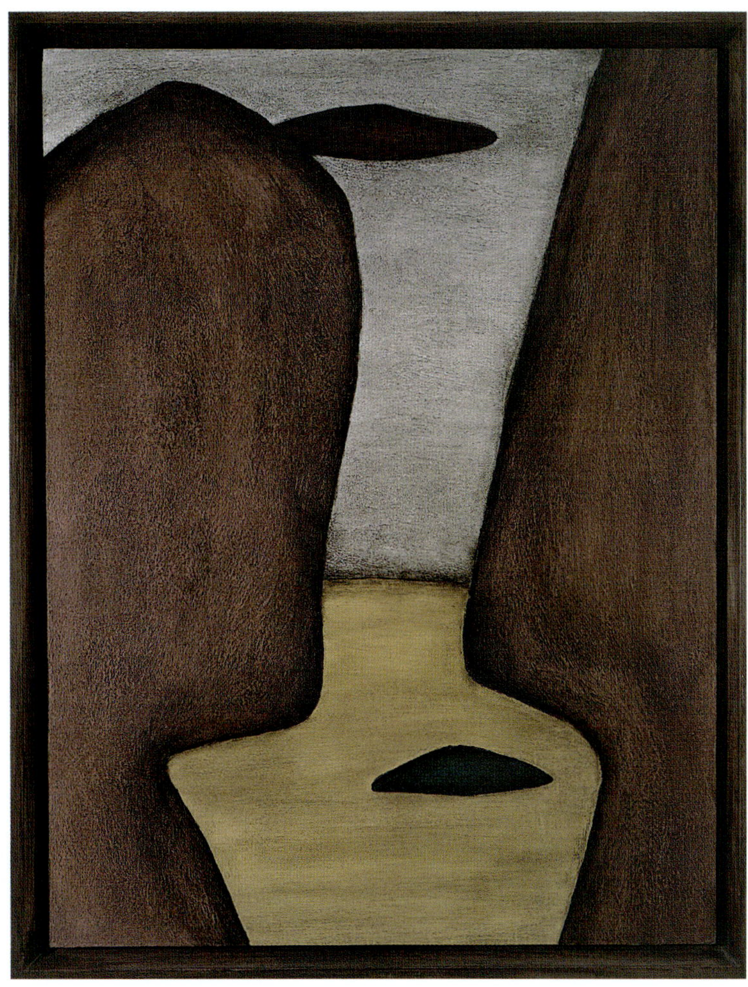

Fig. 33
Zedek II, 1989

Fig. 34
Keba, 1988

Fig. 35
Head and neck figurine, Cycladic period, c. 3000–1000 BCE

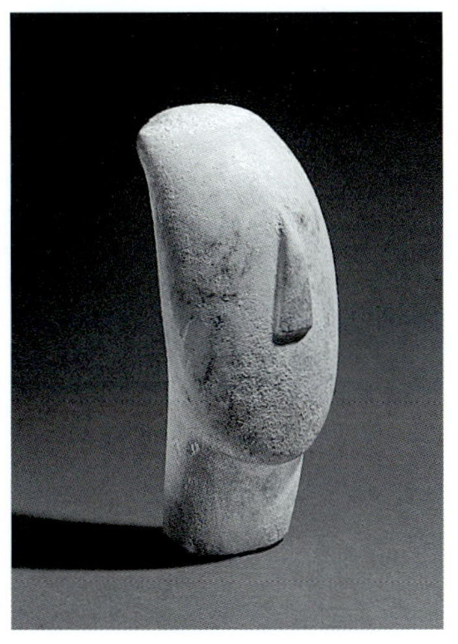

face. This association inspired him to return to the image when creating an alms container the following year for the purpose of collecting charity after the birth of his son, Josh.

Another example of the appropriation of painted imagery for Judaica is in the havdalah tray *Akahr* (1994; Fig. 36). *Akahr* is the only tray Kahn has designed with handles, which emphasize the ceremony of carrying the havdalah implements into the room where his family gathers. The tray was made to accommodate the spice container (*Aruga III*; Plate 11), the havdalah candleholder (*Ma'ohr*; Fig. 99), and a small wine goblet (*Aviya I*; Plate 9). The image painted on the tray—a red "river" flowing through a beige landscape, with a pale blue sky above—is based on the paintings *Seyall* and *Ilica* (Figs. 37, 38). As he was working on the havdalah tray, Kahn recalled his grandfather's words that the wine cup used for havdalah should be overflowing so that the coming week would be full of good things. The vivid red in *Ilica* suggested a river of wine, while its flamelike shape suited a ceremony involving lighting and then extinguishing the braided havdalah candle.

In other instances, the same painted image appears on different works of ceremonial art, but with subtle shifts in meaning. In 1998, Kahn was commissioned to create a Shabbat throne, *Ysai* (1998; Figs. 39, 40, Plate 8),[34] on which he painted images front and back, some drawn from earlier works. The dominant image on the chair front (Fig. 39) consists of three dots suspended above two

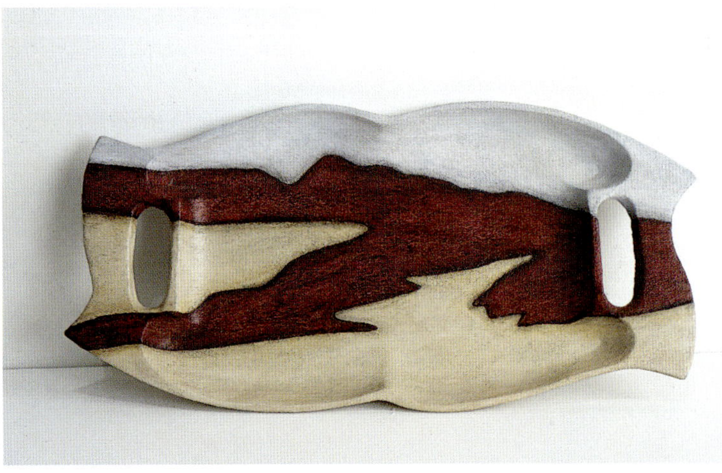

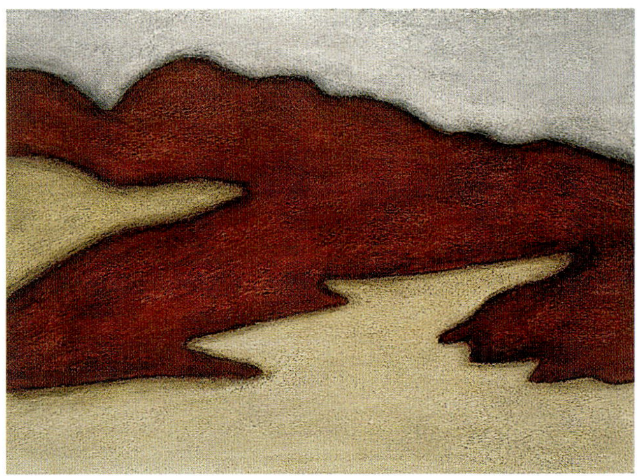

Fig. 36
Akahr, 1994

Fig. 37
Seyall, 1992

Fig. 38
Ilica, 1993

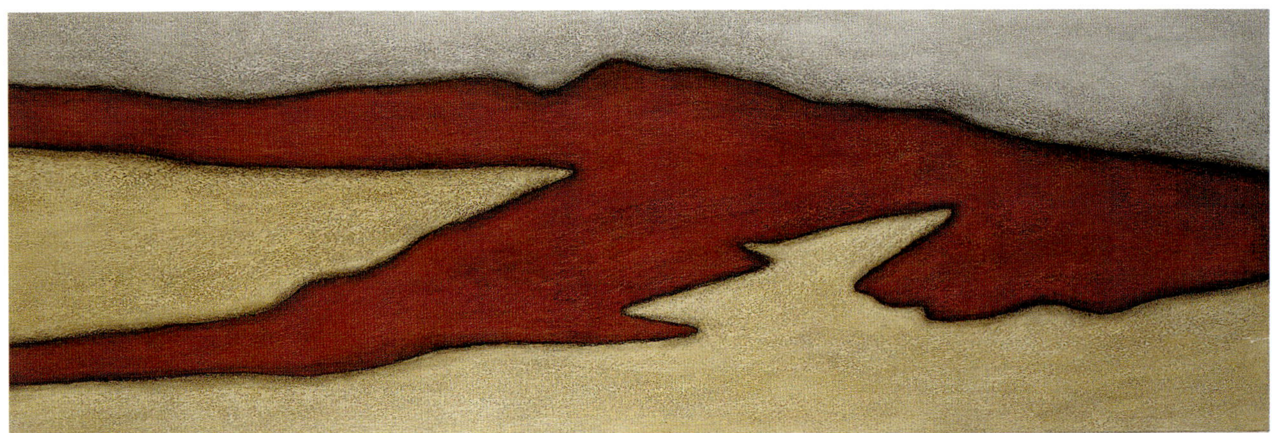

vertical forms that resemble shrouded figures, icicles, or ancient bone fragments, an image that had appeared before in Kahn's paintings (Fig. 41). Read as one image, the five elements suggest the footprint of a primordial creature preserved as a fossil, or two elongated figures, albeit with three heads between them. Both the numbers two and three have associations for Kahn that relate to aspects of the Sabbath. The two elongated forms resemble the two loaves of bread (challot) that are eaten at the beginning of the Sabbath meal. Two challot are a reminder of the Israelites' preparation for the Sabbath in the wilderness, when they gathered a double portion of manna (Exodus 16:22–30). Two also alludes to the lights kindled on Friday evening that usher in the beginning of the Sabbath.[35] In conversation, Kahn also related these two forms to the husband and wife on the Sabbath eve, an interpretation he gives to the recurrent lines that open the hymn *Lekhah Dodi*, with which Jews welcome the Sabbath bride: "Come my friend, to greet the bride." *Dodi* is the same word that appears in the Song of Songs to refer to the beloved.[36] The forms suggested to Kahn figures bowing front and back, as is customary while singing the last stanza of *Lekhah Dodi*.

Though Kahn refrains from using blatant Jewish symbols in his works, the symbolic significance of the number three is one he particularly favors. It derives from the saying of Rabbi Simon the Just: "The world is based on three principles: Torah, worship, and kindliness" (*Ethics of the Fathers* 1:2).[37] Kahn also had in mind another passage from *Ethics of the Fathers* that speaks of the three crowns—the crown of Torah, of priesthood, and of royalty—and indeed, the three dots in *Ysai* "crown" the two vertical elements.[38]

Kahn used this same image in another object created for use on the Sabbath, the challah tray *Ysha* (1995/98; Fig. 42, Plate 10), but here the three dots signify for Kahn his three children.[39] In *Ysha*, the rich copper color evokes the golden brown challot, and the green relates to ideas of

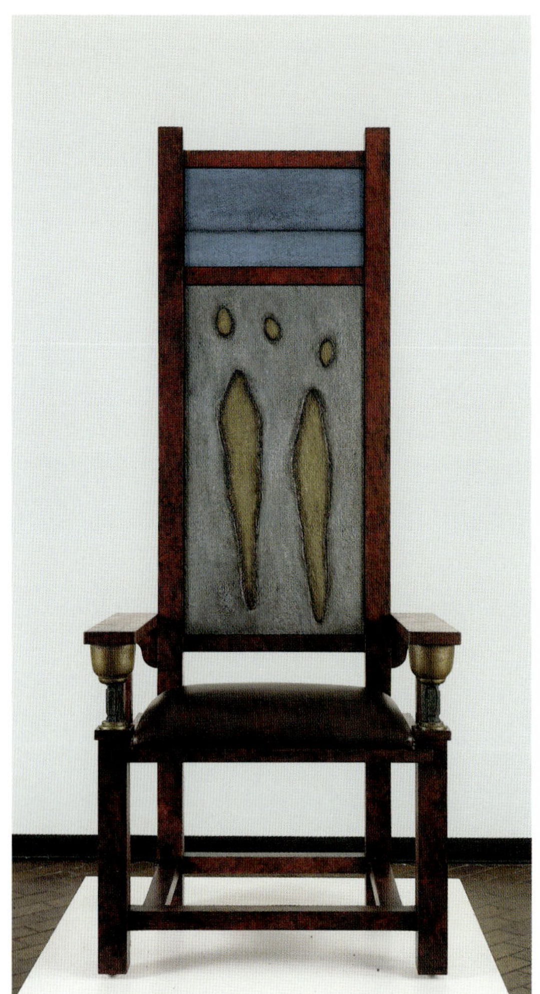

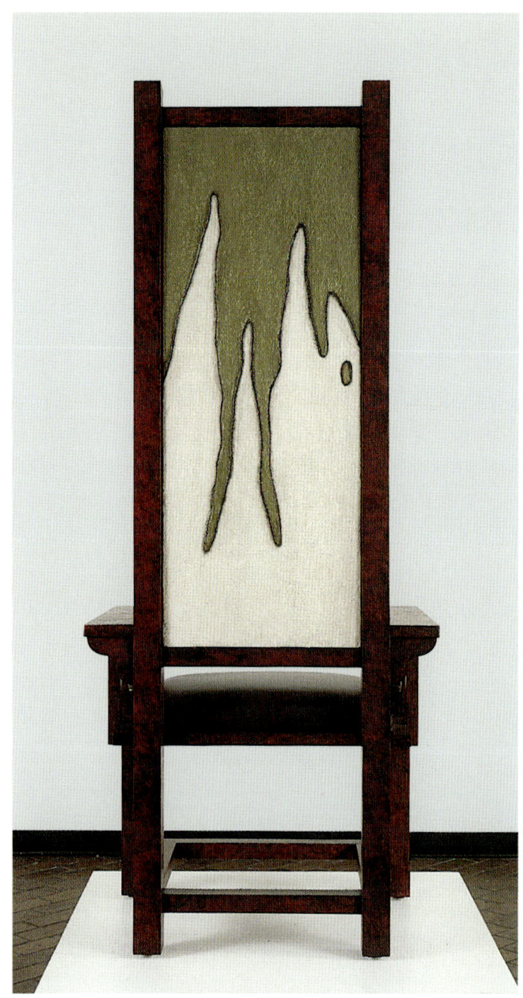

Fig. 39
Ysai, 1998, front view

Fig. 40
Ysai, 1998, rear view

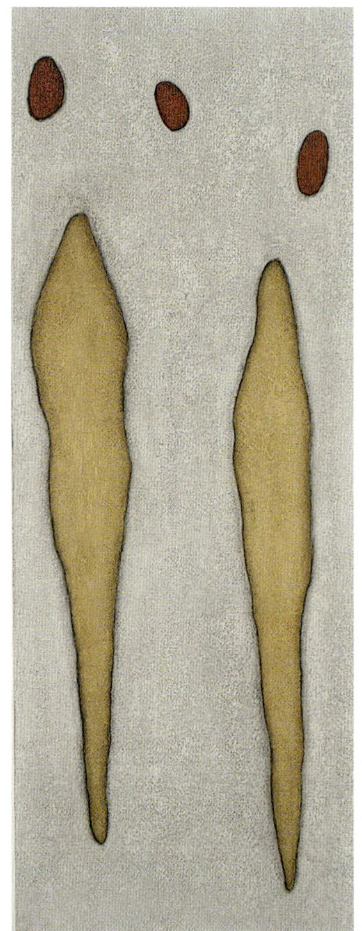

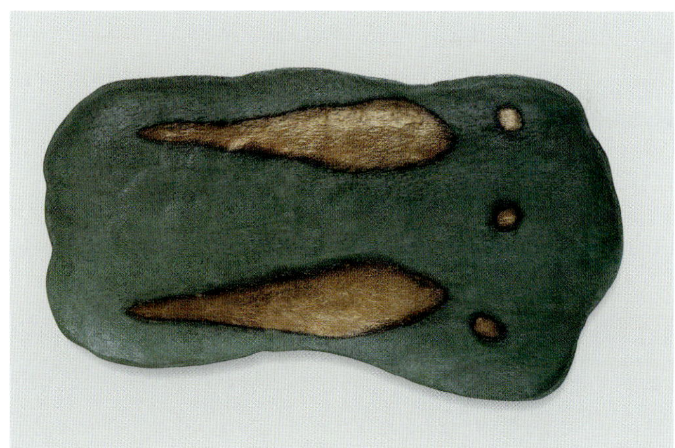

Fig. 41
Jhibu (variation), 1996

Fig. 42
Ysha, 1995/98

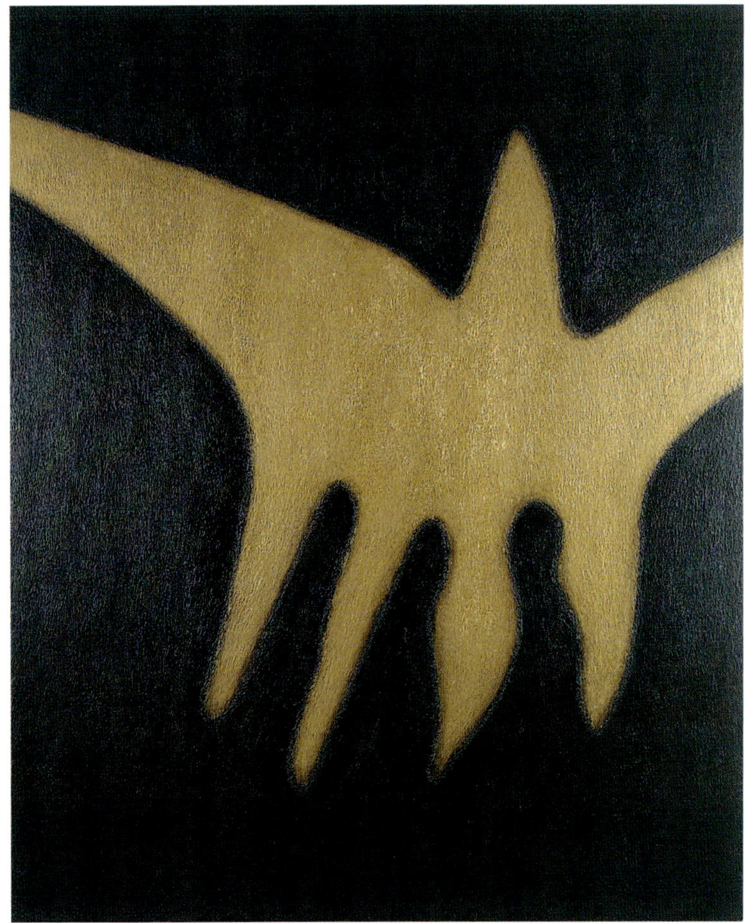

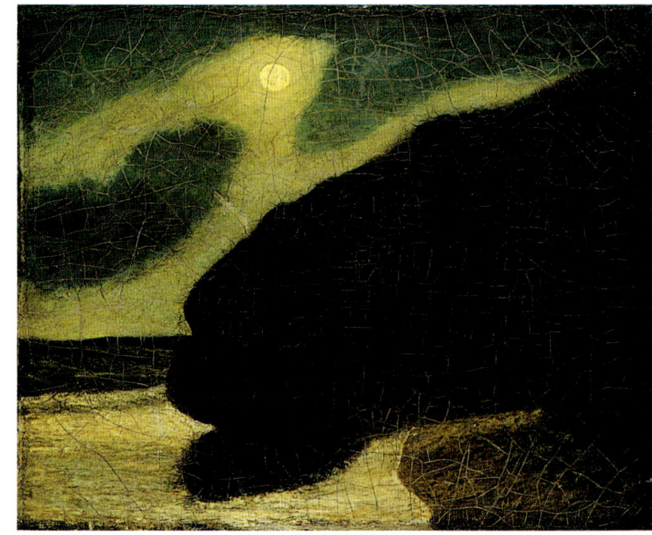

Fig. 43
Luzzan, 1993

Fig. 44
Albert Pinkham Ryder, *Moonlit Cove*, early to mid-1880s

fecundity. As *Ysha* was intended for the festive Sabbath table, the orientation of the image (unlike that of the throne) is constantly shifting, depending on the placement of the viewer at the table. Each person literally sees it differently. In this way, the ambiguity that Kahn desires in his art is built in to many of the "Avoda" objects.

The back of the Shabbat throne *Ysai* (Fig. 40) is devoted to a single image of gold and white, which Kahn has said was inspired by the idea of an angel's wings. This brings to mind Hayyim Nahman Bialik's Hebrew poem describing the onset of the Sabbath, where the Sabbath queen descends along with the "angels of peace and of rest." The image itself relates to a number of earlier canvases, such as *Luzzan* (1993; Fig. 43), which suggests a golden angel spreading its wings within a dark space.[40] On the throne back, only the tips of the wings are in view, as if the angel inhabits a space that lies partially beyond the boundaries of the chair frame, suggesting an infinite expanse extending beyond its borders. Kahn creates a fascinating play between the positive and negative spaces that make up the two color fields of the images.[41] Our reading of the image shifts between white stalagmites reaching up and silhouetted against a gold background and, inversely, gold stalactites hanging down into a white void. Are these white snow-covered peaks against a gold sky, or gold wings on a white ground?

The only element to disturb this perfect separation of gold and white is the gold oval within the white ground. Kahn speaks about this dot as a sign of the *neshamah yeterah*, or "extra soul" that, according to Jewish tradition, each Jew acquires on the Sabbath.[42] Its formal incarnation here, however, is Kahn's homage to the moons that appear in the visionary moonlit landscapes of the nineteenth-century American painter Albert Pinkham Ryder (Fig. 44), in which the natural world is transformed into patterns of suggestive, often mysterious, shapes and rhythms that reveal the soul's communion with some higher principle through a profound experience of the natural world.

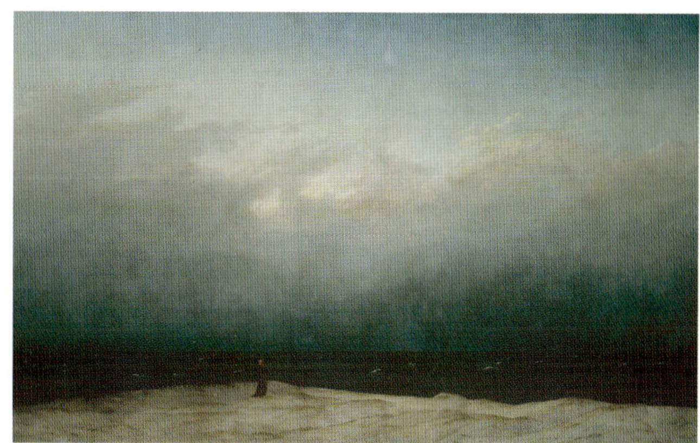

Fig. 45
Ara-Ilam, 1987

Fig. 46
Caspar David Friedrich, *Der Mönch am Meer [The Monk by the Sea]*, 1808–10

Fig. 47
Mark Rothko, *Untitled (Black on Grey)*, 1970

Fig. 48
Barnett Newman, *The Voice*, 1950

But if, in *Ysai*, instead of a gold oval within a white expanse, we see an aperture in the white shape through which is visible the gold background, then the form and placement of the oval resemble the thumbhole on a painter's palette. Individual creativity is linked with the creation of the world, remembered in the observance of the Jewish Sabbath.

The connection between the creation of the world and the sanctification of the Sabbath is made most explicit in the small painting that crowns the front of the throne: a rectangular image divided approximately one-third from the bottom by a thin line into two areas of a subtly related blue-gray color. This sky/water image is a variation on a painting of the previous year, *Ara-Ilam* (1987; Fig. 45). Many of Kahn's works had been organized around a strong horizon line, but here in *Ysai* it is the subject of the painting. In an art-historical context, this radically simplified image reveals many of the important influences on Kahn's art: Caspar David Friedrich, Mark Rothko, and Barnett Newman (Figs. 46–48). In the context of a Shabbat throne, the hermeneutics of the image multiply. According to the Hebrew Bible, one of God's first acts in creating the world occurred on the first day, after the creation of light, with the separation of light from darkness. This was followed on the second day by the separation of the water above from the water below, namely, the creation of sky and water: "God said, 'Let there be an expanse in the midst of the water, that it may separate water from water' " (Genesis 1:6). This inherent "mirroring" of sky and water is linguistically encoded in the Hebrew language, where the words for water and sky—*mayyim* and *shamayyim*—reflect their twinning. Separation is required for the creative act, for wresting life and order from the void and unformed state described in the first sentence of Genesis. Sitting in the Shabbat throne is part of a process of differentiation, separating the Sabbath from the days of the week, when one would sit in a normal chair. The Jewish Sabbath begins at sundown Friday evening, so that the demarcation of sacred time is linked to the cycle of the day, to the natural world. The horizon line becomes an emblem for a whole set of processes central to Judaism and embedded in the meaning of the Sabbath: the sanctification of time and the delineation of the border between the holy and the profane.[43]

EXPLORATIONS IN FORM

Kahn's search for new approaches to the design of Jewish ceremonial objects extends both to painted images and to sculptural forms. Some of the ceremonial objects are fashioned of wood or resin; others are maquettes made of wood, with surfaces painted to simulate the desired patina of the final cast-metal version. In all cases, the form itself conveys Kahn's ideas about the object and its significance; many also relate to the figural and organic imagery found in his paintings.

While Kahn has rejected the common practice of including Hebrew inscriptions that both identify the object and its ritual function and serve as decoration, there is one group of objects in which he incorporates a single Hebrew letter: the series of containers for the mezuzah, each of which bears a stylized version of the letter ש (*shin*), the first letter of the Hebrew word *shaddai*, meaning "Almighty," and traditionally part of the mezuzah design (Figs. 49, 52). Each mezuzah container holds a parchment with the text of the *shema* prayer, and must be ritually fit, or kosher; thus access to the scroll (or *klaf*) is critical to allow checking for any imperfections that would render the scroll unusable. Kahn has included this requirement in the design of his mezuzah containers.[44] On each of the containers, however, the letter *shin* morphs into a human or plant form, suggestive of a variety of physical and emotional states. The initial inspiration for these forms came from an illuminated Hebrew manuscript depicting angels surrounding the Ark of the Covenant (compare Fig. 51). Kahn wanted to base his *shin* on the upturned wings of the angels. In each mezuzah container, Kahn's experiment with the form of the *shin* creates movement and animation in a ceremonial object that is generally static and unobtrusive on the doorposts of Jewish homes and institutions. In the first mezuzah container that Kahn made, *Kelaf I* (1993; Fig. 49, Plate 5), the outstretched arms of the figure/*shin* are particularly dynamic, expressing yearning and struggle; it was a gesture Kahn had begun to explore in the painting *Tura II* (1990; Fig. 50). In *Ymah I* and *Ymah III* (1993; Fig. 52), the *shin* is rendered in a less anthropomorphic manner, suggesting something plantlike, while in *Ymah II*, the *shin* resembles the head and arms of a crucified figure, conveying suffering, which Kahn relates to his study of figures by Georges Roualt and Alberto Giacometti.[45] This powerfully condensed form became the basis for several Kahn projects that express human affliction, all of them associated with acts of personal and communal mourning: paintings made in the aftermath of the death of the artist Juan Gonzalez (a friend of Kahn's), such as *Al'akh* (1995; Fig. 53),[46] as well as the large-scale sculpture integrated into the Holocaust Memorial Garden in La Jolla, California (2000; Fig. 54).[47]

Kahn's expressive use of the human figure takes on another dimension in the *rimmonim* (Torah finials) *Ymahn* (1998; Fig. 55, Plate 3). Each finial is actually a pair of figures, united so as to appear as a single form, either embracing or dancing with upraised arms. The term *rimmonim*

Fig. 49
Kelaf I, 1993

Fig. 50
Tura II, 1990

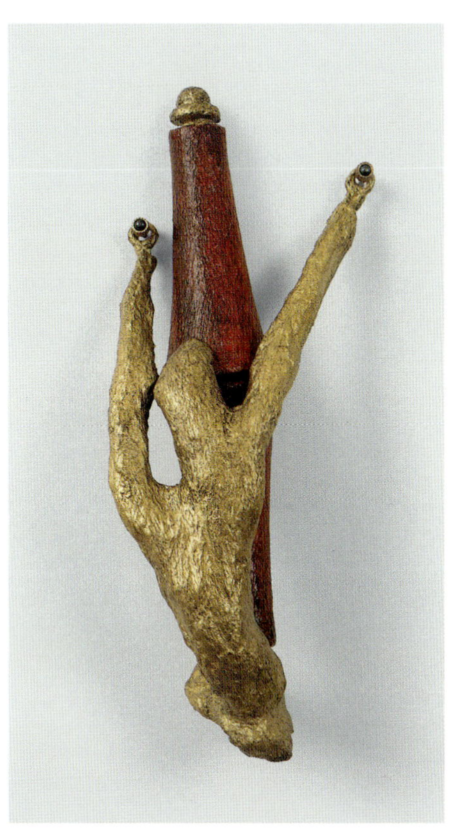

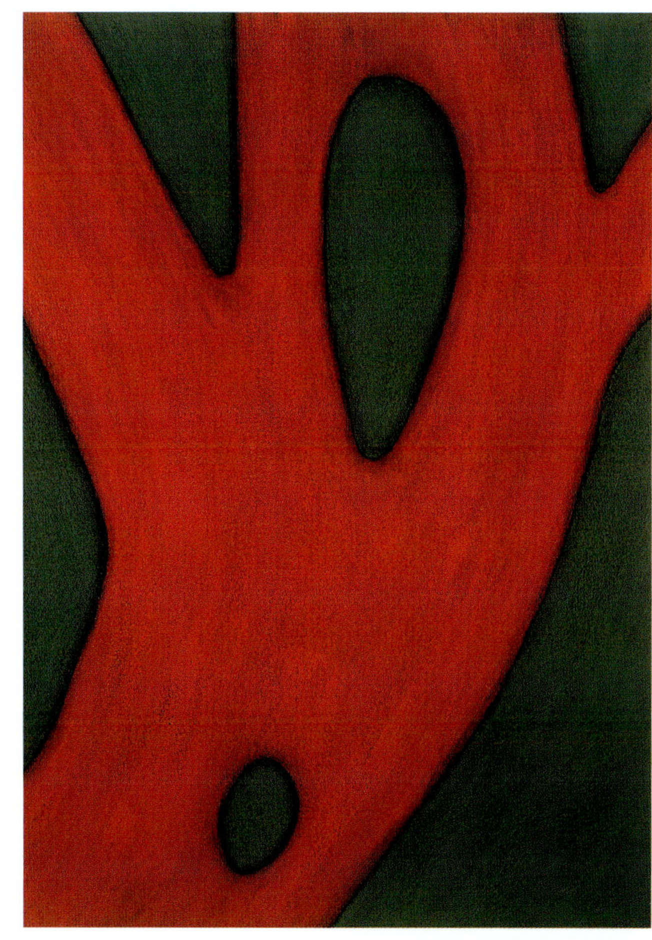

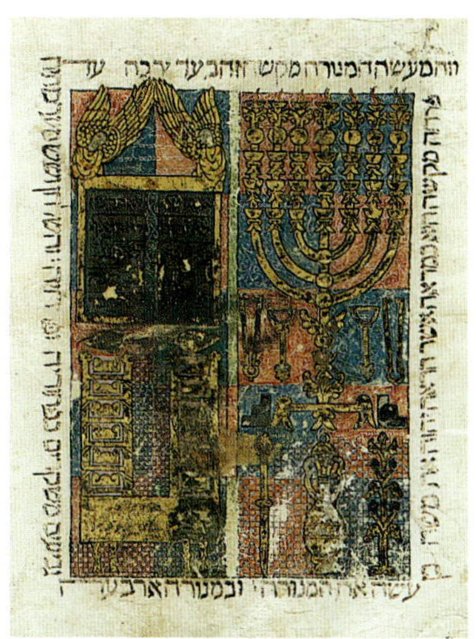

Fig. 51
Illuminated Hebrew Bible, southern France, 1301

Fig. 52
Ymah I, II, III, 1993

Fig. 53
Al'akh, 1995

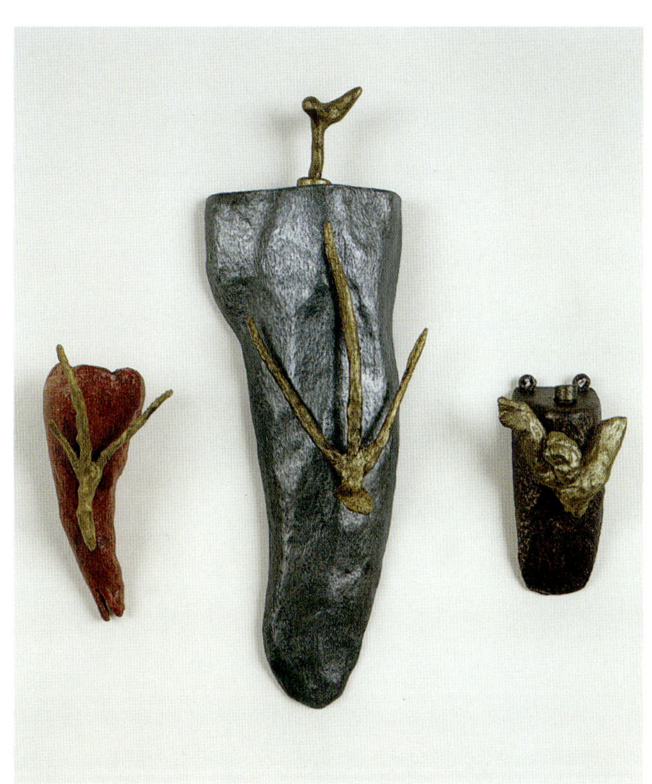

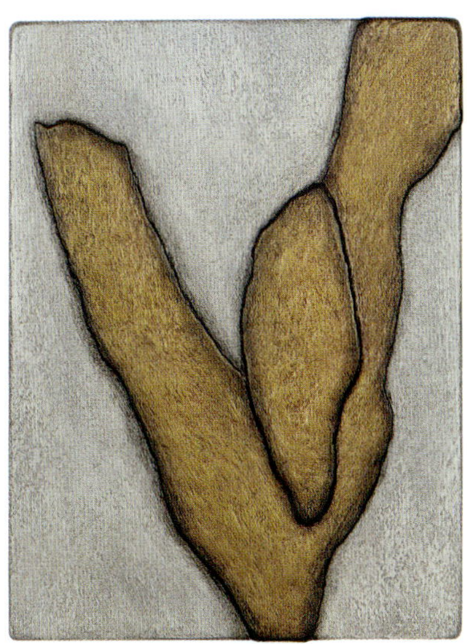

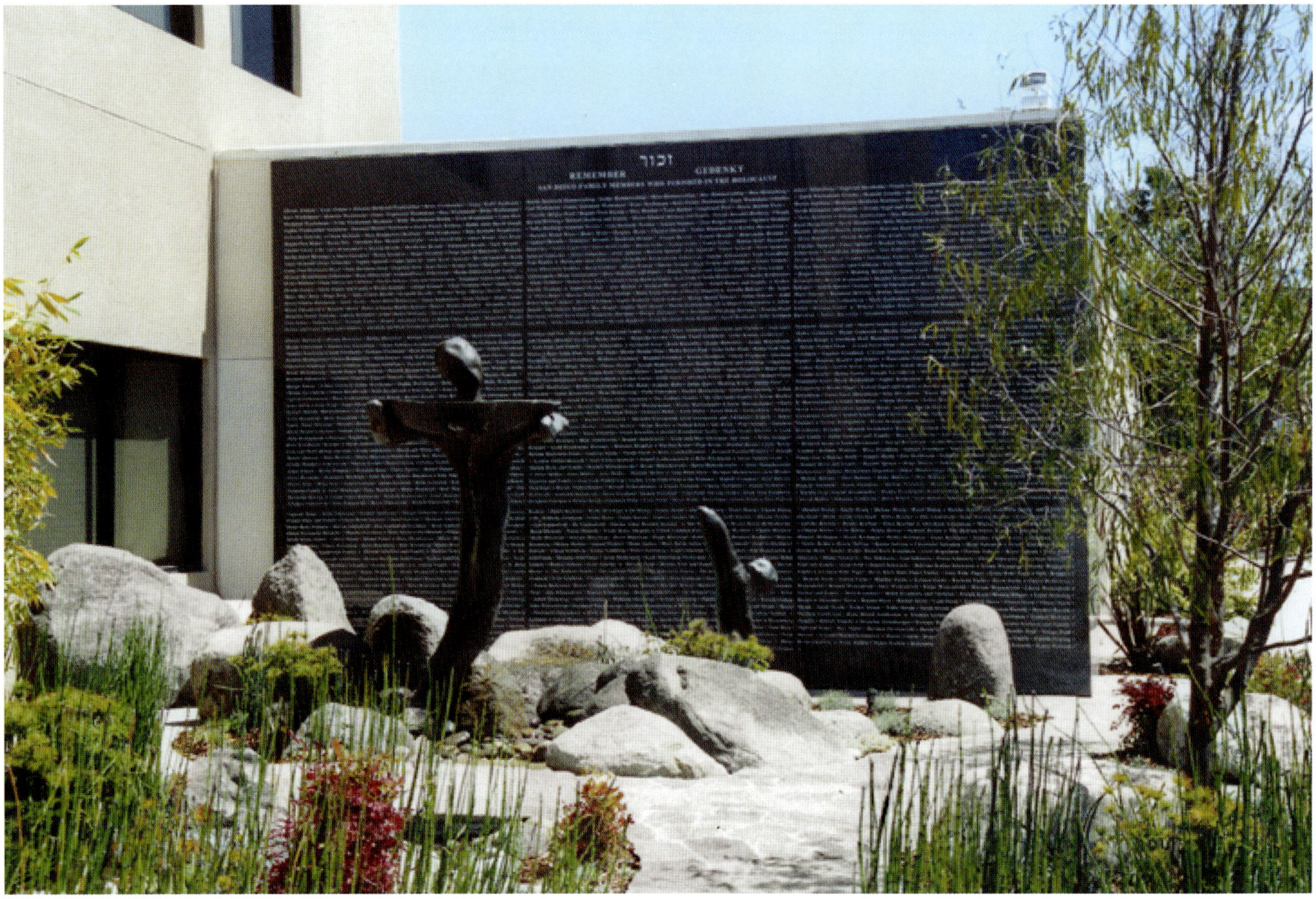

Fig. 54
Holocaust Memorial Garden,
La Jolla, California, 2000

Fig. 55
Ymahn, 1998

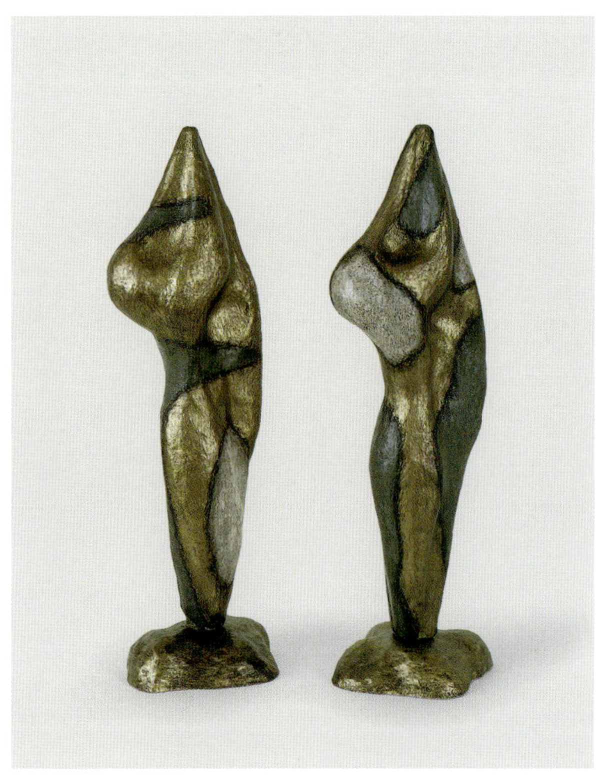

Fig. 56.
Kayom II, 1997

Fig. 57
Kayom III, 1998

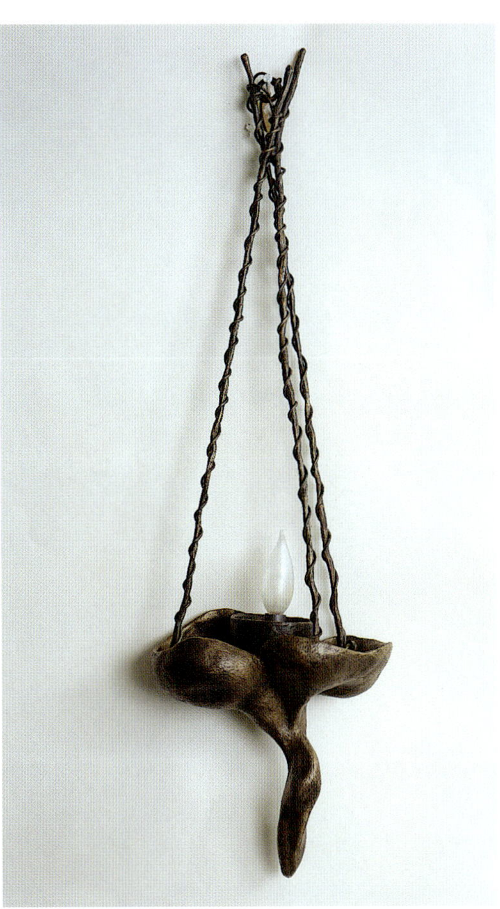

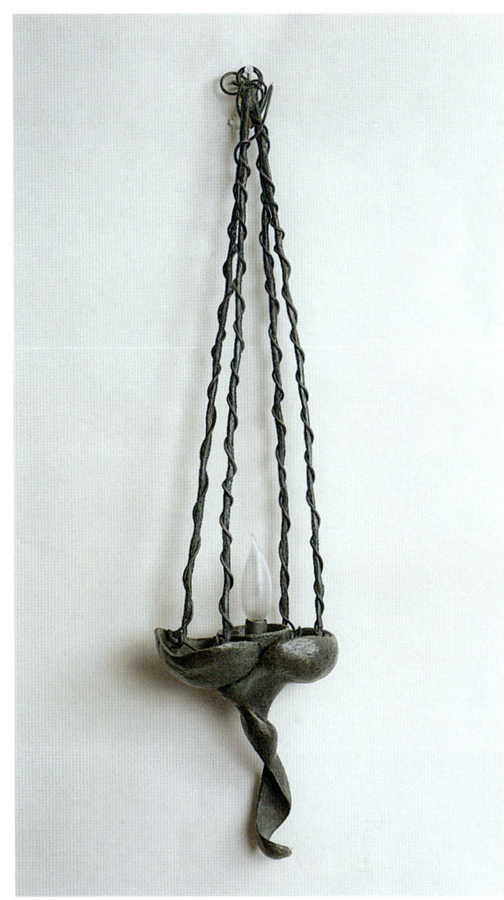

literally means "pomegranates" in Hebrew and is thought to derive from the description of the robes of the high priest.[48] In Jewish tradition, the pomegranate also symbolizes the 613 commandments because it was thought to have 613 seeds. The same abundance of seeds underlies the pomegranate's use as a symbol of fertility. Kahn's evocative form of conjoined figures brings together many elements associated with the pomegranate—sexual union and fecundity, the synagogue Torah service and observing mitzvot—much as our subconscious would in a dream.

We have already seen examples of the influence of late-nineteenth- and early-twentieth-century design movements on Kahn's objects—not surprising, given a shared commitment to objects both functional and beautiful. Kahn's engagement with the organic forms favored by Art Nouveau (see Leora Auslander's essay in this volume) is reflected in a number of his works, many of them lights or candleholders. They are reminiscent of, among other possible sources, Victor Horta's designs for the Hotel Solvay in Brussels (1895–1900), where the lighting fixtures were conceived as flowering plants. In Kahn's series of eternal lights, *Kayom I*, *II*, and *III* (1994, 1997, and 1998; Figs. 56, 57, Plate 2), the vegetal motif extends even to the painting of wires to resemble vines. Originally, as commanded in Exodus, the fuel consumed by the eternal flame (*ner tamid*) was pure olive oil, and this plant derivation provided part of the inspiration for Kahn's choice of motif.[49] In Kahn's eternal lights, the sensuous vegetal forms have a pronounced bulbous quality, verging on the mannerist. This heaviness expresses a visual paradox: though hanging and held aloft, the forms evoke a sense of connection to the earth. The eternal light houses a flame that is meant to burn without interruption; it symbolizes continuity amid the vicissitudes and wanderings of Jewish historical experience. Kahn's visual paradox thus represents the grounding of the Jews in their history and tradition, despite an often peripatetic existence.

Many of the lamps and candleholders Kahn has created are associated, in their ritual function, with women; in these works, the sensuality of the floral forms takes on a joyful air. Lighting candles

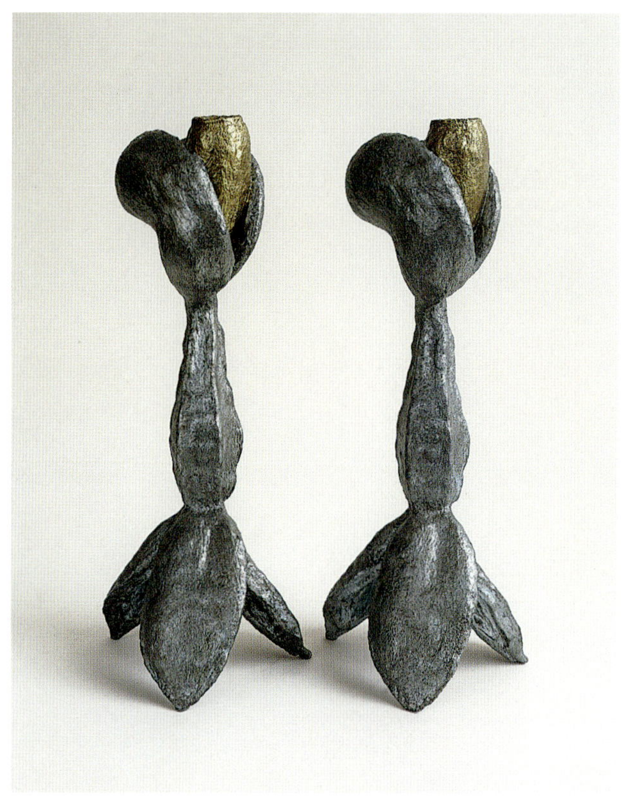

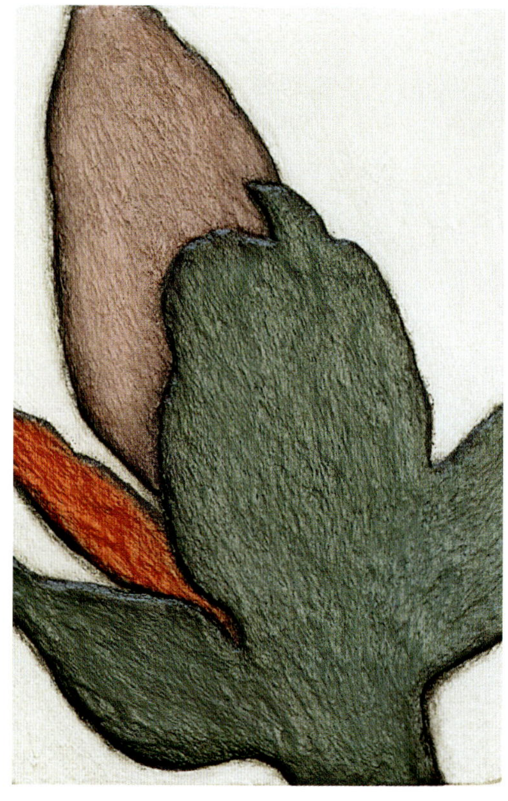

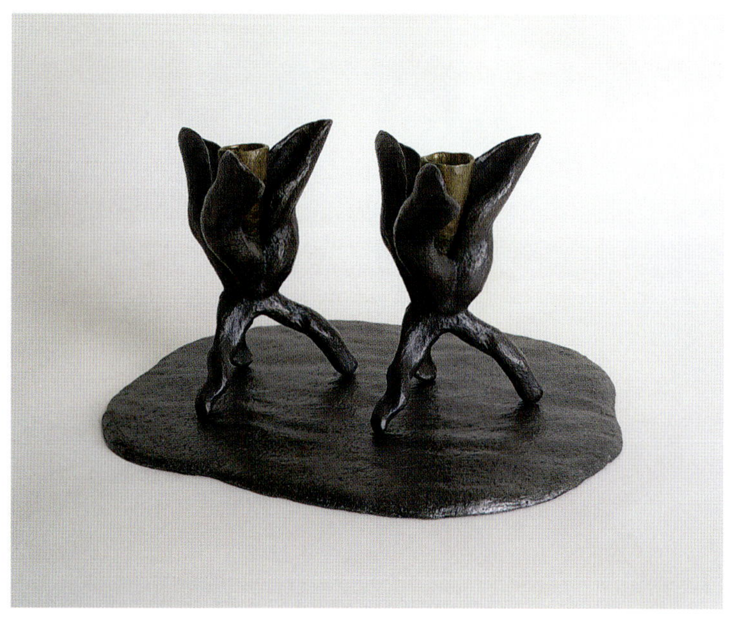

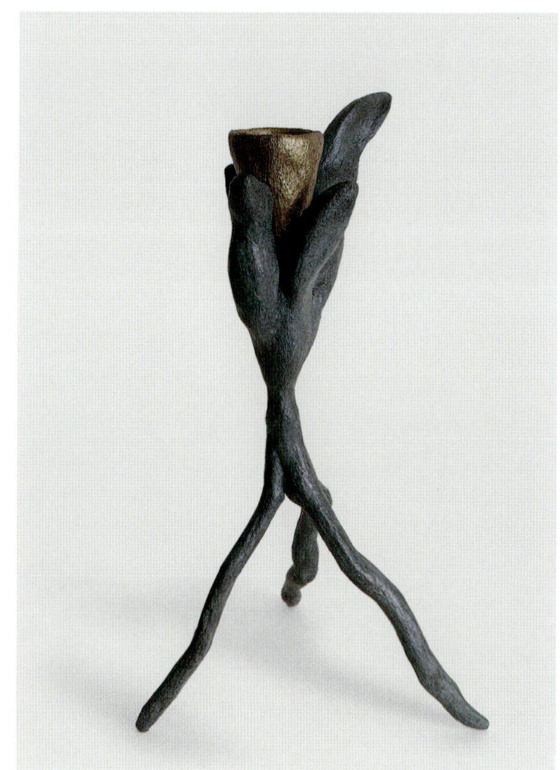

Fig. 58
Lkah, 1994

Fig. 59
Itsan, 1994

Fig. 60
Lkah II, 2000

Fig. 61
Z'chut, 2000

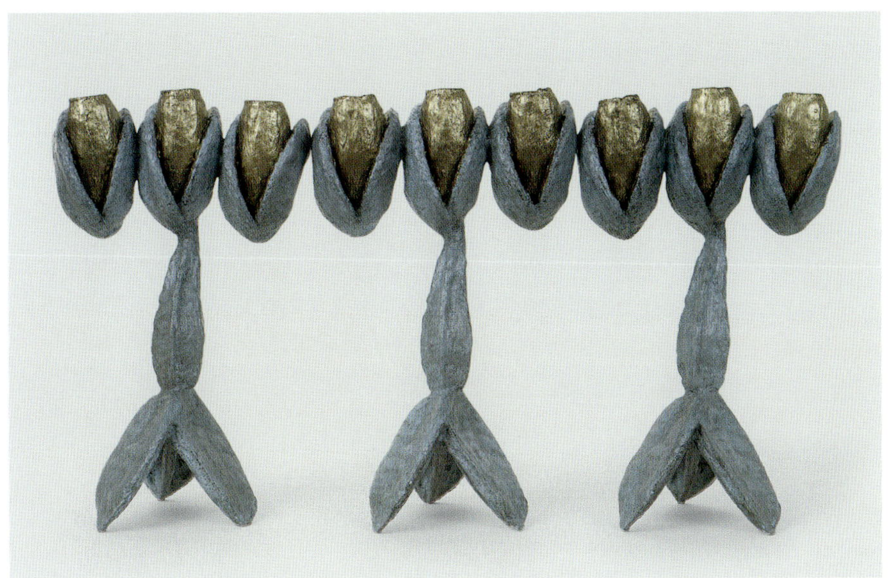

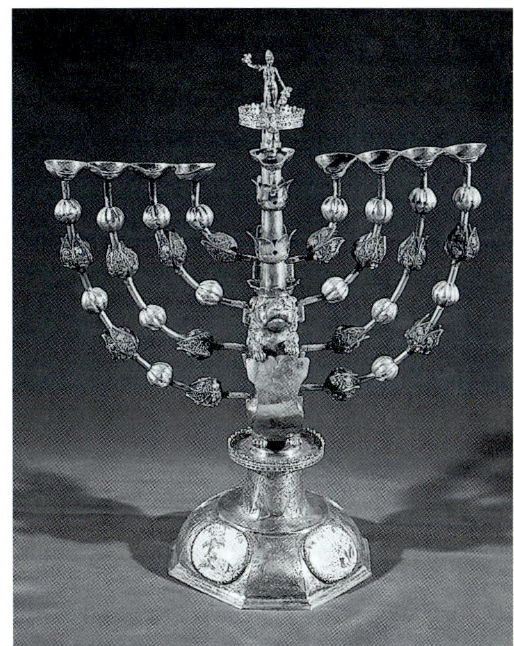

Fig. 62
Quya, 1996

Fig. 63
Johann Adam Boller, Hanukkah Menorah, Frankfurt, 1706–32

on the eve of Sabbath and festivals is not restricted to women, but it is usually the women in a household who perform this ritual. The open petals that form the base of the candlesticks *Lkah* (1994; Fig. 58) and that encase the candleholder have a voluptuous quality, also reflected in related close-up views of blooms in Kahn's paintings from the same period, such as *Itsan* (1994; Fig. 59). Kahn's focus in *Lkah* was on the light itself—how it is generated and what it signifies.[50] Moreover, since he wanted the light to be visible from far away, he based these candlesticks on grand nineteenth-century silver examples from Russia and Germany. Subsequent iterations of candleholders are more delicate and more mannered: for example, *Lkah II* (2000; Fig. 60), created for Kahn's wife; and *Z'chut* (2000; Fig. 61, Plate 12), the candleholder for celebrating Rosh Hodesh, the new moon and beginning of the Hebrew month (*hodesh*), which has become a celebration associated with new feminist rituals.

Kahn made his first Hanukkah lamp, *Quya* (1996; Fig. 62, Plate 15), by expanding on the form he had developed in *Lkah* (Fig. 58), creating a unit of three light holders supported by a stalk and petal base. The lamp can accommodate either candles or oil wicks, and any of the lights can be transformed into the *shamash* (the servitor light used to kindle the other ones) by the attachment of a small additional piece. As in the candlesticks, the vegetal forms here allude to the oil as well, which is central to the miracle that Jews celebrate at Hanukkah. When Antiochus IV Epiphanes conquered Israel, he desecrated the Temple, extinguished the light of the menorah, and broke all the oil vessels. No oil remained. When the Jews, led by Judah Maccabee, eventually defeated their enemies and reclaimed the Temple in Jerusalem, they wanted to rekindle the menorah but found only enough purified oil to last for a single day. But this tiny amount of oil lasted for the eight days that were required to produce a new supply of pure oil for the Temple. The floral motif in *Quya* is a reinterpretation of designs found on many traditional Hanukkah lamps, particularly those made in Frankfurt am Main, where Kahn's family originated (Fig. 63). These, in turn, were inspired by the biblical description of the lampstand made for the tabernacle, with "cups shaped like almond blossoms, each with calyx and petals" (Exodus 25:33).

Having considered traditional, organic, and decidedly more feminine associations in *Quya*, Kahn's second design for a Hanukkah lamp, *Quya II* (1996; Fig. 64), took the opposite direction. *Quya II* explores the historical and military associations of Hanukkah, rooted as it is in the episode of the Jews' successful revolt in 165 BCE against the Greco-Syrian rulers of Judaea. The *shamash* sits

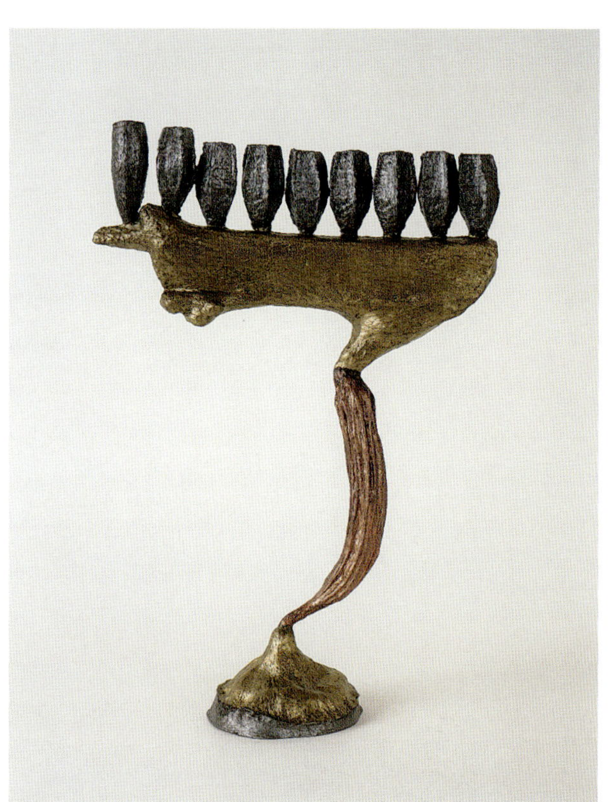

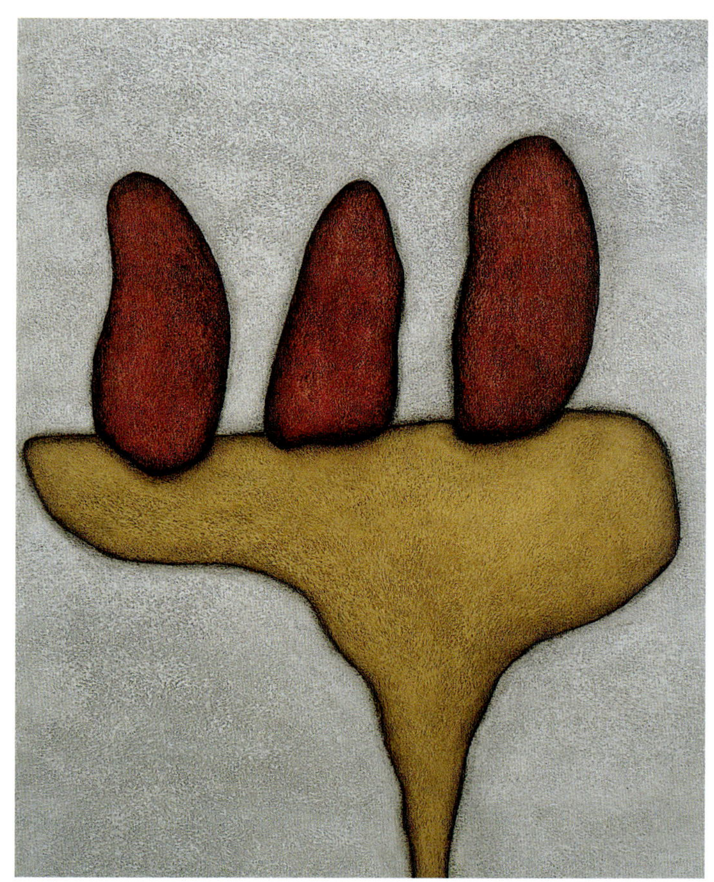

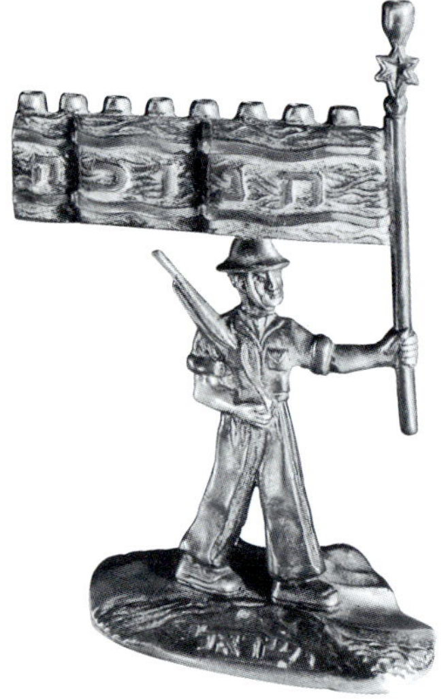

Fig. 64
Quya II, 1996

Fig. 65
Alyz, 1996

Fig. 66
Hanukkah lamp, Israel, 1950s

on the tip of a roughly hewn piece of wood, which resembles driftwood, weathered by time, reinforcing the lamp's evocation of history. This wood has a decidedly aggressive thrust, reminiscent of a rifle.[51] The curving shaft is shaped like a bow, terminating in a shieldlike base. With its military allusions, *Quya II* resembles the Hanukkah lamps produced (most likely for the tourist market) during the first decades after the establishment of the State of Israel (Fig. 66). These lamps featured soldiers, linking the modern Jewish warriors with their freedom-fighting Hasmonean ancestors. Yet *Quya II* also resembles a painting Kahn did that year, *Alyz* (1996; Fig. 65), demonstrating the process of cross-fertilization by which Kahn's paintings and ceremonial objects enrich one another.

Kahn's various solutions to the design of Hanukkah lamps emphasized the different meanings inherent in the festival. Likewise, in the numerous cups he has created, the choice of motifs reflects the cup's particular ritual function. *Rahva* (1998; Fig. 67, Plate 25) is a wedding cup, designed to hold the wine that bride and groom share under the *huppah*, their first joint act as husband and wife. The cup is nestled between two fingerlike branches that join together, reflecting marriage's challenge of union coexisting with individuality. On closer inspection, the figurative elements become clearer, and one notices that the stem supporting the cup takes the form of an abstract angel, one of Kahn's favored motifs.

Rkadh (1998; Fig. 68, Plate 20) is a Miriam's cup, a new type of ceremonial object for the Passover seder, developed by Jewish feminists in their effort to introduce ritual practices that express an egalitarian Judaism.[52] The Miriam's cup is filled with water to symbolize Miriam's miraculous well that, according to the midrash, accompanied the Israelites and sustained them during their wanderings in the desert. The Bible describes Miriam, sister of Moses and Aaron, as she led the Israelite women in song and dance after the crossing of the Red Sea: "Then Miriam the prophetess, Aaron's sister, took a timbrel in her hand, and all the women went out after her in dance and with timbrels. And Miriam chanted for them: Sing to the Lord, for He has triumphed gloriously; horse and driver He has hurled into the sea" (Exodus 15:20–21). It is this image that Kahn has presented in

Fig. 67
Rahva, 1998

Fig. 68
Rkadh, 1998

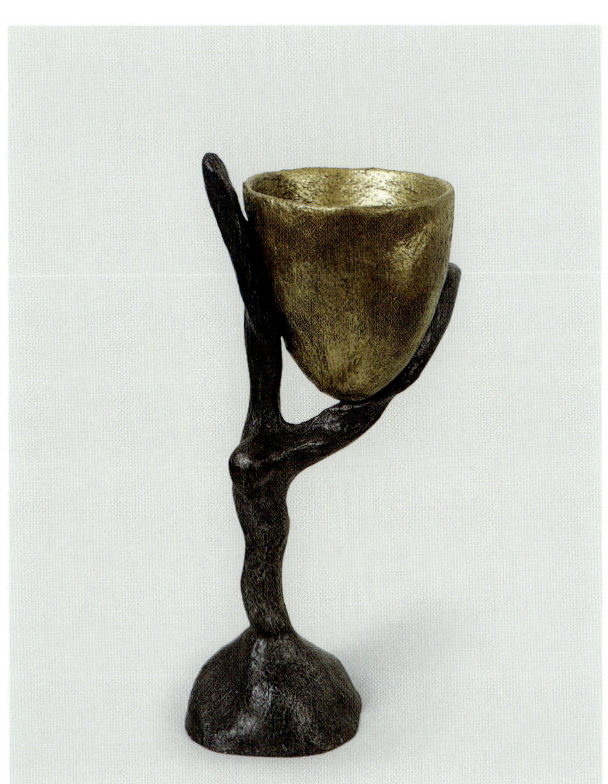

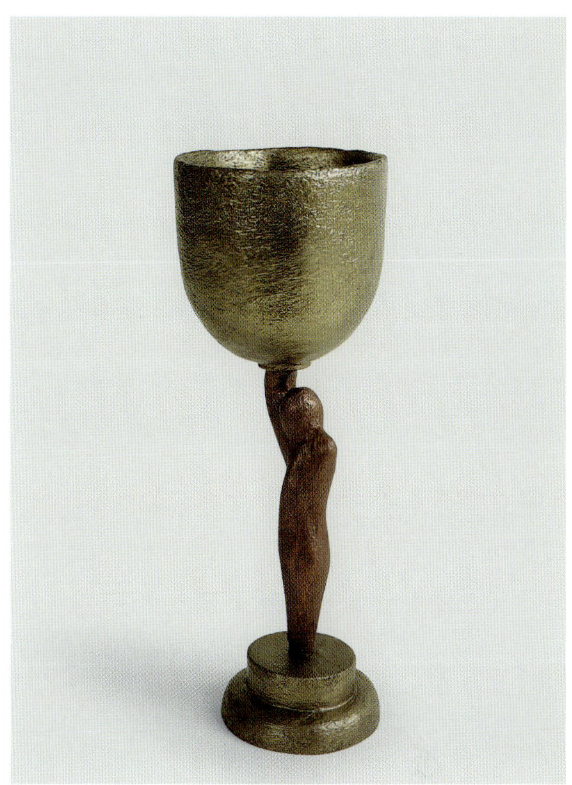

Rkadh, the cup's stem consisting of a female figure with her hands raised over her head, holding a tambourine.

The Miriam's cup was conceived to complement the traditional Elijah's cup, so Kahn linked it visually to an Elijah's cup he had created two years earlier (Fig. 69) by incorporating a similar stepped base. *Vayti* was inspired by Egyptian motifs and designed to work as an ensemble with *Erhu* (1996; Fig. 70, Plate 18), a three-tiered seder plate. Each tier holds one of the matzot (unleavened bread), with groups of three stylized Egyptian figures resting on the top tier, holding aloft dishes for the symbolic foods of the seder meal. Similar stylized figures serve as the feet and interim supports of the three levels. *Erhu* is derived from a particular type of traditional silver German and Austrian seder plate (Fig. 71). Kahn has radically simplified the caryatid figures, basing them on Egyptian sculptures he studied at the Metropolitan Museum of Art. Thus he enlisted the Israelites' former enslavers to help "carry" the ceremony celebrating freedom.[53] Instead of the round trays, Kahn substituted square ones, whose texture simulates that of the matzot.[54]

The ancient roots of much Jewish practice are expressed in a number of "Avoda" objects. The series of Torah pointers (*yads*) (Plate 4) Kahn created over the years resemble pieces of ancient bone or utensils found at an archaeological site. *Tyla* (1996; Fig. 72, Plate 7), Kahn's hand-washing set, was inspired by the biblical episode in which Abraham washes the feet of the angels who visit the patriarch incognito, to inform him that he and Sarah will have a son (Genesis 18). "What would Abraham have used to wash the feet of his visitors?" Kahn wondered. The forms of the set resemble archaeological artifacts excavated in Israel (Figs. 73, 74) but also relate to Kahn's student experiments in ceramics (Fig. 77).

In *Dahsa* (1998; Fig. 76, Plate 16), the bird finial on Kahn's case for the Purim megillah (scroll with the text of the Book of Esther) was also inspired by archaeological finds (Fig. 75). At the same time, there is a painted design of playful forms that seem to play tag with one another around the cylindrical case. The "Avoda" objects created for the celebration of Purim share this whimsical

Fig. 69
Vayti, 1996

Fig. 70
Erhu, 1996

Fig. 71
Three-tiered seder plate, Vienna, 1807

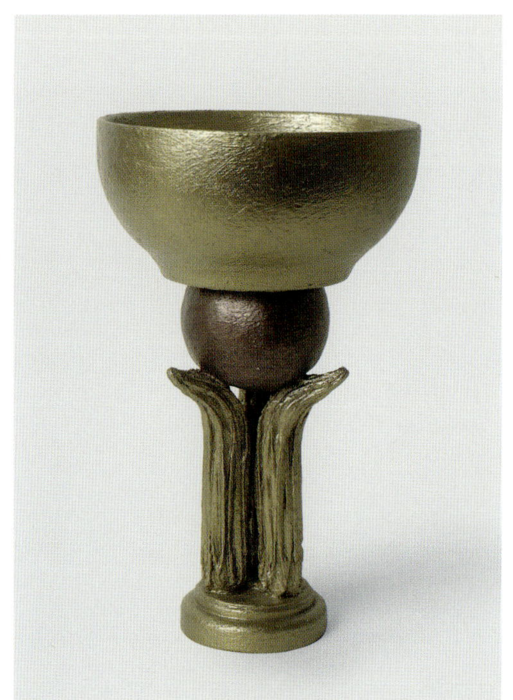

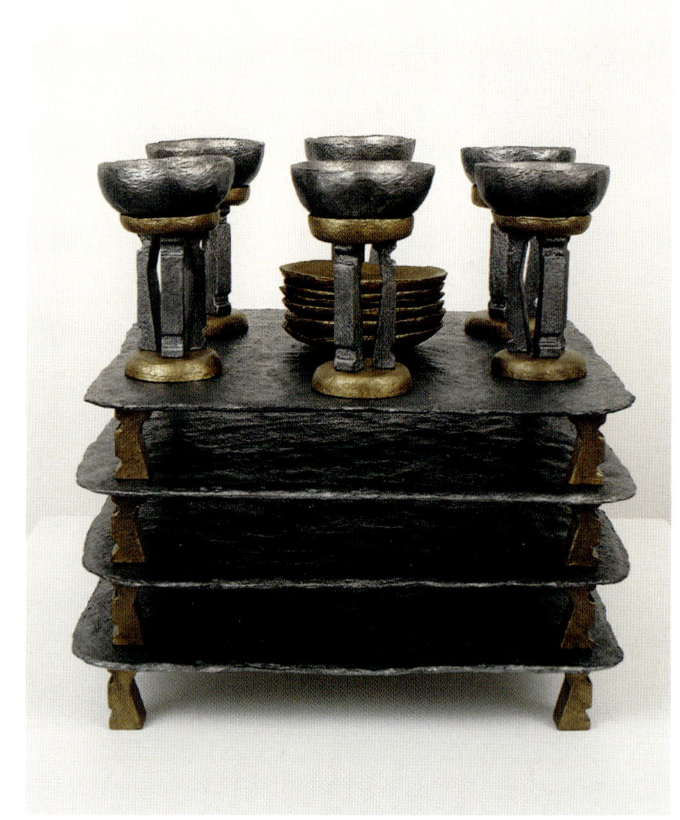

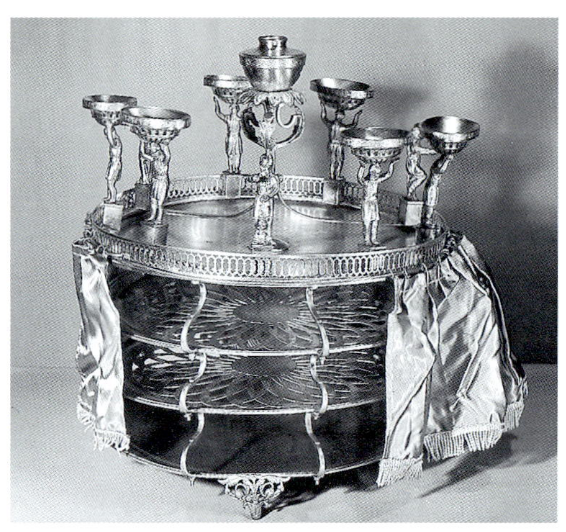

Fig. 72
Tyla I, II, III, IV, 1996

Fig. 73
Wide-mouth juglet or cup, ancient Israel, Hasmonean or early Roman period, third century BCE–first century CE

Fig. 74
Bowl, ancient Israel, Hasmonean or early Roman period, mid-second century BCE–mid-first century CE

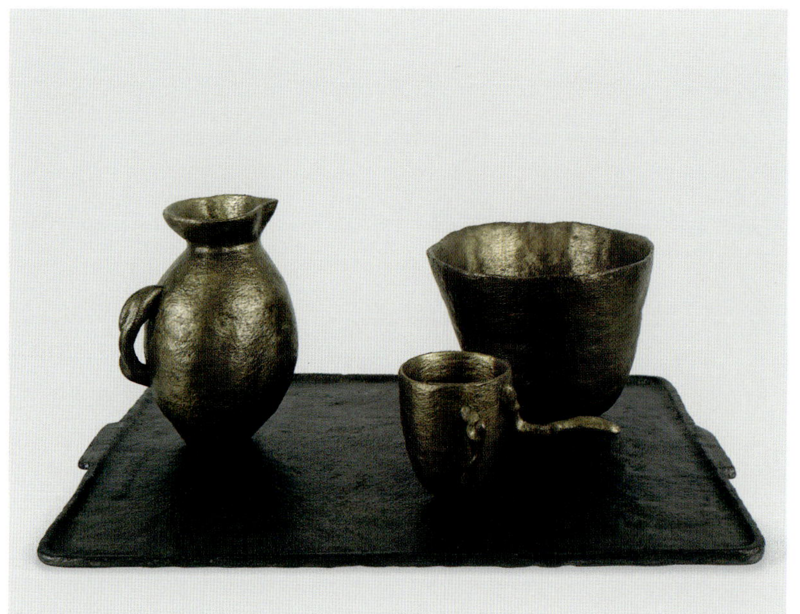

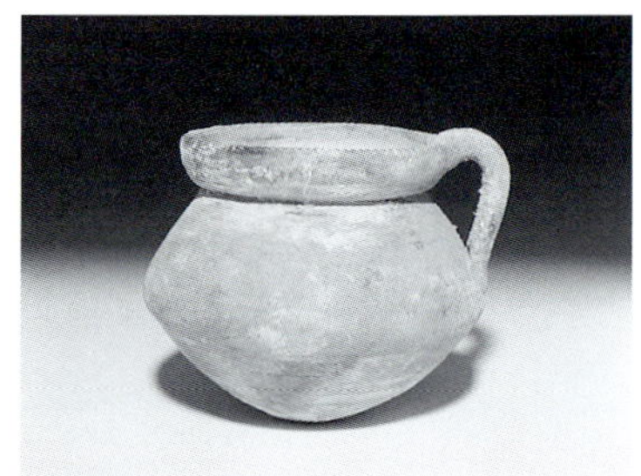

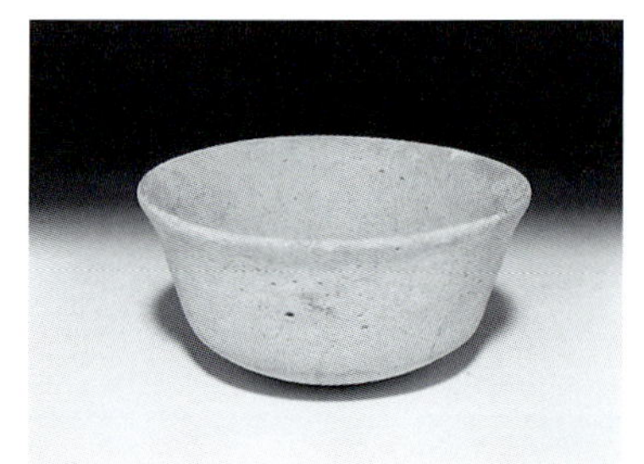

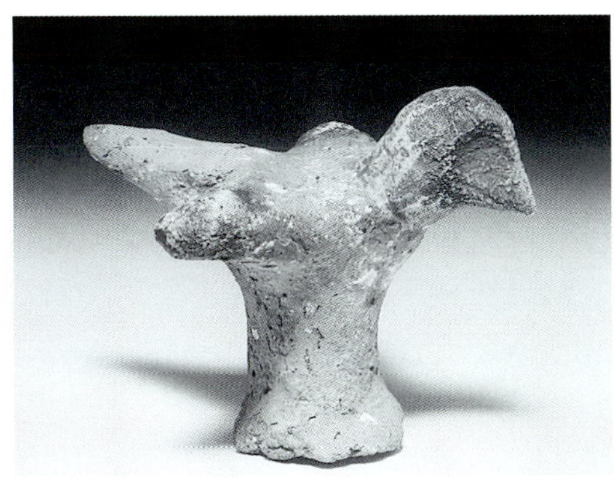

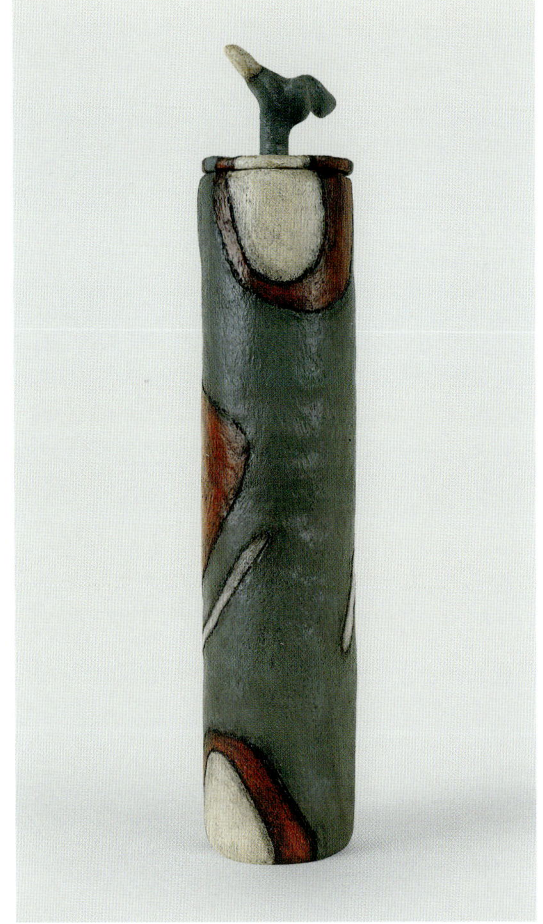

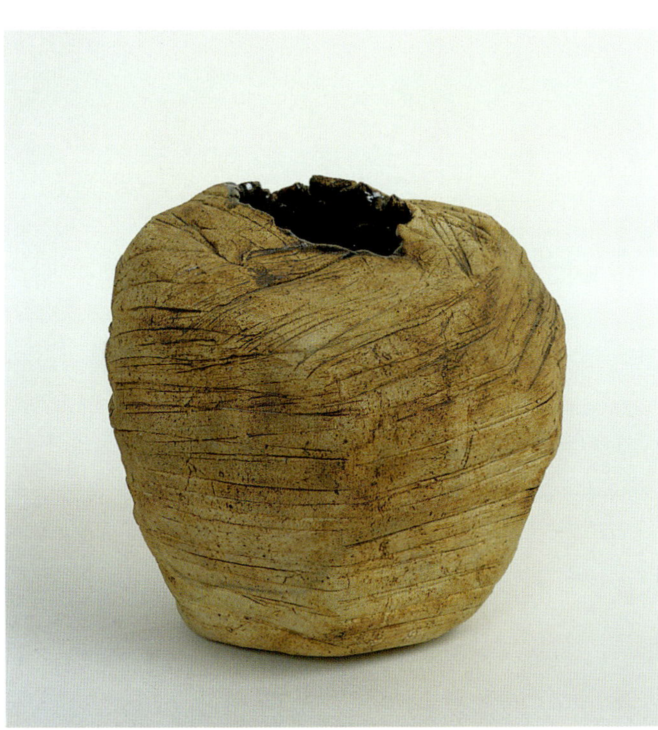

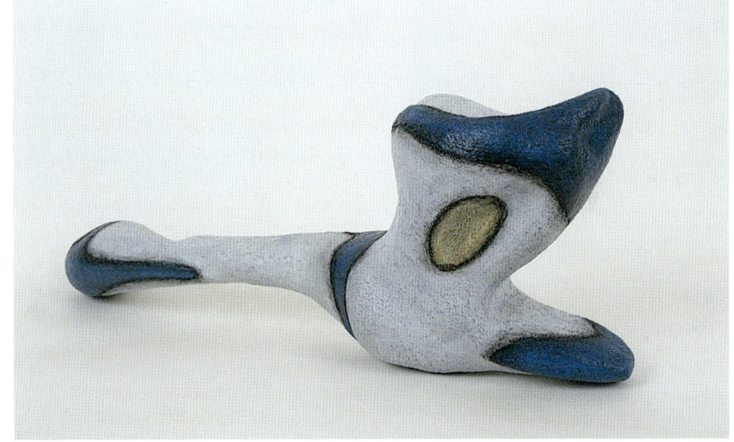

Fig. 75
Bird figurine, ancient Israel, Iron II A-C, 1000–700 BCE

Fig. 77
Enclosure VII, 1975

Fig. 76
Dahsa, 1998

Fig. 78
Aasha II, 1999

Fig. 79
Gal-Gal, 1993

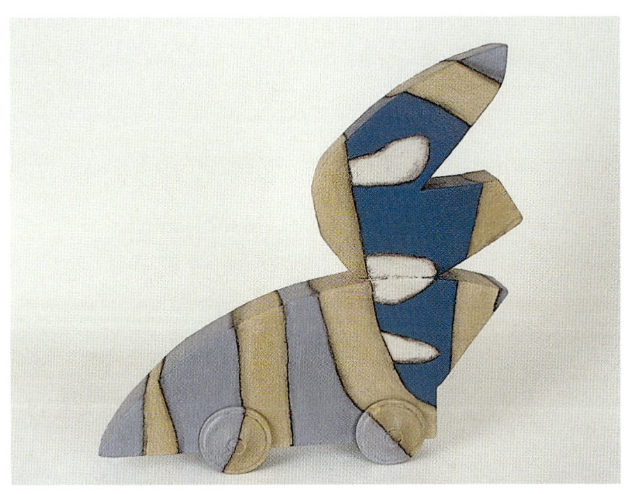

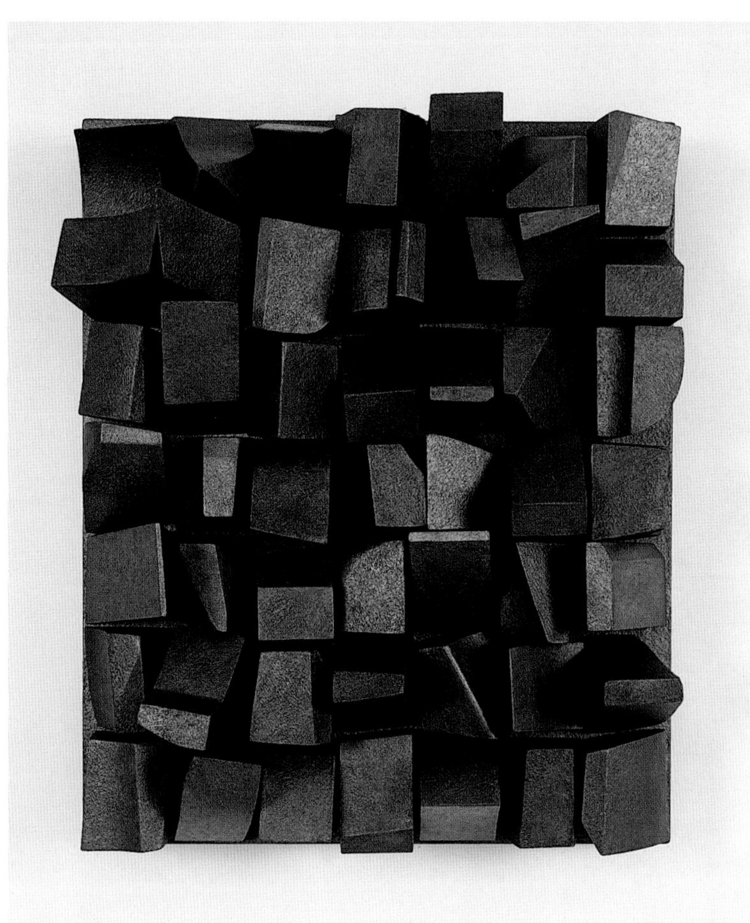

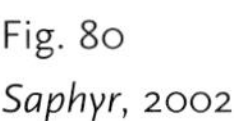

Fig. 80
Saphyr, 2002

quality, in keeping with the spirit of the holiday, and rely on strategies of shape and decoration similar to those Kahn employed in his children's toys; compare, for example, the Purim grogger (noisemaker) *Aasha II* (1999; Fig. 78) and the pull-toy *Gal-Gal* (1993; Fig. 79). *Aasha II*'s hammerlike shape is a reference both to the contemporary Israeli custom of bonking people with plastic hammers on Purim, and to the comical browbeating of Haman, the villain of the Purim story, by his wife, Zerash. Kahn's Purim pieces also recall some of the outdoor sculptures created by Nikki de St. Phalle in their joyful exuberance allied with a touch of the sinister, a combination that seems particularly appropriate for Purim.[55] This festival commemorates the deliverance of the Jews of Persia from the evil Haman, who had planned to annihilate them. But in the celebratory aftermath, as described in the Book of Esther, all is turned on its head by means of costume, drunken revelry, and the violent revenge the Jews took on their enemies. Even today's peaceful celebrations take on a raucous edge, as Jews are commanded to drink until they cannot tell the difference between the evil Haman and the hero of the story, the righteous Mordecai.

A NEW APPROACH

Kahn's most recent ceremonial objects have been influenced by his increasing involvement in designing and constructing sacred spaces (see below), as is evident in his omer counter *Saphyr* (2002; Fig. 80). An omer counter is used to mark each of the forty-nine days between the second day of Passover and the first day of Shavuot (the Feast of Weeks), between the first spring grain harvest of barley and the second spring grain harvest of wheat in ancient Israel.[56] The agricultural basis was augmented by the historical and spiritual transitions associated with the events commemorated by the two festivals: Passover celebrates the passage from slavery to freedom, and Shavuot recalls the receiving of the Law at Mount Sinai. This period of seven weeks is characterized by abstinence: observant Jews refrain from cutting their hair, and marriages are generally not performed. It is a

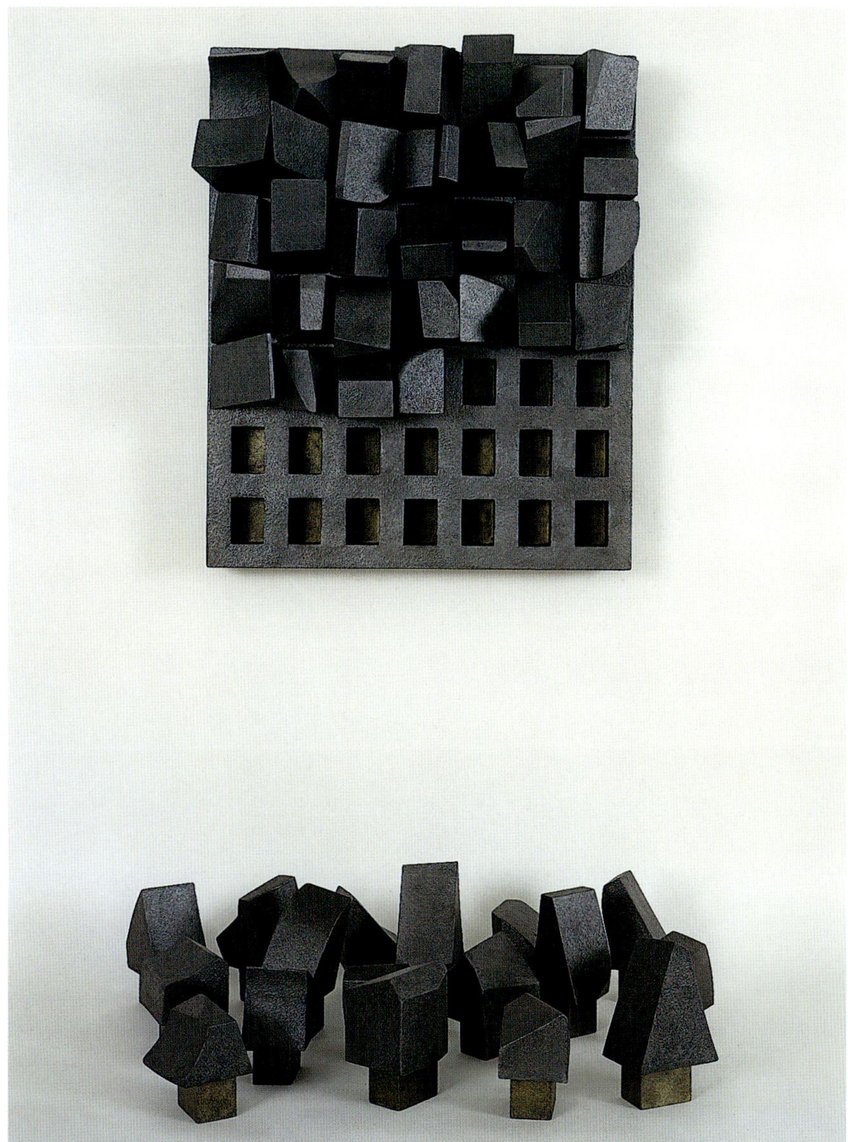

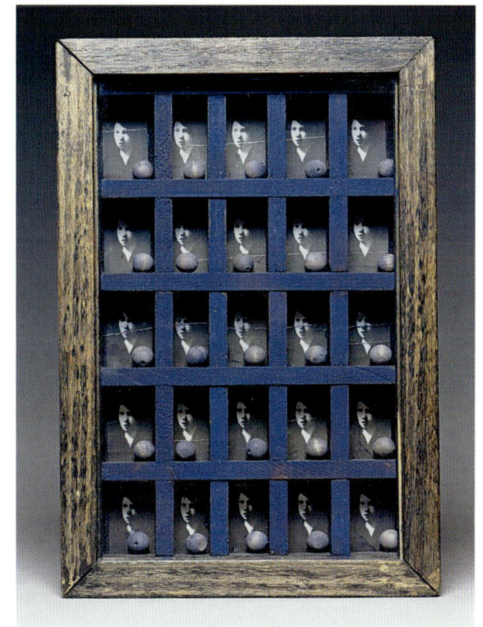

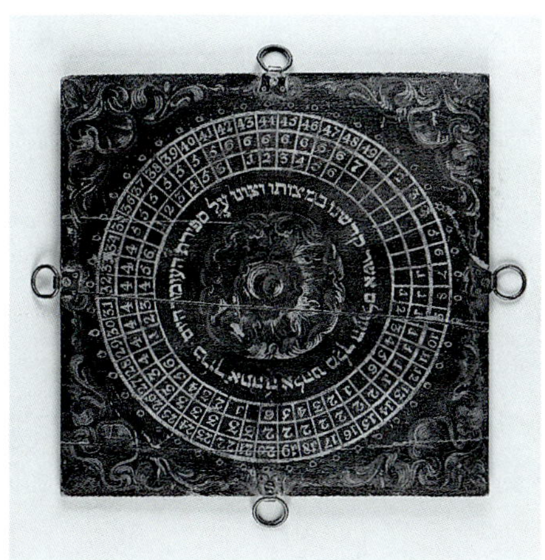

Fig. 81
Saphyr, 2002

Fig. 82
Joseph Cornell, *Untitled (Caravaggio Boy)*, c. 1953

Fig. 83
Omer calendar, Holland, eighteenth century

time of moral gravity, emphasizing the link between freedom and the acceptance of responsibility, between the liberation from Egyptian bondage and the receiving of the Law.

Kahn's omer counter is conceived as a large rectangular grid, with seven rectangular apertures running along each of the seven rows. Each of these forty-nine openings represents one of the days of the period of the omer and is fitted with a sculptural peg. Though each sculptural unit is unique, they are machine-cut and later sanded and shaped, not whittled, as is Kahn's usual practice. Kahn conceived of each piece as a little house, and some are ominous, even threatening, with sharp, pointy edges. Perceiving the work with all pegs in place, one senses movement across its surface, like a wave.

There is an insistent heaviness and seriousness in the work, befitting the mood associated with this period in the Jewish year. Kahn mobilizes the grid—practically an icon of cool and detached Minimalism—and infuses it with the literal and spiritual weight of each day of counting the omer. A grid loaded with such resonant forms has a spiritual affinity with Joseph Cornell's box constructions, filled with everyday found objects that evoke childhood memories and personal associations (Fig. 82).[57]

Traditional omer counters generally consist of a box holding a scroll marked with each of the forty-nine days; with each passing day, the scroll is turned to the next day. In Kahn's counter, each day is marked by removing the appropriate peg from its slot and placing it between the fittings along the top edge of the grid (Plate 21). The closest forerunner of Kahn's system is an eighteenth-century Dutch example, consisting of a wood tablet with the days marked in boxes arranged around the circumference

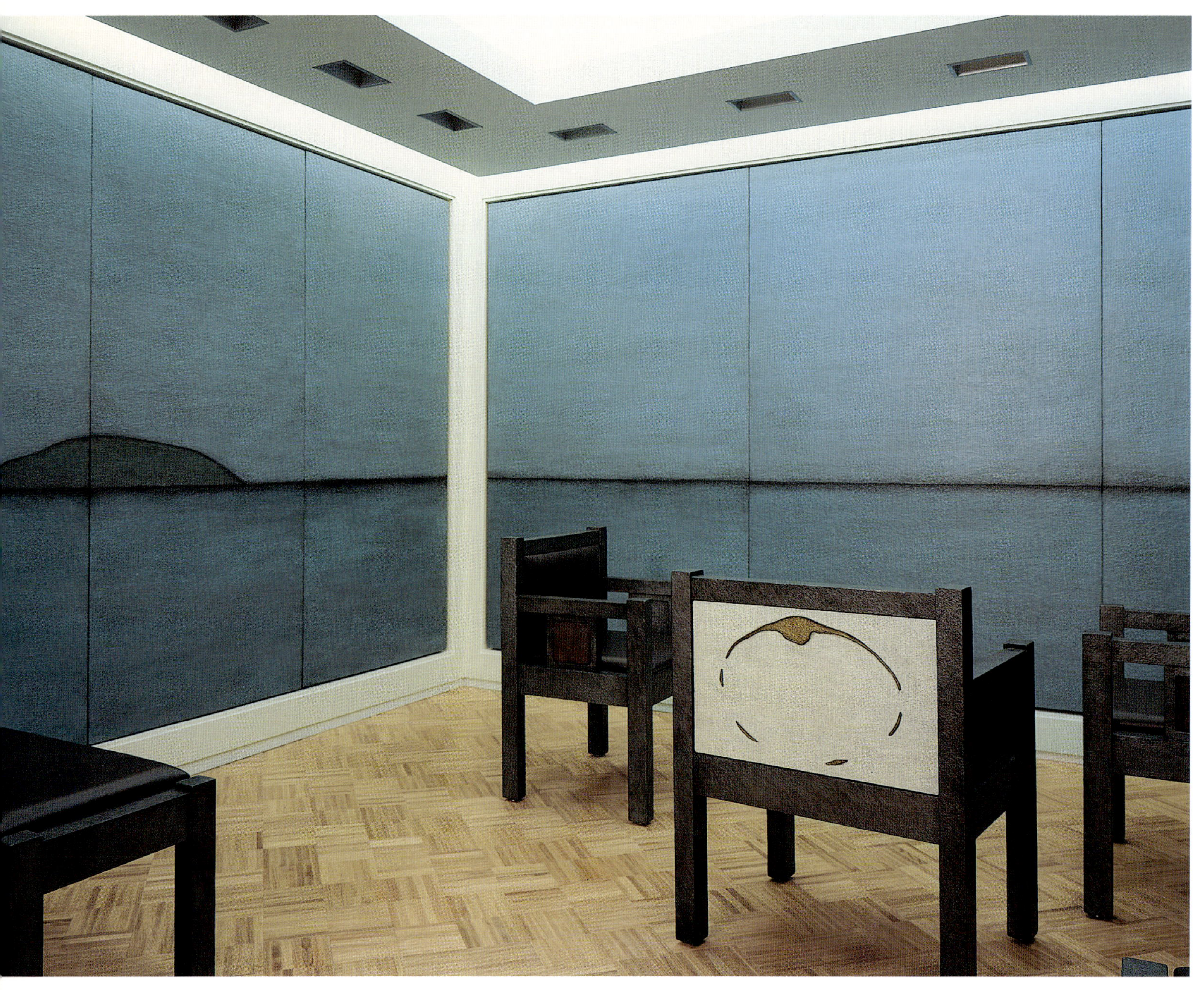

Fig. 84, 85
Meditative Space,
HealthCare Chaplaincy,
New York, 2002

of a circle; each day is counted by moving a small pin around the outer edge of the circle and placing it in the hole appropriate for that day (Fig. 83).

Among Kahn's innovations is his insistence on "seeing" all forty-nine days at once in the grid. He has described this piece as a "Jewish abacus," and the analogy is apt. In touching and moving the beads of an abacus, we "feel" each number. Whoever uses Kahn's omer counter has a tactile encounter with time as each day passes and each peg is removed and placed along the top edge. The visualization of time's passage is both linear, as the seven weeks are marked out, and circular, as the process repeats itself year after year. When it is not in use, the omer counter remains on the wall like a sculpture, awaiting the next Passover to resume the counting.

Like so many of Kahn's ceremonial objects, the omer counter emphasizes the participation of the user; it requires activation. After Kahn had finished the piece, a new way of using it occurred to him: arranging all the pieces on the floor and placing each peg in its allotted slot day by day over the seven weeks (Fig. 81). This alternate use would require devoting an entire room to the process of counting the omer, transforming the work from a single object into an installation/performance piece, with an added emphasis on the "performer's" interaction with the space.

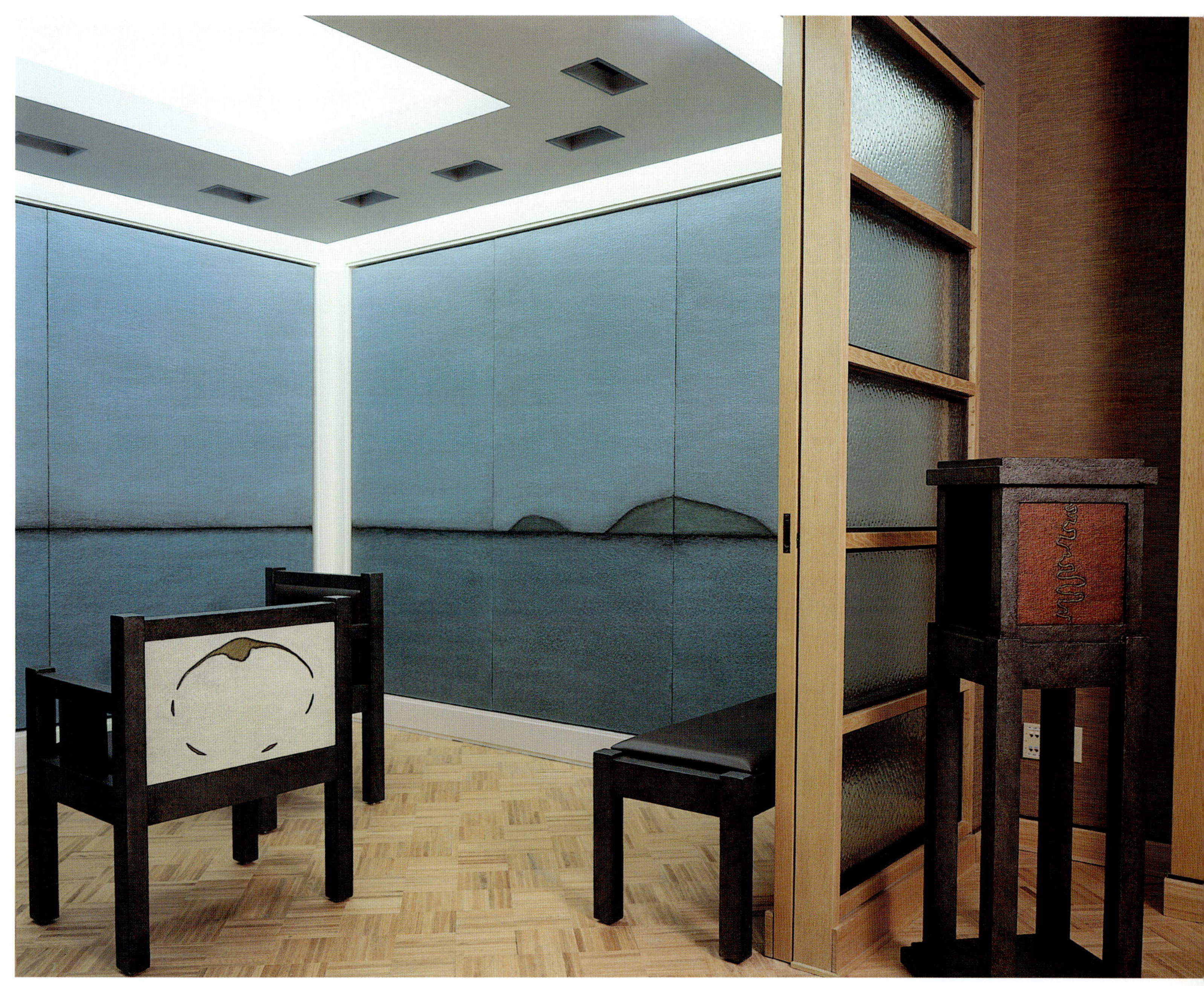

CREATING SACRED SPACE

Most recently, Kahn's artistic focus has been the creation of a number of site-specific sacred spaces.[58] The first, completed in 2002, is a meditative space for the HealthCare Chaplaincy in New York City, a place of retreat and quiet reflection for the clergy of many faiths who serve the city's hospitals, hospices, and clinics (Figs. 84, 85, Plate 27). This commission provided an opportunity for Kahn to integrate many of the elements that had preoccupied him in his painting, sculpture, and ceremonial objects, but now in the context of a total environment. The space is dominated by painted murals on three walls. Kahn collaborated on elements of the interior design, such as flooring, ceiling, and the sliding glass doors that constitute the fourth wall, and he created seating and a stand for holy books just outside the entrance. (See Terrence Dempsey's description of this project, p. 68.)

The primary theme of the HealthCare Chaplaincy murals is sky and water, imagery that Kahn has been developing in many guises over the years (Figs. 39, 45). Kahn had already begun to envision this motif as the basis of a series, and in 1999 he developed it for an installation at the Albright-Knox Art Gallery in Buffalo as part of an exhibition entitled "Landscape at the Millennium."[59] The Buffalo installation (Fig. 86), like the HealthCare Chaplaincy that followed, involved coordinating sky/water imagery within a specific space and taking into account the visitor's shifting view and

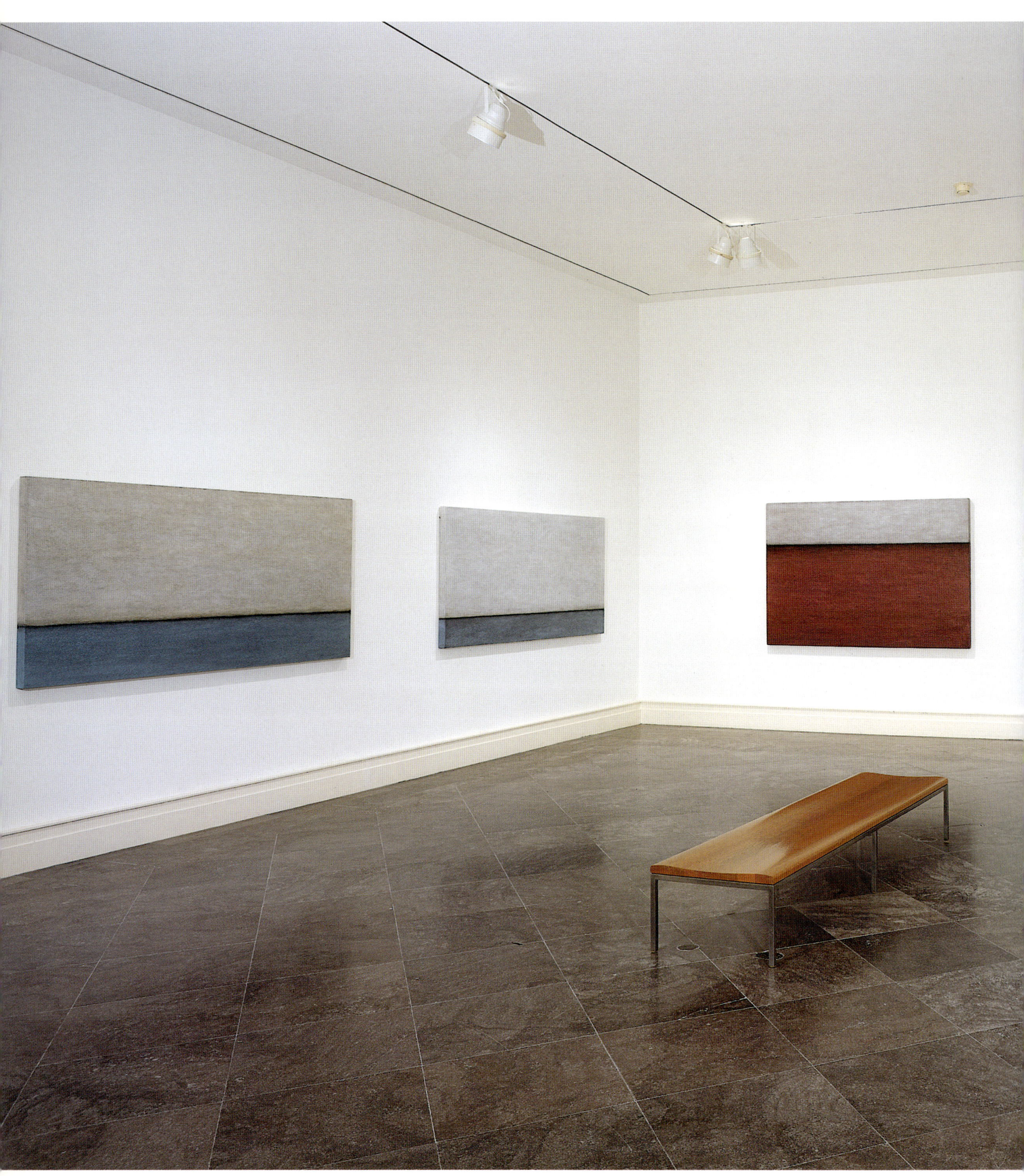

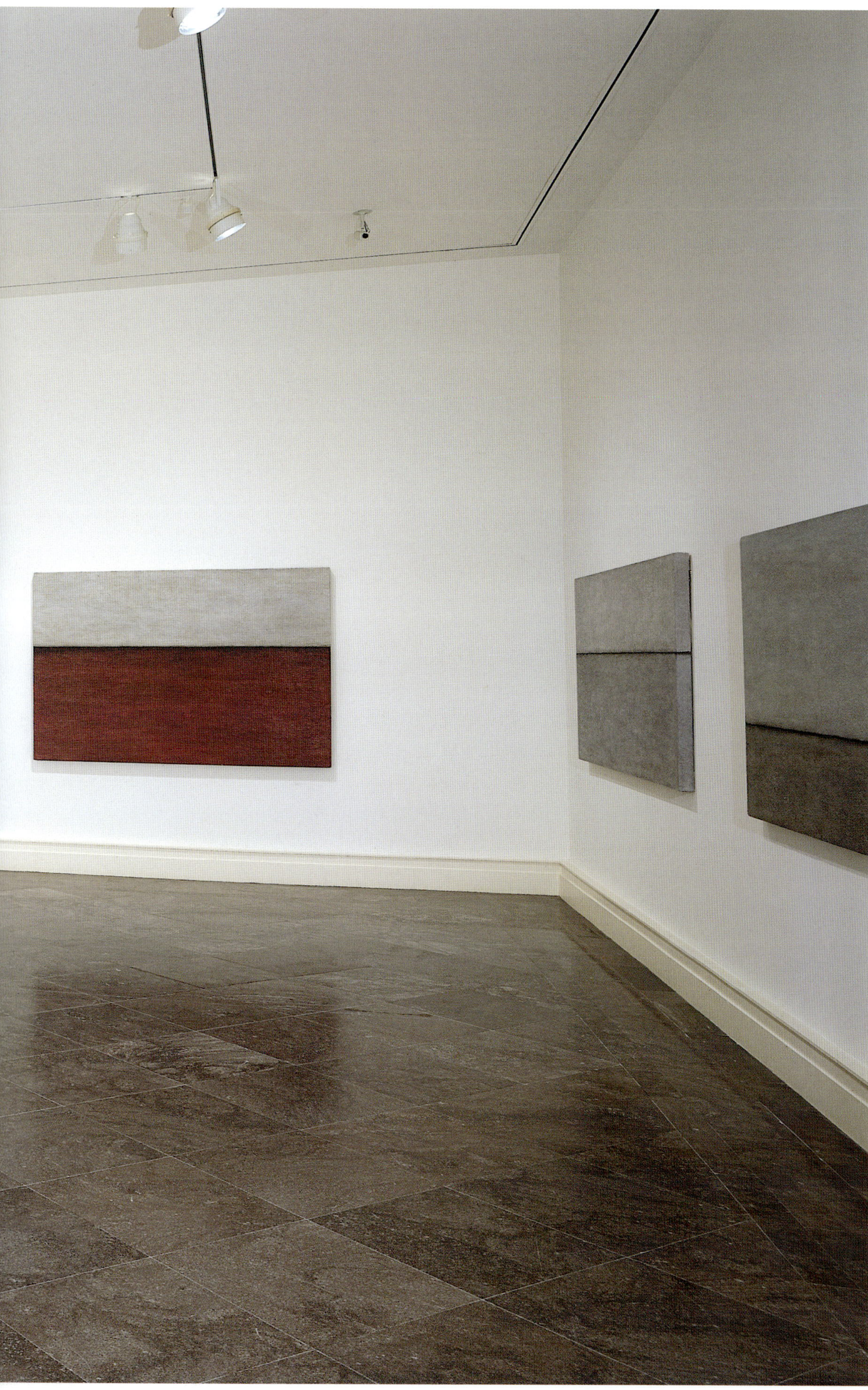

Fig. 86
Sky and Water, for "Landscape at the Millennium" exhibition, Albright-Knox Art Gallery, Buffalo, New York, 1999

responses while moving about the gallery. The paintings installed in Buffalo employ a range of colors, with blues, grays, and even red for the water. The demarcation of the horizon varies greatly in each painting, and with these modulations, the viewer's relationship to the paintings and to the space changes as well.

Kahn has commented on the way the series developed: "Unlike other series I've done, the sky, the land, and water images are indeed reductive. Yet they're complicated in the sense that as color varies with time of day, the possibilities become endless. At a certain point, in its most minimal form, the image becomes something else, more abstract, more suggestive."[60] In the Buffalo installation, Kahn explored the effects of shifts in orientation and color on the viewer's emotional responses: "I would like the installation to embody a range of emotions, from tranquil to turbulent, based on the same place seen at different times of the day and year. I'm also interested in what people bring to the work and the power of landscape to act as a vehicle for some kind of emotional transformation."[61] Kahn's comments about observing the same place under varying conditions reveal an affinity with Claude Monet's series and the mural projects on the theme of his water garden at Giverny.[62]

Kahn's desire to initiate an emotional transformation in the viewer through the sky/water motif became a key element in creating a meditative room for the HealthCare Chaplaincy. The goal was to foster a sense of calm and well-being for the chaplains, ministers, rabbis, and imams using the space, to provide a respite from the emotionally depleting work of ministering to the city's sick and troubled. The even horizon line and Kahn's choice of palette for the room, focusing on closely related hues of a soothing blue, result in an experience at once cleansing and transcendent.

One is reminded again of the blue seascapes of Caspar David Friedrich (Fig. 46). The effect is similar to Friedrich's work, which Hugh Honour has described as "timeless moments of frozen tranquility."[63] Sitting in the meditative space, we are like figures in Friedrich's paintings, looking out toward the horizon. Mark Rothko's hovering veils of color and the works of Barnett Newman can be seen as catalysts for Kahn's murals. Indeed, in creating a sacred space, the precedents of the Rothko Chapel in Houston and Newman's *Stations of the Cross* are inescapable.[64]

It is important to note that in the meditative space, unlike the Albright-Knox installation, Kahn retains recognizable and tangible forms. He does not abandon us to the abyss, but provides an anchor in the islands visible on the horizon. If we look straight ahead, the view is of an infinite void; but looking to either side, we sight land, a metaphor perhaps for the mission and good works of the HealthCare Chaplaincy itself. In the end, human beings need not be alone. That is the message of community, and it is what endows so much ritual with its power. One can relate this message to the utopian vision of modern art movements that strive to marry the functional and the beautiful, to make works of art that are also utilitarian objects, and to enhance life by creating meaning through ritual and ennobling ritual by honoring it with beautiful and meaningful objects.

Kahn is an inherently optimistic artist, and art has a role to play in *tikkun olam*, repairing or perfecting the world. Kahn's objects of the spirit are life-affirming. As Jews are commanded: "I have put before you life and death. . . . Choose life" (Deuteronomy 30:19).

1. Paul Gauguin, letter to Emile Schuffenecker, August 14, 1888; cited in John Rewald, *Post-Impressionism from Van Gogh to Gauguin* (New York: Museum of Modern Art, 1956), p. 196.

2. Kurt Hiller, "Ausstellung der Pathetiker," *Die Aktion*, 2 (November 27, 1912), col. 1515. All translations are by the author, unless otherwise indicated.

3. Secular objects have been transformed into Jewish ceremonial art by the addition of Hebrew inscriptions. Thus, wine goblets or vodka shot beakers have become kiddush cups, and sugar boxes have become etrog containers.

4. In this regard, Kahn is part of a much larger trend in the development of modern art, what James Hall has described as "the rise of object-based art in the twentieth century." See James Hall, *The World as Sculpture: The Changing Status of Sculpture from the Renaissance to the Present Day* (London: Chatto & Windus, 1999).

5. Tobi Kahn, quoted in Dominique Nahas, *Sacred Spaces*, exh. cat. (Syracuse, New York: Everson Museum of Art, 1987), pp. 14–15.

6. All translations from the Bible are taken from *Tanakh—The Holy Scriptures: The New JPS Translation According to the Traditional Hebrew Text* (Philadelphia, New York, and Jerusalem: Jewish Publication Society, 1988).

7. Jules Harlow, "Jewish Textiles in Light of Biblical and Post-Biblical Literature," in *The Fabric of Jewish Life: Textiles from The Jewish Museum Collection*, exh. cat. (New York: The Jewish Museum, 1977), p. 34.

8. *Shabbat* 133b.

9. In western Europe, where silversmiths and other artisans were controlled by the guild system, Jews were forbidden entry to the guilds. Thus, in Europe, Jews commissioned their ritual objects from non-Jewish craftsmen. In many Muslim lands, by contrast, Muslims were forbidden by their religion from engaging in these crafts, so the metalworkers were often Jews. See Vivian B. Mann, ed., *Morocco: Jews and Art in a Muslim Land*, exh. cat. (New York: The Jewish Museum, 2000), pp. 35 and 131ff.

10. See Martin Gilbert, *The Holocaust: A History of the Jews of Europe during the Second World War* (New York: Henry Holt and Company, 1985), p. 37.

11. Conversation with the artist, February 10, 2000; transcript, p. 14. In recent years, Kahn has been commissioned to create a number of Holocaust memorials; see Fig. 54.

12. Unless otherwise indicated, all quotations by Tobi Kahn are taken from a series of conversations between the author and the artist held between January 2001 and February 2002.

13. Isamu Noguchi, *A Sculptor's World*, with foreword by R. Buckminster Fuller (New York and Evanston: Harper & Row, 1968), p. 18.

14. When Kahn was working on the *huppah*, he turned to his father for an appropriate midrash. His father told him that one is the most holy on one's wedding day, and linked this state to the special sanctity of the altar in the ancient Temple. The absence of metal in the altar's construction is derived from the conviction that nothing that could be used to fashion a weapon should be incorporated into this most holy of sites.

15. After his wedding, Kahn made this *huppah* available to friends for their own nuptials.

16. See Norman Kleeblatt and Vivian B. Mann, eds., *Treasures of The Jewish Museum*, exh. cat. (New York: Universe Books, 1986), p. 52.

17. Compare the interior doors of a Renaissance Torah ark from Urbino, Italy, in Vivian B. Mann, "The Recovery of a Lost Work," *Jewish Art*, 12–13 (1986/87), pp. 269–78, esp. Fig. 8. The motif of the tablets of the Law also appears frequently on Torah ark curtains, as in the example from Venice, 1698/99 (Fig. 10, above), where the golden hues of the tablets of the Law, and the whitish blue clouds above, find an echo in the color of mountains and sky in *Orah*.

18. The abundant use of gold in the ancient tabernacle as described in Exodus 25–27 is related by the Rabbis as underlining the tabernacle's role as expiation for the sin of creating the golden calf; see Harlow, "Jewish Textiles," p. 31.

19. The Bible refers to water descending from Mount Sinai, into which Moses threw the remains of the golden calf after he had ground it down into dust: "the brook that comes down from the mountain" (Deuteronomy 9:21). A river descending from Mount Sinai is depicted in an Italian Torah curtain from Venice dated 1634, and the image most likely derives from a tradition of Byzantine icons. See David Cassuto, "A Venetian *Parokhet* and Its Design Origins," *Jewish Art*, 14 (1988), p. 43, who notes the significance of the river: "The Torah is often figuratively identified with water, and if Mount Sinai signifies the giving of the Torah, the river flowing from it . . . symbolizes the flow of Torah to the entire world.

20. See midrash *Tehillim* 68:9 and parallels. *The Midrash on Psalms*, vol. 1, trans. from the Hebrew and Aramaic by William G. Braude (New Haven: Yale University Press, 1959), p. 543. In the seventeenth-century Venetian Torah curtain mentioned above (n. 19), tablets of the Law are depicted above three golden mountains. See Cassuto, "A Venetian *Parokhet*," pp. 35–43. Cassuto, however, does not see three separate mountains, but "Mount Sinai tak[ing] the form of three summits side by side" (p. 35).

21. Peter Selz, "Tobi Kahn: Metamorphoses," in *Tobi Kahn: Metamorphoses*, exh. cat. (Lee, Massachusetts, and New York: Council for Creative Projects, 1997), p. 14.

22. See Charles C. Eldredge, "Nature Symbolized: American Painting from Ryder to Hartley," in *The Spiritual in Art: Abstract Painting 1890–1985*, exh. cat. (Los Angeles: Los Angeles County Museum of Art, 1986), pp. 113–29.

23. Quoted in Hugh Honour, *Romanticism* (New York: Harper & Row, 1979), p. 80.

24. See Joseph Leo Koerner, *Caspar David Friedrich and the Subject of Landscape* (London: Reaktion Books, 1990, 1995), p. 16. For an illuminating discussion of the *Tetschen Altarpiece*, see pp. 47ff.

25. Randall Suffolk, "The Seduction of Memory: Paintings by Tobi Kahn," exh. brochure (Glens Falls, New York: The Hyde Collection, Hoopes Gallery, 1997), n.p.

26. See, for example, a nineteenth-century double-seated bench from Bohemia, reproduced in David Altshuler, ed., *The Precious Legacy: Judaic Treasures from the Czechoslovak State Collections* (Washington, D.C.: Smithsonian Institution Traveling Exhibition Service, 1983), p. 198; and an eighteenth-century chair from northern Italy, reproduced in Vivian B. Mann, ed., *Gardens and Ghettos* (Berkeley: University of California Press, 1989), no. 118, ill. p. 266.

27. On Kahn's shrines, see Michael Brenson, "Survival Rites," in *Tobi Kahn: Metamorphoses*, pp. 34–37.

28. See *Robert Wilson's Visions*, exh. cat. (Boston: Museum of Fine Arts, 1991).

29. *Golg* is one of several works Kahn created related to the theme of the golem, the mythical Jewish figure formed of clay and animated by means of mystical incantations. The word "golem" is derived from the verse in Psalms 139:16: "Your eyes did see my 'golem,' " understood as God speaking to Adam, where the word "golem" refers to a being in the process of formation. The connections between this "golem" and a developing fetus create a conceptual link to support the visual relationship between *Golg* and *Natyh*. See Emily D. Bilski, *Golem! Danger, Deliverance and Art*, exh. cat. (New York: The Jewish Museum, 1988), esp. pp. 96 and 106–7 for Kahn's golem works.

30. Quoted in Lisa Dennison, *New Horizons in American Art: 1985 Exxon National Exhibition*, exh. cat. (New York: Solomon R. Guggenheim Museum, 1985), p. 58.

31. The photographs of Polish synagogues come from George Loukomski, *Jewish Art in European Synagogues (From the Middle Ages to the Eighteenth Century)* (London: Hutchinson & Co., 1947), pp. 76, 117—a book that Kahn keeps in his studio and whose influence he has acknowledged.

32. On tower-shaped spice containers, see *Towers of Spice*, exh. cat. (Jerusalem: Israel Museum, 1982).

33. Christos Doumas, *Cycladic Art: Ancient Sculpture and Pottery from the N. P. Goulandris Collection* (London: British Museum, 1983).

34. Although the Shabbat throne is not a traditional object type, it refers to the royal associations of the Sabbath as a queen.

35. The requirement is to light two or more lights to usher in the Sabbath, and Jews often employed hanging lamps with six lights. But for those lighting candles, two has become the customary number.

36. The emphasis placed on the marital relationship on Friday evening is expressed by the husband's recital of *Eshet Hayil* from the Book of Proverbs (31:10ff: "What a rare find is a capable wife! Her worth is far beyond that of rubies") and in the traditional custom of enjoying conjugal relations on Friday night.

37. The Hebrew word for the second principle, worship, is *avodah*, the overall term that Kahn chose for his works of ceremonial art. Other works in "Avoda" that incorporate the symbolic resonance of the number three include the etrog container *Hadahr* (Plate 14), with its three-tiered top and depiction of three fruits; the Hanukkah lamp *Quya* (Plate 15), constructed of three units with three lights each; and the tripartite division of each of the three wall paintings in the Healthcare Chaplaincy (Figs. 84, 85, 92).

38. "Rabbi Simon said: 'There are three crowns: the crown of Torah, the crown of priesthood, and the crown of royalty; but the crown of a good name excels them all' " (*Ethics of the Fathers* 4:17).

39. The challah tray *Ysha* has a complicated history, which reveals much about Kahn's working methods and the associative way in which his mind operates. It was first made in 1995 without the three dots. The image with the three dots as Kahn had developed it in the Shabbat throne took on an additional connotation with the birth of his third child, Doria, in 1998. For this reason, Kahn reworked the tray in 1998, adding the three dots as a reference to his three children.

40. The same image rendered in different colors appears elsewhere—for example, in *Takhula* (1992).

41. See Dore Ashton's discussion of what she terms "a figure-ground challenge" in Kahn's *Ohalim* (1995), in "Tobi Kahn's Matter and Memory," in *Tobi Kahn: Metamorphoses*, p. 33.

42. *Baytzah* 16a. This "extra soul" has been interpreted as increased spirituality and peace of mind, which enable the Jew to forget the cares of the week, and relax, enjoy, and draw sustenance from experiencing the Sabbath.

43. This notion of separation is central to Judaism. The prayer recited at havdalah (which literally means "separation"), the service concluding the Sabbath, makes this clear: "Blessed art thou, O Lord our God, King of the universe, who distinguishes between sacred and profane, between light and darkness, between Israel and other nations, between the seventh day and the six days of labor."

44. Kahn's mezuzah containers were also influenced by the traditional art of Japanese packaging, though here the relationship is more conceptual than purely formal. Hideyuki Oka, *Tsutsumu: An Introduction to an Exhibition of the Art of the Japanese Package*, exh. cat. (New York: Japan Society and the American Federation of Arts, 1975), has pride of place among the books in Kahn's studio. Conceptually, the relationship between this packaging art and the mezuzot can be discerned from Oka's book, which presents the utilitarian, aesthetic, and ritual aspects of a practice of packaging, once a part of everyday life in Japan: "The act of packaging an object becomes, then, a ritual of purification, of distinguishing the contents of the package from all similar objects that have not been purified" (p. 14).

45. *Ymah II* originated as a possible design for a mezuzah container commissioned by the Holocaust Museum in New York City (Museum of Jewish Heritage: A Living Memorial to the Holocaust), although the museum ultimately chose another of Kahn's mezuzah containers.

46. A variation of this image was included as the seventh canvas in the installation *Eyda*, seven paintings on the creation of the world, commissioned by Mitchell & Company, Boston, where it seems to refer to the creation of humanity.

47. For the adoption of the crucified figure as a motif used to express the suffering of Jews during the Holocaust, see Ziva Amishai-Maisels, *Depiction and Interpretation: The Influence of the Holocaust on the Visual Arts* (Oxford: Pergamon, 1993), pp. 178–97.

48. Exodus 28:33–34: "On its hem make pomegranates of blue, purple, and crimson yarns, all around the hem, with bells of gold between them all around: a golden bell and a pomegranate, a golden bell and a pomegranate, all around the hem of the robe."

49. An eternal light hangs in the synagogue, suspended before the Torah ark, and houses a light that is never extinguished. This derives from the biblical instruction: "You shall further instruct the Israelites to bring you clear oil of beaten olives for lighting, for kindling lamps regularly. Aaron and his sons shall set them up in the Tent of Meeting, outside the curtain which is over [the ark of] the Pact, [to burn] from evening to morning before the Lord. It shall be a due from the Israelites for all time, throughout the ages" (Exodus 27:20–21).

50. As with the eternal lights, Kahn associated the light with the olive oil that provided the fuel, developing the connection to the land and nature in his choice of forms.

51. In order for a Hanukkah lamp to be kosher—ritually fit—all of the eight lights (not including the *shamash*) must be on the same level. Though it appears that the last light on the end, next to the *shamash*, is higher than the other seven, the holder actually sits more deeply, ensuring that the light itself will be level with the other lights.

52. Passover, with its theme of passing from slavery to freedom, has been at the center of much feminist reinvention.

53. There are many precedents in the European decorative arts of the past centuries for basing caryatid figures on Egyptian prototypes. See, for example, *Egyptomania: L'Egypte dans l'art occidental 1730–1930*, exh. cat. (Paris: Musée du Louvre, 1994), no. 165, and pp. 284ff.

54. Kahn was familiar from childhood with another type of three-tiered plate, though without caryatid figures to support the food dishes: the carved olive-wood plates made in Palestine that were popular in Jewish homes in Germany during the first half of the twentieth century.

55. See, for example, Nikki de St. Phalle's *Golem*, a sculpture/children's slide installed in a Jerusalem neighborhood, featured in an exhibition on the golem, which also included examples of Kahn's works; Bilski, *Golem!*, esp. pp. 94, 97–98 for St. Phalle, and pp. 96, 106–7 for Kahn.

56. The word *omer* refers to the dry measure of barley that was brought as an offering to the Temple in Jerusalem every day during this seven-week period between the two pilgrimage festivals of Passover and Shavuot. The practice of counting each of the forty-nine days and reciting blessings each day is derived from Leviticus 23:15: "And from the day on which you bring the sheaf of elevation offering—the day after the Sabbath—you shall count off seven weeks. They must be complete."

57. There are many personal associations for Kahn connected with the period of counting the omer. He was born during this season of the Jewish year, and recalls how the talk he gave at his bar mitzvah focused on the question of whether the counting of the omer constitutes a single act or forty-nine separate acts. This analysis was in order to determine whether someone who attained the age of responsibility for performing mitzvot—the age of thirteen for a Jewish male, celebrated by the bar mitzvah ceremony—during the period of the omer was required to begin counting from the day he turned thirteen, or whether he would only be obligated to do so beginning the following year. (If counting the omer constitutes a single act, the latter would be true; if it consists of forty-nine individual acts, then the former would hold.) Kahn's omer counter could be understood as a visual response to this question in the interpretation of Jewish law. In a more lighthearted vein, Kahn also recalls how his grandmother encouraged each of her grandchildren to properly count all forty-nine days by rewarding those who complied with a cheesecake at the beginning of Shavuot (cheesecake being a traditional food associated with the festival).

58. Kahn is currently working on the design for a small chapel for Jane Blaffer Owen and the Blaffer Trust in New Harmony, Indiana.

59. The sky/water motif as the basis for a series and its relation to a primordial and biblical landscape can be related to the photographic *Seascape* series of Hiroshi Sugimoto: "The legend of the Tower of Babel says that all human beings once spoke the same language, but because we tried to reach the divine, we were punished and our languages were separated. My seascapes are before this happened"; interview with Sugimoto in *Sugimoto*, exh. cat. (Madrid: Fundación "La Caixa," 1998), p. 18.

60. Douglas Dreishpoon, "Interview with Tobi Kahn," in *Landscape at the Millennium: Installations by Tobi Kahn and Pat Steir*, exh. cat. (Buffalo: Albright-Knox Art Gallery, 1999), p. 21.

61. Ibid., p. 22.

62. Though Monet may not readily come to mind in relation to Kahn, there are other connections as well. Like Monet, Kahn is concerned with all aspects of his living environment. Moreover, a number of Kahn's paintings appear to constitute an homage to Monet's paintings of the cliff at Étretat (le Manneporte); see, for example, *Otza II* (1987), illustrated in *Tobi Kahn: Metamorphoses*, p. 46.

63. Honour, *Romanticism*, p. 82.

64. The spiritual affinities of Kahn's work to artists from Friedrich to Rothko, as well as their shared formal strategies, can be discerned in Robert Rosenblum's description of the northern Romantics: "The sense of divinity in boundless voids, where figures, objects, and finally matter itself are excluded, belongs to a Romantic tradition primarily sustained by non-Catholic artists—Protestants, Jews, or by members of such modern spiritualist sects as Theosophy—for the iconoclastic attitudes of these religions were conducive to the presentation of transcendental experience through immaterial images, whether the impalpable infinities of horizon, sea, or sky or their abstract equivalents in the immeasurable voids of Mondrian or Newman"; Rosenblum, *Modern Painting and the Northern Romantic Tradition: Friedrich to Rothko* (New York: Harper & Row, 1975), p. 212.

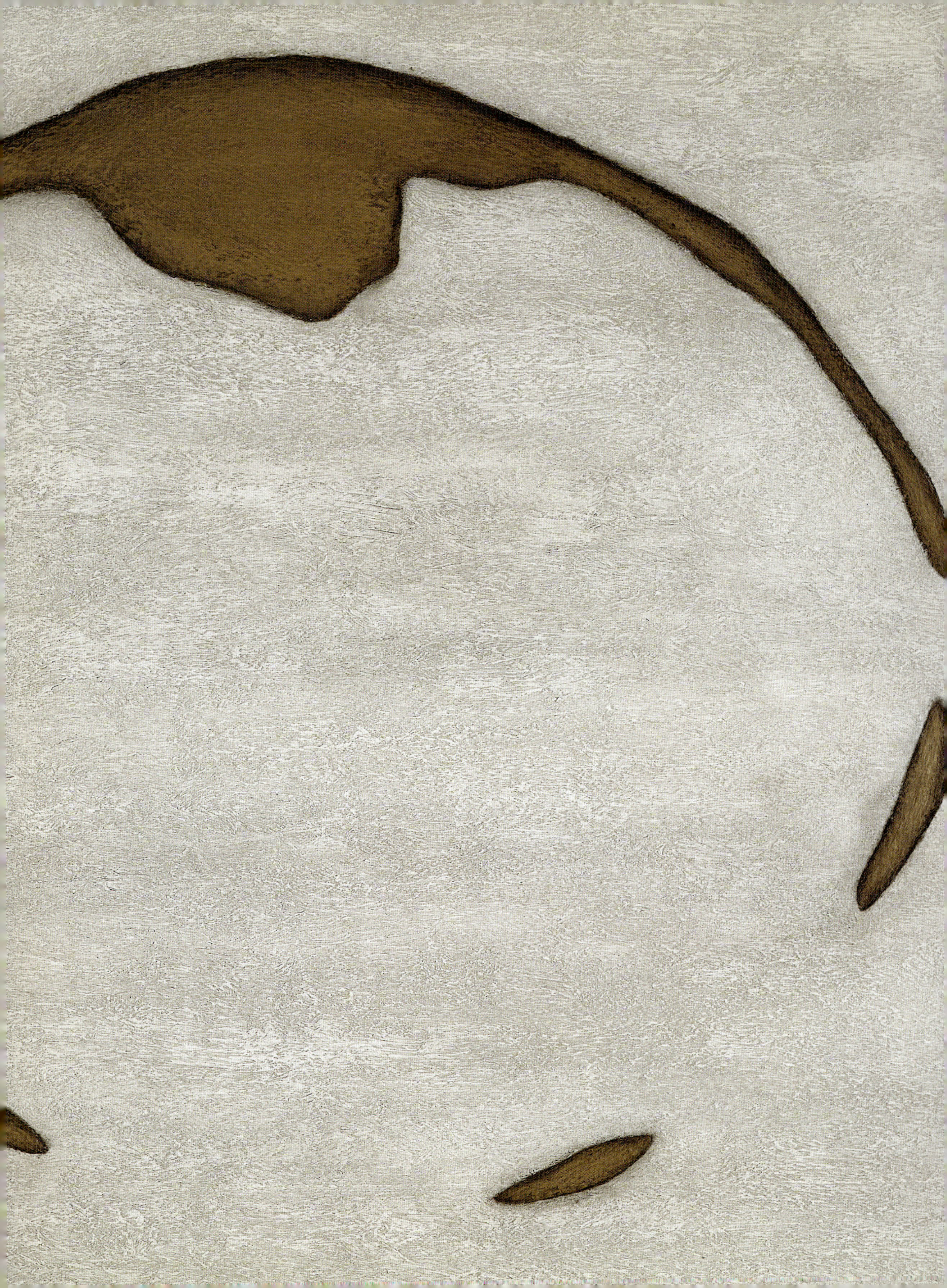

TERRENCE E. DEMPSEY, S.J.

Shaping the Sacred in Contemporary Art

In her January 7, 2001, *New York Times* article, "The Impenetrable That Leads to the Sublime," art critic Amei Wallach, writing on the Wolfgang Laib retrospective at the Hirshhorn Museum, states that "a sense of the sacred is alive and well in contemporary art."[1] Wallach concludes her article by remarking: "There is nothing new about art as spiritual practice except how hot the topic is becoming as the art world wakes up to its significance."[2]

Although many members of the art community have come to agree with Wallach's declaration, such an appreciation was not to be heard from the major critics, curators, and scholars in the 1970s, 1980s, and early 1990s. Yet during those years, artists—well known and little known—were involved in "art as spiritual practice." In spite of the radical formalistic art rhetoric espoused by Clement Greenberg and others that read all meaning out of a work except its materiality, many artists of our time are doing what great artists have done for centuries: fashioning forms that call upon our innate sense of metaphor to give meaning that goes far beyond the object being experienced. For some artists it is a departure from their normal interests, but for many it has become the substance of their work.

These artists are tapping into what anthropologist Ellen Dissanayake calls "artifying," the "shaping and enhancing [of] ordinary objects so that they are no longer ordinary but somehow extraordinary."[3] Dissanayake speaks of the making of art as necessary for human development because it sustains and enhances the species, and she speaks of its necessary connection to the emotions "since emotion is nature's way of making sure we care about and thus pay attention to vital subjects."[4] And the vital subjects to which Dissanayake refers have been the essential themes throughout human history: "love, birth, death, the body, the divine order, the moral order, the forces of nature, the unknown, the feared or the forbidden."[5]

Contemporary artists have continued that legacy. The styles vary from folk art to Minimalism, and the works are executed in a number of different media; some are accessible, while others maintain a hermeticism about them. What these artists all share, however, is a desire to engage with those themes that touch the deepest core of our humanity.

A significant number of artists involved in this "spiritual practice" have incorporated a sense of ritual into their works, and a major artistic dynamic in ritual is the creation of sacred objects and sacred environments. In their own works, these artists reflect the insights of Mircea Eliade, who, in his classic book *The Sacred and the Profane*, speaks of the culture of the Achilpa, a nomadic aboriginal tribe of Australia, and its need to link its world to the cosmos. What Eliade says about the Achilpa could also apply to people living in the modern world: "Life is not possible without an opening toward the transcendent; in other words, human beings cannot live in chaos."[6] In today's world, we can readily see the enormous toll that chaotic situations take on people when there is no sense of teleology. In contrast, artists have shaped ritual objects and spaces as means of entering into dialogue with mystery, of addressing the concerns of our mortality, of realizing some connection to a reality greater than ourselves, and of feeling inner peace.

Meditative Space,
HealthCare Chaplaincy,
New York, 2002
(detail, Figs. 84, 85; Plate 27)

THE BREACHING OF BOUNDARIES

Among the boundary walls erected by the world of modern art are two of major importance. The first is a bias against decorative or applied arts, those arts associated with objects that have a practical purpose. Often these arts are relegated to the second tier of prestige in the art world, giving way to the dominance of fine art that "exists as an end in itself."[7] As Thomas P. Campbell, curator of the highly successful 2002 Metropolitan Museum of Art exhibition "Tapestry in the Renaissance: Art and Magnificence," has said, such thinking is a modern construct. In the exhibition catalogue, Campbell states that "the tapestry medium has suffered from the emphasis placed by most schools of art history during the nineteenth and twentieth centuries on the fine arts at the expense of the decorative arts and from the associated emphasis on connoisseurship in the realms of painting and drawing."[8] Campbell speaks of the prestige of the tapestry in fifteenth- and sixteenth-century Europe: "If tapestry was the most widely commissioned figurative art form in the courts and chapels of the [Renaissance] period from Scandinavia to the Italian peninsula, it was also, in its finer forms, one of the most expensive."[9]

The terms "decorative arts" and "applied arts" are also misleading. To understand an object existing purely as an end in itself without a more pragmatic purpose is to discount much of art history. The greatest works by Grünewald, van Eyck, Campin, Giotto, Raphael, Michelangelo, Leonardo, El Greco, Caravaggio, and Rubens were "used to embellish an object that had a practical purpose"—namely, a chapel, an altar, or a refectory. They were not disembodied works of art floating in a modernist white box. They were not ends in themselves but functioned quite practically in a larger program. Objects from antiquity such as *Zeus Throwing the Thunderbolt* or the *Aphrodite of Knidos*, or the Panathenaic processional frieze on the Parthenon or the Buddhas and Bodhisattvas of Asia or the ancient burial figures in China, Egypt, and nearly all the known art of Mesoamerica —all these were intended to function within a very well thought-out and pragmatic context and not as ends in themselves. Today, however, boundaries are being broken. It was not so long ago that many objects from non-Western areas such as Africa and Oceania were relegated to anthropological museums; now encyclopedic museums such as New York's Metropolitan Museum of Art have created new galleries for these objects, where they are given the same dignity accorded to Western art.

The boundaries have also been breached in a second, related direction, in the realm of religious art—territory that, as we have seen, often coincides with the territory of the decorative and functional. This change exposes the long-standing discomfort, embarrassment, and even outright hostility of the modern art world toward religious art, especially religious art with personal or communal devotional or liturgical connections. Admittedly, much modern and contemporary liturgical art is uninspiring (although the same could quite legitimately be maintained about many objects claiming to be "fine art"), but a growing number of gifted artists have made "art as spiritual practice" by invoking the traditions in which they were raised or to which they have been drawn, honoring those traditions but articulating them in modern terms, not slavishly imitating a style from the past. Some artists have pursued a more syncretistic approach in their spiritual journeys by incorporating art and iconography from a variety of backgrounds. At times this can become a facile pastiche, a "cafeteria approach" often associated with New Age spirituality and against which world-religions scholar Huston Smith has spoken.[10] At other times, syncretism simply underscores the fact that no tradition is completely isolated from outside influences, whether it be the Hellenistic influences on the wall paintings of the third-century synagogue at Dura-Europos, or the incorporation of Roman river gods and the ancient Syrian custom of veiled hands in the fifth- and sixth-century Christian mosaics of Ravenna.

The modern art world's preference for opaqueness over clarity, inaccessibility trumping comprehension, is an understandable bias: art that is too clear, too obvious, can become reduced to a form of illustration and may trivialize that which is rich and complex. As the artist James Rosen has said, "I hope that my work illuminates rather than illustrates." There is much to be recommended in this approach. Often, art that becomes too literal tends to reduce the realm of mystery to a one-dimensional experience. Theologian David Tracy speaks of the religious experience in a similar way—that this experience is best described in terms of metaphor, of revelation and concealment. He encourages analogical language as a way of remaining open to a conversation and dialogue and thereby being open to the possible. Those expressions that are voiced with clarity and certainty close the door to the possible. The possible emerges through the language (whatever form it takes) of "scandal and mystery."[11]

Does this kind of analogical, metaphorical imagination close the door to accessibility? How are people to understand what they are seeing if they do not have some access to it? Is it so buried in mystery as to be hermetically sealed to most people? This is a dilemma that has been exacerbated by the variety of traditions—and the lack of traditions—that make up our society. In the art of the northern Renaissance, for example, viewers of works by Jan van Eyck, Rogier van der Weyden, and Robert Campin would see a continuity of color symbolism as well as the symbolism of objects, animals, and plants. This commonly understood visual vocabulary that was closely linked to a commonly held religious faith helped underscore the principal understandings of that faith. Ours is a pluralistic culture where one cannot depend on a commonly understood visual vocabulary. Contemporary artists who have explored the spiritual and religious dimensions have had to face this dilemma. Some have, indeed, seen themselves in a prophetic mode, but sometimes the prophecies become so obscure as to be unintelligible to the general public. The visual vocabulary determined by the artist is often so privatized that one needs a type of lexicon in order to gain access to the work's meaning. Indeed, a number of artists have flourished in a vocabulary accessible to very few. Clearly, a communal involvement that incorporated a basic understanding of what was occurring was not the intention. Yet the great altarpieces, frescoes, and private devotional works of the past did have this intention—great art did not have to be inaccessible to people, but it always had the capacity to lift people to a new level of understanding or, as David Tracy says, to a sense of possibilities.

TOBI KAHN: THE BRIDGING OF TWO WORLDS

The discussion above is important in understanding the work of contemporary New York artist Tobi Kahn. Since the early 1980s, Kahn has created a body of work—paintings, drawings, and sculptures—that has been praised by the mainstream art community. At the same time, he has been fabricating miniature shrines and ceremonial objects. The ceremonial objects, in particular, are based on the practices of his Jewish faith, designed with a careful appreciation of the Jewish tradition but rendered in a visual vocabulary that brings the tradition to the present day. The objects are intended to be used by a community, whether that community be his immediate family or a larger worshiping community. Until recently, these objects have not been publicly exhibited. To the mainstream art world, there is a great separation between the "fine" artworks and the "decorative" or "applied" artworks, and especially "decorative" or "applied" art that is religious in nature. To Kahn, there is no separation. As Kahn has stated in the *New York Times*, "I've always been committed to the notion that modern art and ancient ritual can enhance, rather than exclude each other."[12]

Kahn's ceremonial work is being made public at a time when some highly placed people in the mainstream art world are accepting the fact that many works in their own collections were part of a common faith experience in a particular tradition. In 2000, Neil MacGregor, director of the National Gallery in London, organized an exhibition entitled "Seeing Salvation" based on this very premise. Recognizing that at least a third of the paintings in the National Gallery are of Christian subjects, MacGregor also acknowledged that the religious significance of these paintings is unknown to many visitors, mainly because they are not Christian themselves. If they are Christian, they may no longer be practicing their faith, they may come from one of the denominations of Christianity in which art is not perceived as a value, or they simply have lost touch with the rich visual tradition of Christianity.[13]

As a result, MacGregor and his colleagues created an exhibition and catalogue "to focus on the purpose for which the works of art were made, and to explore what they might have meant to their original viewers."[14] In a word, these art objects were presented as vessels of belief. Clearly, MacGregor sensed an interest among the British people and the gallery's many visitors from abroad, for "Seeing Salvation" became one of the most well-attended exhibitions in the National Gallery's history, and the best-attended exhibition (over 355,000 visitors in its ten-week run) in the United Kingdom for 2000. It also attracted the highest number of first-time visitors of any exhibition held at the National Gallery.

MacGregor had his finger on the pulse of a phenomenon present in the art world as well as the general world—there is a hunger for ritual, for meaning, for tradition, for mystery in a world that is seemingly more fragmented. Kahn and many other artists have perceived this as well. In a very real sense, they are prophetic in their artistic vocations, but their sense of prophecy is at the service of a larger community.

PRINCIPAL THEMES IN KAHN'S CEREMONIAL ART

Among Kahn's concerns in his ceremonial art, there are four that emerge with great frequency: light; rites of passage; community and hospitality; and the text.

LIGHT Light has been a central theme in the work of many contemporary artists. James Turrell has created ineffable Minimalist installations using light. The late Dan Flavin, noted for his fluorescent tube sculptures that have an iconic presence, also used fluorescent lighting in the Chiesa Rossa in Milan (Fig. 87), a church designed in the 1930s by Italian architect Giovanni Muzio. In the Chiesa Rossa, Flavin concealed the lighting but employed it to define the barrel-vaulted nave ceiling in soft blue and the sanctuary apse in yellow. The result is a sacred space of great tranquillity. Stephen

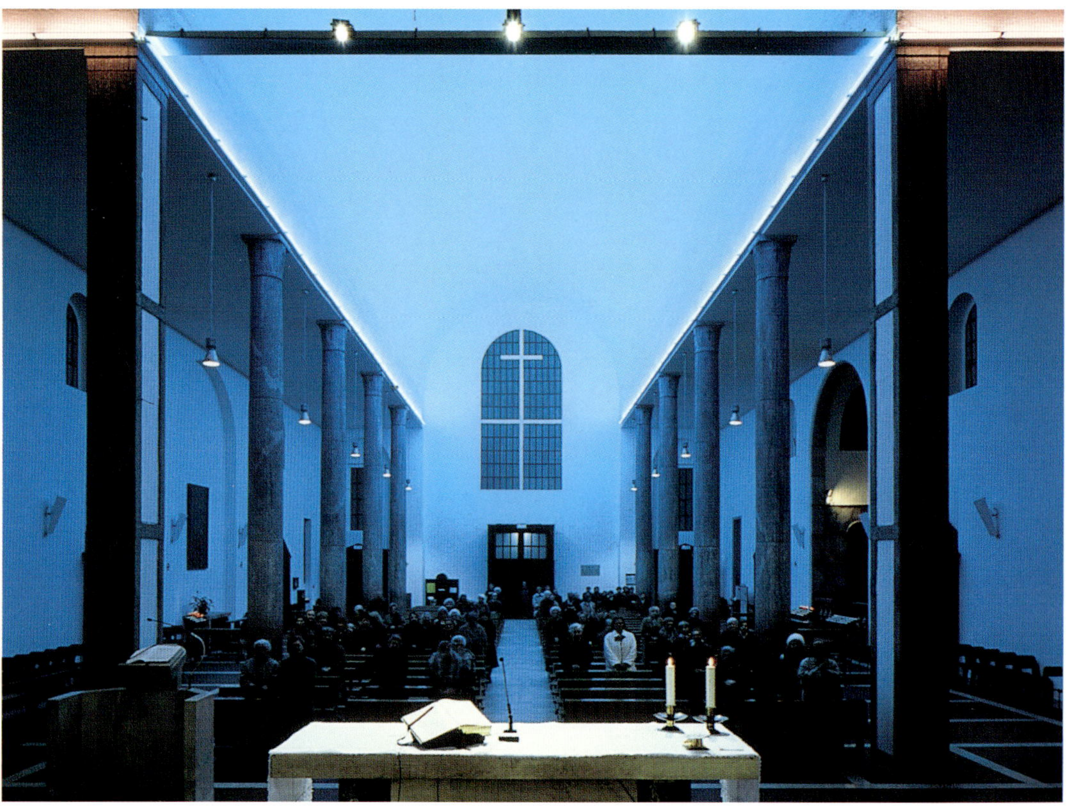

Fig. 87
Dan Flavin, Santa Maria in Chiesa Rossa, Milan, 1997

Antonakos has created Minimalist wall panel paintings, often brushed with gold and backlit by neon in such a way that the neon tubing remains unseen, thus creating a halo or corona around the work. In the spring of 2002, light was used on an epic scale at the site of the World Trade Center. Entitled *Tribute in Light*, forty-four searchlights created two vertical shafts of light, forming a memorial not only to the twin towers that were targets of terrorist attacks on September 11, 2001, but also to all those who died during the attacks. Other artists have used a natural source of light, flame, to evoke a sense of commemoration and of prayer. Iranian-born Seyed Alavi, who now resides in Oakland, California, fashioned 120 candlesticks out of nickel and placed a candle in each holder. Over 8 feet in length, this raked display of candles spells the word "forever," the flames realizing the word in light and the dark nickel bases serving as a shadow version of the word. When lit, the candles engage four of our senses—sight, touch, hearing, and smell—as Alavi uses one of the most ephemeral substances, melting wax being consumed by flame, to express the eternal.

Among Kahn's ceremonial objects are artifacts that have light as their chief theme. As is characteristic of all his art, there is an organic quality to these containers of light. In Kahn's Yahrzeit candle (Plate 26), traditionally lit on the anniversary of a loved one's death as a gesture of memory and respect, he has created an object whose base is anthropomorphic and seems to suggest the gesture of offering. He has also fashioned a Hanukkah lamp that seems to grow out of three plant forms, each one carrying three budding shapes that hold the candles (Plate 15).

RITES OF PASSAGE If the Yahrzeit light is lit to commemorate the passage of a loved one from this life, Kahn has created other objects to honor the transitions within our mortal life.

For his own wedding, Kahn designed a *huppah* (Plate 24), the ceremonial canopy under which the bride and groom stand. Representing the dwelling place of the married couple, this canopy shares a tradition with many cultures of offering reverential shelter for people or objects of special importance, whether it be a canopy over the throne of royalty or the baldachino found over the altar in many Christian cathedrals and churches or the umbrella-shaped Chatra in Buddhism, symbolizing the tree under which the Buddha sat to reach Nirvana. The baldachino not only protects; it

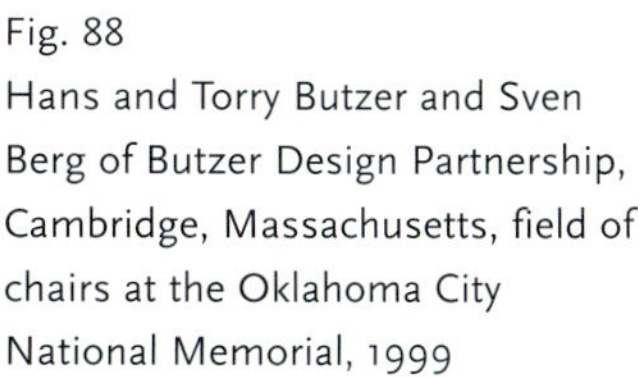

Fig. 88
Hans and Torry Butzer and Sven Berg of Butzer Design Partnership, Cambridge, Massachusetts, field of chairs at the Oklahoma City National Memorial, 1999

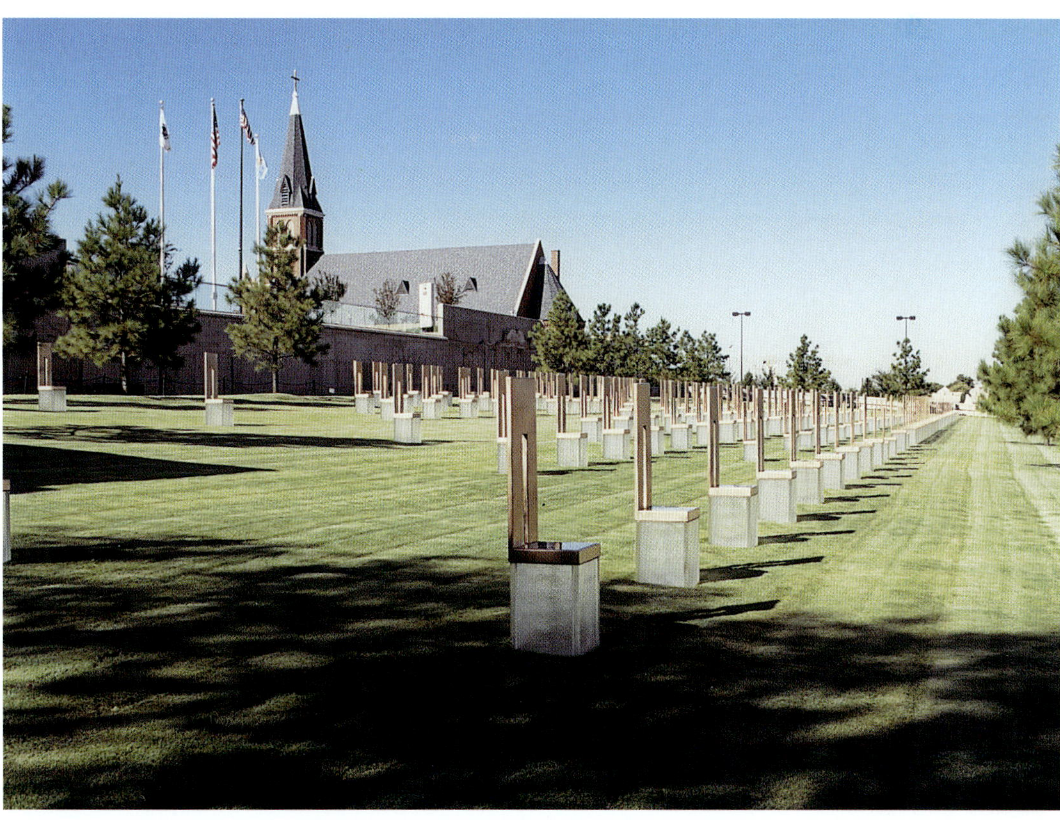

sets aside and marks as special those who are beneath it. How appropriate such symbolism is with the *huppah*, as the two people standing beneath it begin their married life together.

For Kahn's two daughters' naming ceremonies, he created three high-back chairs (Plate 23), "in which his wife, mother and mother-in-law welcomed the next generation of female children into the family."[15] He also created a high-back chair for his son's circumcision ceremony (Plate 22). Chairs have a long history in many religious traditions. In the Roman Catholic tradition, for instance, the chair known as the *cathedra* is used by the bishop of the diocese and symbolizes the appointed temporary representative who occupies it until its true occupant (Christ) returns. On ancient Roman and Greek stele, the deceased person was often presented sitting in a chair. This tradition has resonances with the Oklahoma City National Memorial (Fig. 88), dedicated to the 168 victims of the 1995 terrorist bombing. Arranged in nine rows, symbolic of the nine floors of the destroyed Murrah Federal Building, are 168 high-back chairs, made of bronze, granite, and glass, each bearing the name of one of the victims. The chair offers rest, and in this lineup of chairs, the overall effect is solemn, liturgical, and compassionate.

COMMUNITY AND HOSPITALITY In many Jewish ceremonies, the meal is central, as it is in other religious traditions. It is a meal not to be consumed in isolation but rather to be shared with the community. In Kahn's work, this sense of the shared meal is quite evident. He has created a series of kiddush cups, used with the blessing at the beginning of Sabbath observances and other Jewish ceremonies. His seder plate is compact and beautiful. On top of a three-tiered platform base used for the three matzot, Kahn has placed three cups and three plates, all of his own design. The ritualistic sharing of beverages and foods is a custom that is a part of many religious faiths. In the Catholic and Christian Orthodox traditions, it is central in the form of the Eucharist, in which

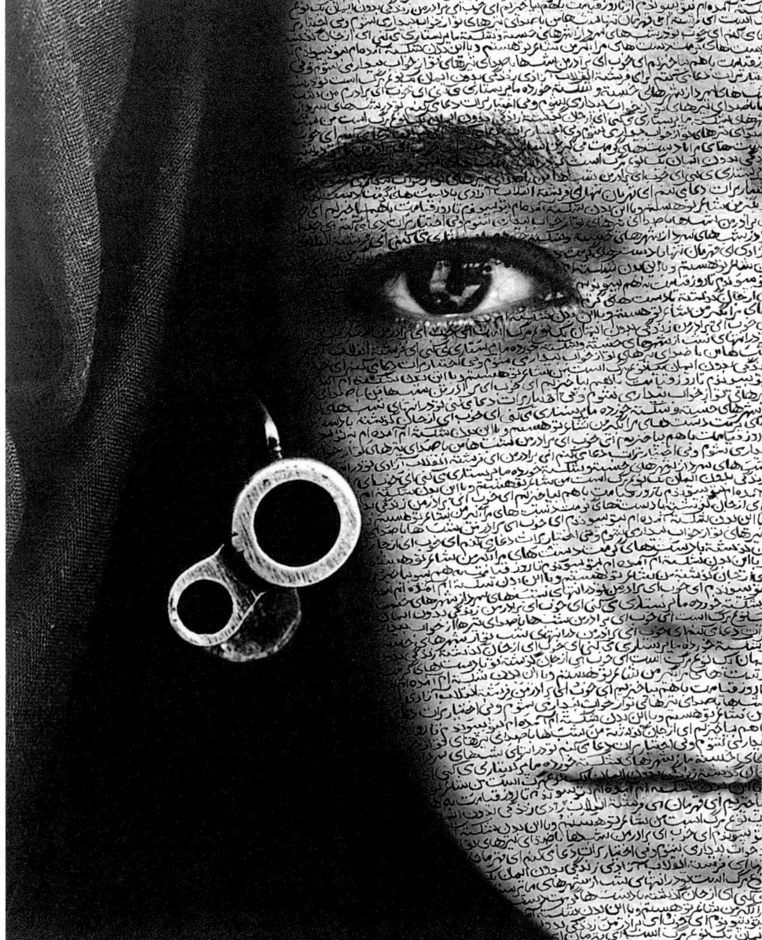

Fig. 89
Shirin Neshat,
Speechless, 1996

bread and wine are consecrated to become the sacramental body and blood of Jesus Christ. In many mainstream Protestant traditions, the bread and the wine are also a part of liturgical practice. The ritual hospitable sharing of drink appears in non-Western traditions, too, as was demonstrated in a stunning 2002 exhibition at New York's Asia Society and the Japan House entitled "The New Way of Tea," which focused on the meaning of the tea ceremony in Zen Buddhism.

Hospitality and regard for others also extend beyond one's immediate community. In Judaism, there is the custom of the *tzedakah* container, used to gather funds for the poor. Kahn has approached this custom by fashioning a series of containers that have expressed in their design a sense of dignity, generosity, and hope.

THE TEXT Jews, Christians, and Muslims are people of the book, and in each of these traditions, sacred scripture is considered the revealed word of the Almighty. Saint John's Gospel opens with "In the beginning was the Word." Text plays a major role in these traditions, and interestingly, text has become a greater part of contemporary art. Some of today's artists use text with an ironical sensibility, but there are artists for whom text is a link with the spiritual. Bernard Maisner, arguably the finest contemporary maker of illuminated manuscripts, has studied Christian, Jewish, Islamic, and Hindu manuscripts and has combined their designs with quoted passages from such diverse figures as William Blake, Anaïs Nin, John Cage, Patti Smith, Heraclitus, and Marcus Aurelius. While not religious in intent, these works express Maisner's delight in being in the presence of mystery without any need for a resolution.

Likewise, text is important to Iranian-born artist Shirin Neshat, who incorporates passages from the Koran into her photographic work. Often serving as her own subject, the artist has photographically superimposed these texts on her hands, her face, and even her eyes in so convincing a manner that they resemble tattoos (Fig. 89). These passages, literally and metaphorically, fully absorb the subject.

In the Jewish tradition, the Torah scroll is so highly regarded that one does not touch it, but instead uses a *yad*, or pointer, when reading from it. The traditional *yad* is often made of silver and has a little hand with a pointing finger at the end of the shaft. Relying on his love of organic forms, Kahn has created a series of *yad*s that have branch or vinelike curves in them and that taper to a point (Plate 4). The mezuzah container, holding a miniature scroll inscribed with excerpts from the Torah, makes touch possible. Placed at the entrance to Jewish homes, this small, narrow, rectangular object contains parchment with lines from a passage in Deuteronomy as well as one of the mystical names of God. Upon entering and leaving the house, the believer is invited to touch the mezuzah and the mystical name of God while calling to mind a special prayer: "May God watch over my going out and my coming in from now and evermore." It is a tactile experience that tangibly puts the person into contact with the word of God. In his mezuzah-container design, Kahn has created an organic form that looks treelike as well as anthropomorphic (Plate 5). This object invites touch, as the form wraps itself around the parchment in both a gesture of protection and of reverence and praise.

SACRED SPACES Artists of considerable reputations have been invited to create sacred spaces or to modify already existing spaces (Dan Flavin, mentioned earlier, modified a traditional church in Milan with his fluorescent lighting) or to create art for a sacred space specifically designed for their work (the Rothko Chapel in Houston comes immediately to mind). Some artists have created the sense of sacred spaces, but on a temporary basis. Video artist Bill Viola, for example, in his *Room of Saint John of the Cross*, creates an installation that juxtaposes the frightening, noisy, and chaotic outer world with a peace-filled interior world of a monastic cell. For most individuals, this art object is observable only in traveling exhibitions. Other artists have sought to design their own

Fig. 90
Michael Tracy, Emmanuel Chapel for the Corpus Christi Cathedral, Texas, 1985

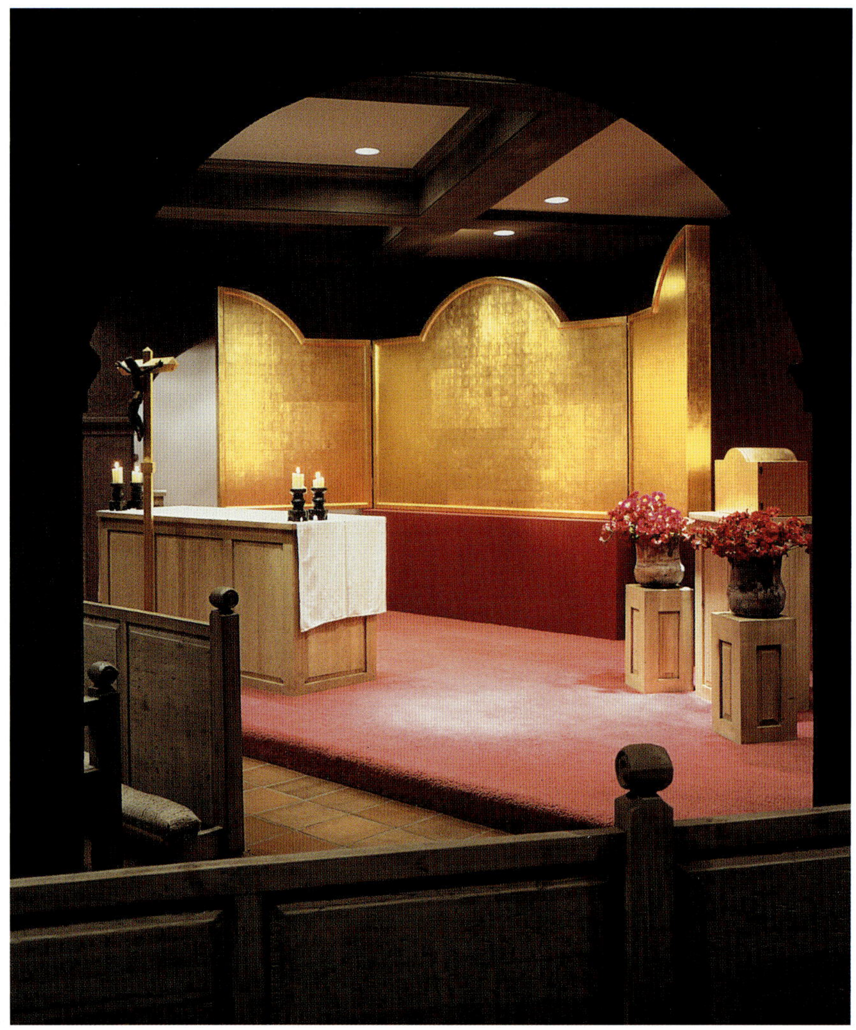

Fig. 91
Louise Nevelson, Errol Becker Chapel of the Good Shepherd in Saint Peter's Lutheran Church, Citicorp Center, New York, 1977

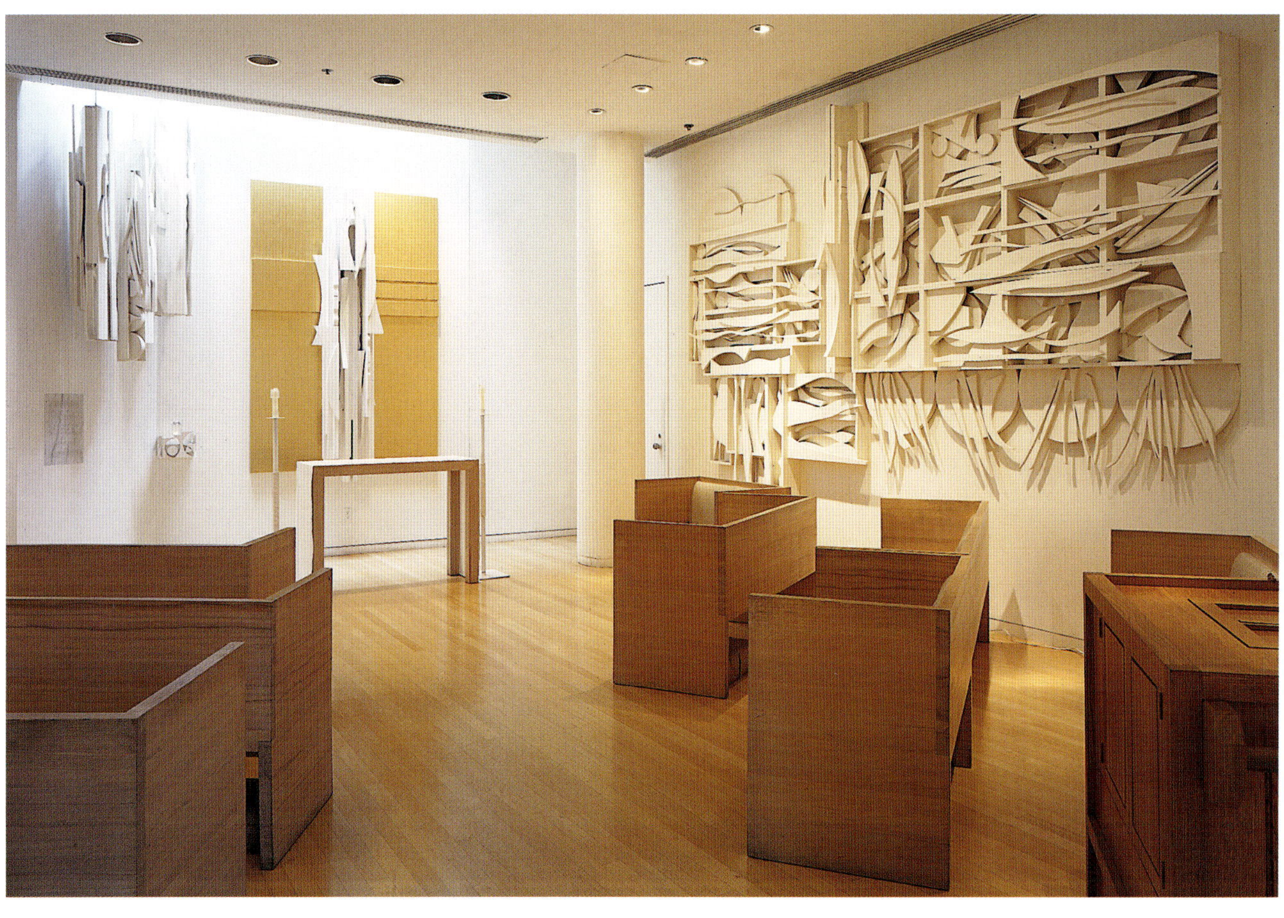

intimate spaces. New York–based artist Stephen Antonakos has created a series of chapel maquettes that could be translated into full-size sacred spaces, although even at full scale, the chapels would still be of intimate proportions, no larger than 15 x 26 x 26 feet. The few of Antonakos' full-scale chapels that have been built to date were constructed within the context of the art world, not commissioned by religious institutions. Nevertheless, there have been numerous examples of serious engagement between religious leaders and contemporary artists in the last several decades. I will mention only three.

Texas-based artist Michael Tracy, long concerned about the suffering and oppression in Latin America, has created works of passionate empathy that are strongly liturgical. In 1985, Tracy was commissioned to design the Emmanuel Chapel in the undercroft of the Corpus Christi Cathedral in Corpus Christi, Texas (Fig. 90). With a splendid gold imageless reredos, a rich rose-colored carpet, and handcrafted altar and pews, Tracy created an intimate sacred space of great warmth and radiance.

The Errol Becker Chapel of the Good Shepherd in Saint Peter's Lutheran Church, beneath the towering Citicorp Center in midtown Manhattan, engages in an interesting dialogue between the sacred and profane (Fig. 91). Louise Nevelson was commissioned to do the wall sculptures for each of the five walls in this small (28 x 21-foot) room. The subtle play of shadow and light, as well as the lyrical shapes within the sculptures, creates a quiet space of embracing prayerfulness and warmth. While the dominating Citicorp building, hiked up on stiltlike 127-foot-high columns, straddles Saint Peter's Church like some architectural Goliath, the beautiful sacred space of the church and its small Chapel of the Good Shepherd nevertheless seem to hold their own quite well.

Fig. 92
Meditative Space,
HealthCare Chaplaincy,
New York, 2002

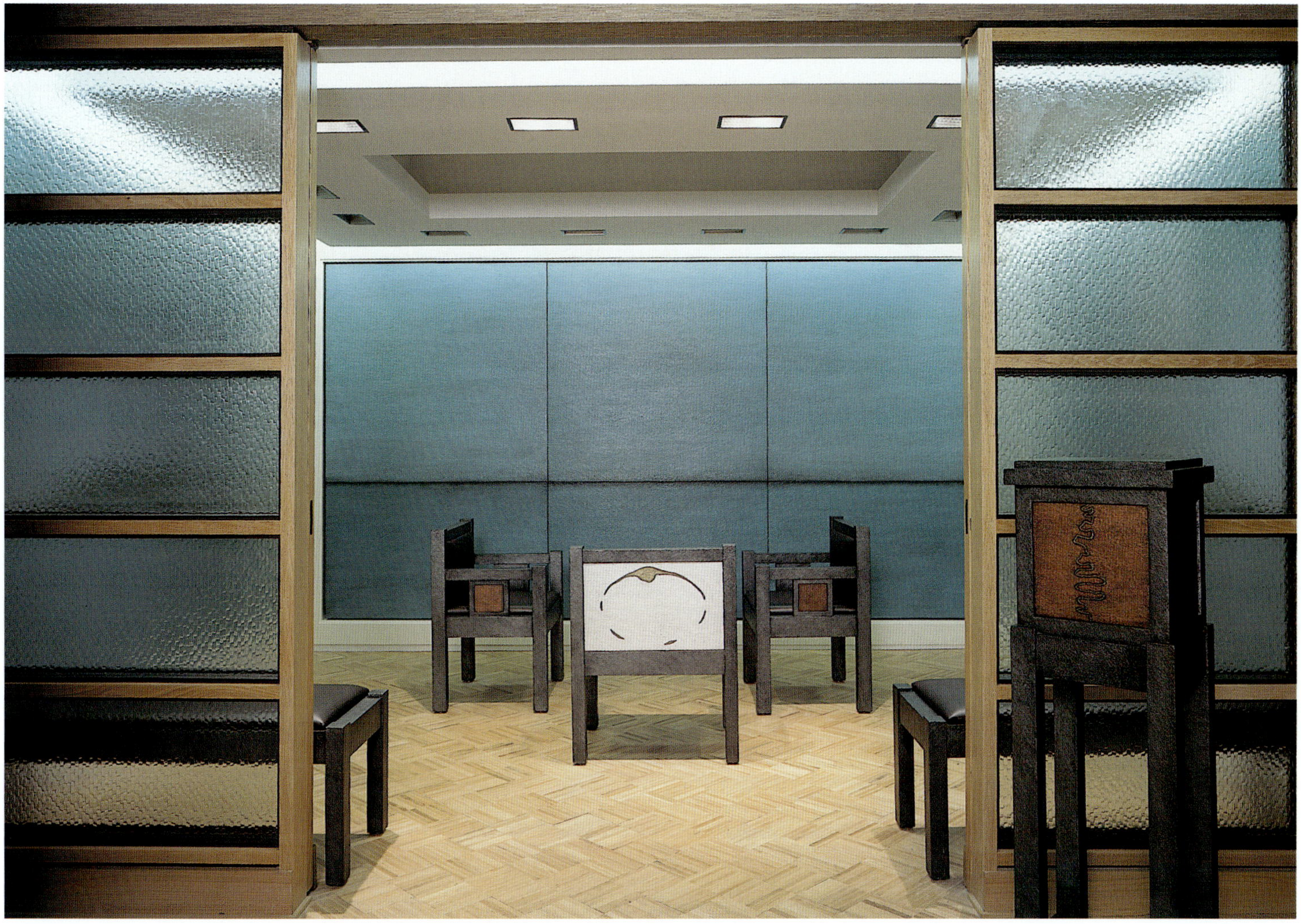

Just several blocks north of the Nevelson-designed chapel is another chapel-like space, which was dedicated in June 2002. Tobi Kahn was commissioned to create a contemplation space within the fourth-floor offices of New York's HealthCare Chaplaincy, located on East Sixty-second Street (Figs. 84, 85, 92; Plate 27). The entire floor was gutted and redesigned. Near the elevator entrance to the Chaplaincy offices is the space designed by Kahn. In the 1980s, Kahn created a series of miniature shrines and sacred spaces—microcosms of larger spaces. The HealthCare Chaplaincy contemplation space was Kahn's first chapel-like space that could actually accommodate people, but even this space had a microcosmic-macrocosmic dynamic. The meditative room is physically quite small (10 x 14 feet with 8-foot ceilings), but Kahn designed the room to give it a sense of expansiveness, with floor-to-ceiling paintings on three of the four walls. The fourth wall is the wall separating the space from the outer offices. It is made up of two sliding doors with opaque glass framed in light wood, which give the room a distinctly Japanese feel and, because of the glass, allow diffused light to enter, lending what is an intimate space the quality of expansiveness. The paintings that line the remaining three walls are done in Kahn's signature technique—gesso built up on wood panel with many layers of acrylic on top of the gesso. The central suggested image is a vast horizon line above which is sky and below which is water. The colors are two dominant shades of blue that are richly nuanced and textured. The two side walls contain images of similar simplicity, with the addition of a solitary island on one wall and two islands on the opposite wall. These paintings are perhaps Kahn's most minimal; they strongly suggest the seascapes of Caspar David Friedrich and the hovering rectangles of Mark Rothko, and they have affinities to Ingmar Bergman's and Federico Fellini's use of the sea as a symbol of eternity in their films. Kahn returns to his fondness for the ceremonial chair by placing in the center of the room three large straight-back chairs at right angles to one another, so that three people can have a conversation or engage in group prayer. Like the Nevelson chapel, this meditative space provides a quiet refuge from the chaos of the outer world, and, more specifically, it offers a calming environment for private meditation, group prayer, or serious conversations regarding health matters.

Ritual objects and sacred spaces have emerged as art forms that have gained greater acceptance in mainstream art communities. The embarrassment once felt by the art establishment when faced with contemporary art objects that were clearly spiritual and religious in content is gradually fading. This can only be good for all concerned, as Tobi Kahn and many other gifted artists continue in their efforts to reconnect with religious and spiritual experiences, in part as a rejection of the materialism, narcissism, and cynicism of much of the contemporary art world, but also as a desire to rediscover the original link between art and the religious dimension—not as an investment, nor as power or prestige, but as a way to connect to those "vital subjects" that are the enduring themes of human experience.

1. Amei Wallach, "The Impenetrable That Leads to the Sublime," *The New York Times*, January 7, 2001, sec. 2, p. 37.

2. Ibid., p. 41.

3. Ellen Dissanayake, "Darwin and Everyday Aesthetics," unpublished lecture given in the session "Examining the Theoretical and Art Historical Possibilities of Everyday Aesthetics," College Art Association, 85th Annual Conference, New York, February 12–15, 1997.

4. Ibid.

5. Ibid. One need look no further than New York City and Washington, D.C., to see the truth of Dissanayake's thoughts. After the attacks on the World Trade Center and the Pentagon on September 11, 2001, many spontaneous "shrines" appeared near the attack sites and elsewhere. If one walked around either site, one encountered pictures of lost loved ones, sometimes solo portraits, but more often in photographs of celebratory events with family or friends, and messages, flowers, votive candles, and objects of personal significance. Other shrines appeared in Grand Central Terminal and Union Square, and as one walked by the various fire stations and police stations throughout New York, one encountered still more shrines dedicated to the lost colleagues who were members of those particular units. People from all walks of life still pause and take time to look at these memorials.

6. Mircea Eliade, *The Sacred and the Profane: The Nature of Religion*, trans. Willard R. Trask (San Diego: Harcourt Brace Jovanovich, 1959), p. 34.

7. Michael Clarke, *Oxford Concise Dictionary of Art Terms* (Oxford and New York: Oxford University Press, 2001), p. 74.

8. Thomas P. Campbell et al., *Tapestry in the Renaissance: Art and Magnificence*, exh. cat. (New York: The Metropolitan Museum of Art, 2002), p. 9.

9. Ibid., p. 4. Campbell cites Giorgio Vasari to corroborate his claim of the tapestry's prestige and value. According to Vasari, the ten tapestries that constituted the *Acts of the Apostles*, commissioned by Pope Leo X and designed by Raphael, cost more than five times the amount given to Raphael's contemporary Michelangelo for his fresco painting of the Sistine Chapel ceiling.

10. Huston Smith, in a 1997 interview with Marilyn Snell of *Mother Jones* magazine ("The World of Religion According to Huston Smith," *Mother Jones*, November–December 1997; www.motherjones.com/news/qa/1997/11/snell.html), responded to Snell's question about New Age practices:

> *What you describe as New Age, and what I call the cafeteria approach to spirituality, is not the way organisms are put together, nor great works of art. And a vital faith is more like an organism or work of art than it is like a cafeteria tray.*
>
> *The New Age movement looks like a mixed bag. I see much in it that seems good: it's optimistic; it's enthusiastic; it has the capacity for belief. On the debit side, I think one needs to distinguish between belief and credulity. How deep does New Age go? Has it come to terms with radical evil? More, I am not sure how much social conscience there is in New Age thinking. If we think, for example, that we are drawing closer to transcendence or God but are not drawing closer in compassion and concern for our fellow human beings, we're just fooling ourselves. Do New Age groups produce a Mother Teresa or a Dalai Lama? Not that I can see. So, at its worst, it can be a kind of private escapism to titillate oneself.*

11. David Tracy, *The Analogical Imagination* (New York: Crossroad Publishing Company, 1981), p. 173.

12. Susan Kleinman, "Blending Modern Art with Objects of the Spirit," *New York Times*, April 26, 2000, p. E2.

13. Neil MacGregor, introduction to Gabriele Finaldi et al., *The Image of Christ*, exh. cat. (London: National Gallery, 2000), p. 6. MacGregor talks about a further difficulty—the loss of religious context—when he says that "the pictures made to inspire and strengthen faith through public and private devotions have been removed from the churches or domestic settings for which they were intended and hang now in the chronological sequences of the Gallery, not to the glory of God, but as part of a narrative of human artistic achievement. Worse, addressing questions of slender concern to those of other—or no—beliefs, they seem to many irrecoverably remote, now best approached in purely formal terms."

14. Ibid.

15. Kleinman, "Blending Modern Art."

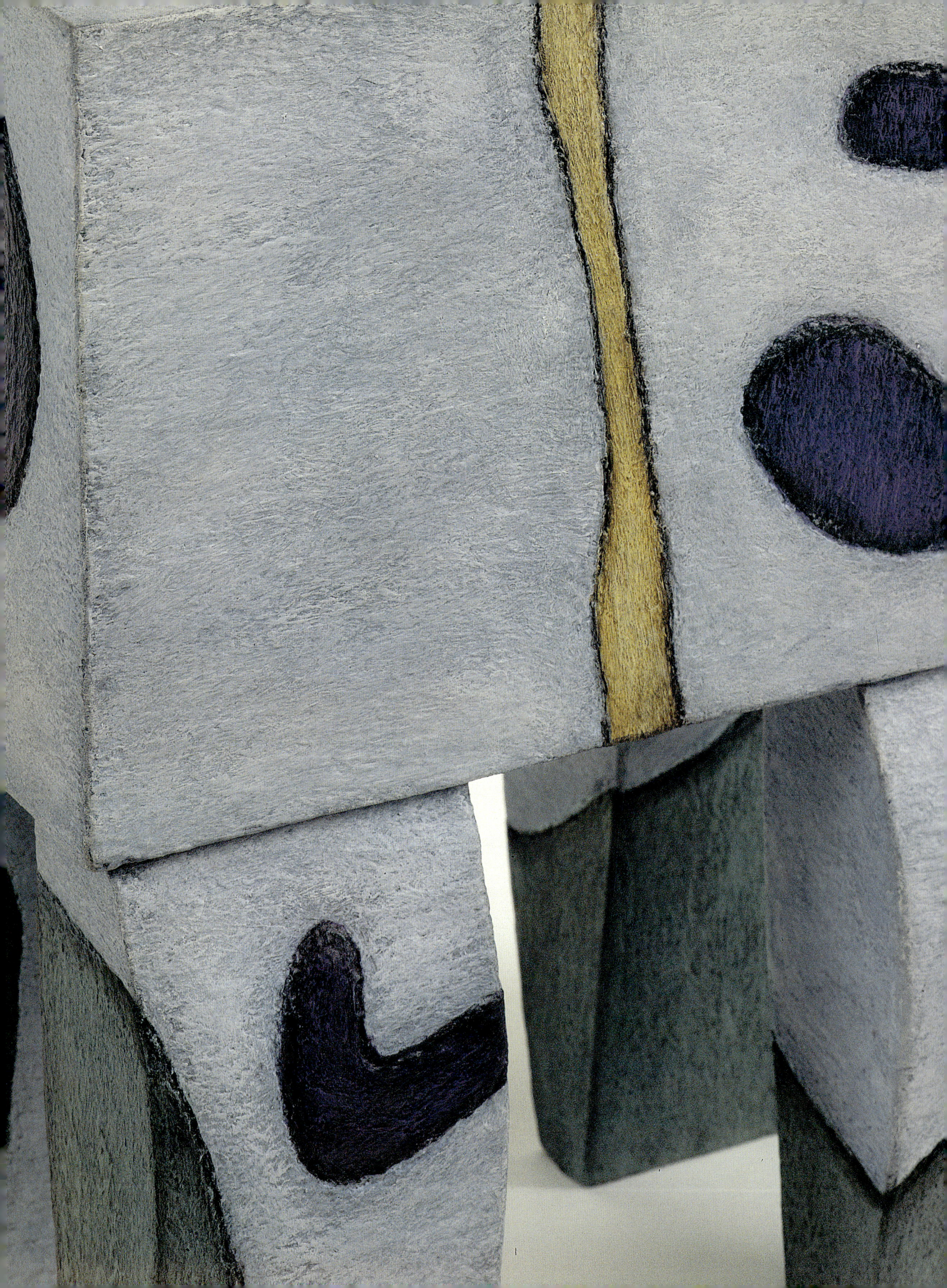

LEORA AUSLANDER

Resisting Context: The Spiritual Objects of Tobi Kahn

The origins of the installation "Avoda: Objects of the Spirit" (Fig. 97) lie not in a decision made by Tobi Kahn to create Jewish ritual objects for exhibition, but rather in his production of Judaica for himself and his family, with no intent to sell or display it (Fig. 93). Some of the objects in the installation come from that original impulse, some were commissioned later, and some were made even more recently, with this installation in mind. In a sense, then, Tobi Kahn started the project as a Jew seeking to express his spirituality, and is now displaying the results as an artist. Yet he is always both Jew and artist as well as a human being without religious or professional designation, simultaneously participating in diverse communities with varying expectations, possibilities, and constraints.[1] This threefold identity is, of course, one long experienced by Jewish artists. Some have responded to it by producing only Jewish work, that is, work with Jewish themes or for Jewish purposes. Others have chosen the opposite route by never giving aesthetic expression to their religious, ethnic, or spiritual identification.[2]

Tobi Kahn seems to have chosen to do some of each. Neither the work displayed in the group show "Landscape at the Millennium" nor the interview in that catalogue refers to Kahn's Jewishness.[3] He participated in the exhibition "simply" as a landscape painter. Likewise, the "Avoda" installation represents "simply" the Jewish artist, while his earlier traveling show, "Metamorphoses," explicitly incorporated both facets of his identity.[4] Yet despite the seemingly tidy division between *Sky and Water* (the 1999 series of paintings displayed in "Landscape at the Millennium") and the clearly Jewish ritual objects of "Avoda," I am loathe to impose such a division. The work itself and the mode of display fight against the dichotomy thematically, aesthetically, and technically.

Thus "Avoda" expresses, like much of Kahn's work, preoccupations with the passage of time and with the relationship between the human and the natural. Aesthetic reminders of his *Sky and Water* series (Fig. 86) are found in the landscapes painted on many of the larger pieces. Furthermore, like some of his other work, Kahn's Judaica uses the materials and technique of "craft" to make "art." In his sculptures and some of his sacred objects, for example, he uses construction-grade wood and furniture-building techniques. His work often requires a kind of mechanical labor and repetition more often associated with artisanry than with artistry. The everydayness of some of the materials and practices links his work to the domesticity, privacy, and particularity of the home rather than to the publicness and universality of the art museum. By contrast, the display techniques and labeling practices are more typical of exhibitions of art than of religious objects. This essay seeks to think through the meanings borne by these objects, how they emerge out of and relate to Kahn's "secular," "artistic," and "public" training and work, and how the context of production and consumption (production for self-use, on commission, or for display in a gallery to strangers) matters.

The "Avoda" project, as represented by the "Objects of the Spirit" installation, comprises a wide variety of Jewish ritual objects for use at home and in the synagogue. They fall into two broad categories, marked by distinctive techniques and styles, although sharing an unconventional use of materials and a carefully ambiguous location between art and craft. On the one hand are small pieces,

Zedek X, 2000 (detail, Fig. 97)

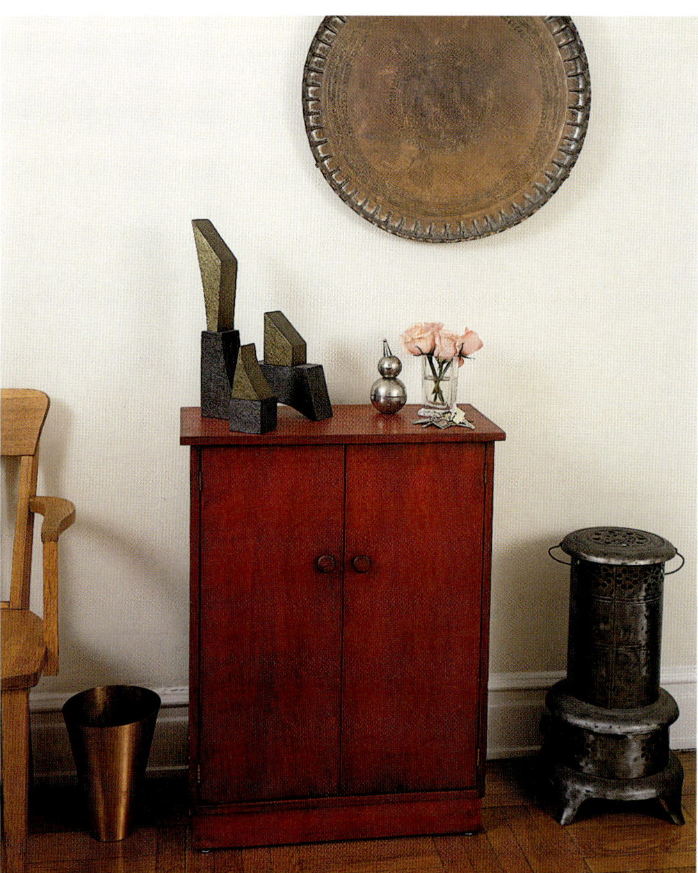

Fig. 93
The artist's home, with *Kinamon* (spice containers) on the cabinet top, 2003

including candlesticks, lamps, *yads*, mezuzah containers, and kiddush cups. On the other, one finds large architectonic pieces—arks, ceremonial chairs, and a *huppah*.

A viewer first encountering the smaller objects would expect them to be made of silver and bronze and will be surprised to find that many of the objects are crafted from acrylic on wood (for example, Fig. 95), a significant minority from acrylic on polyester resin, with others cast in bronze. Whatever the material, the objects on display seem to be completed and ready to use. The eternal light for the ark is equipped with electrical wiring and a lightbulb (Plate 2), the wood kiddush cup is beautifully finished and outfitted with hand-blown glass inside to make it safe for drinking (Plate 9), and the resin candlesticks are decoratively painted. Many of these seemingly completed objects are forms from which molds for bronze castings are to be made (and some have, in fact, been cast). They are thus simultaneously finished and in process. Kahn's choice to exhibit "finished" forms rather than the cast objects is an interesting and significant one. Part of the explanation may, of course, be pragmatic: casting is expensive. I would like to suggest, however, other reasons for using casting as a technique and for exhibiting the wood and resin forms rather than the limited-edition metal castings.

Casting is a labor-intensive process involving the work of the hands, concentration, and repetition. A mold is made from a form that has been carved or built up by hand. Molten metal is then poured into the mold; when the metal has cooled, the mold is removed. Some processes involve breaking the mold after a single cast; more often the mold is used again. It is a symbolically paradoxical process that melds hand labor with reproduction and repetition. The forms from which the molds are made bear the unique mark of the artist's hand, but the resulting casts are identical copies. Casting is, as a result, also a process that lies between "art" and "craft" as they are conventionally understood: sculpting the forms is the work of the artist, while making the casts is the work of an artisan.

Casting may be seen as a process mirroring Jewish ritual practice, which also involves a melding of individual and collective acts, of singularity and commonality, and repetition. Each lighting of the Sabbath candles, for example, is unique, but each recalls other lightings and blessings. Each time

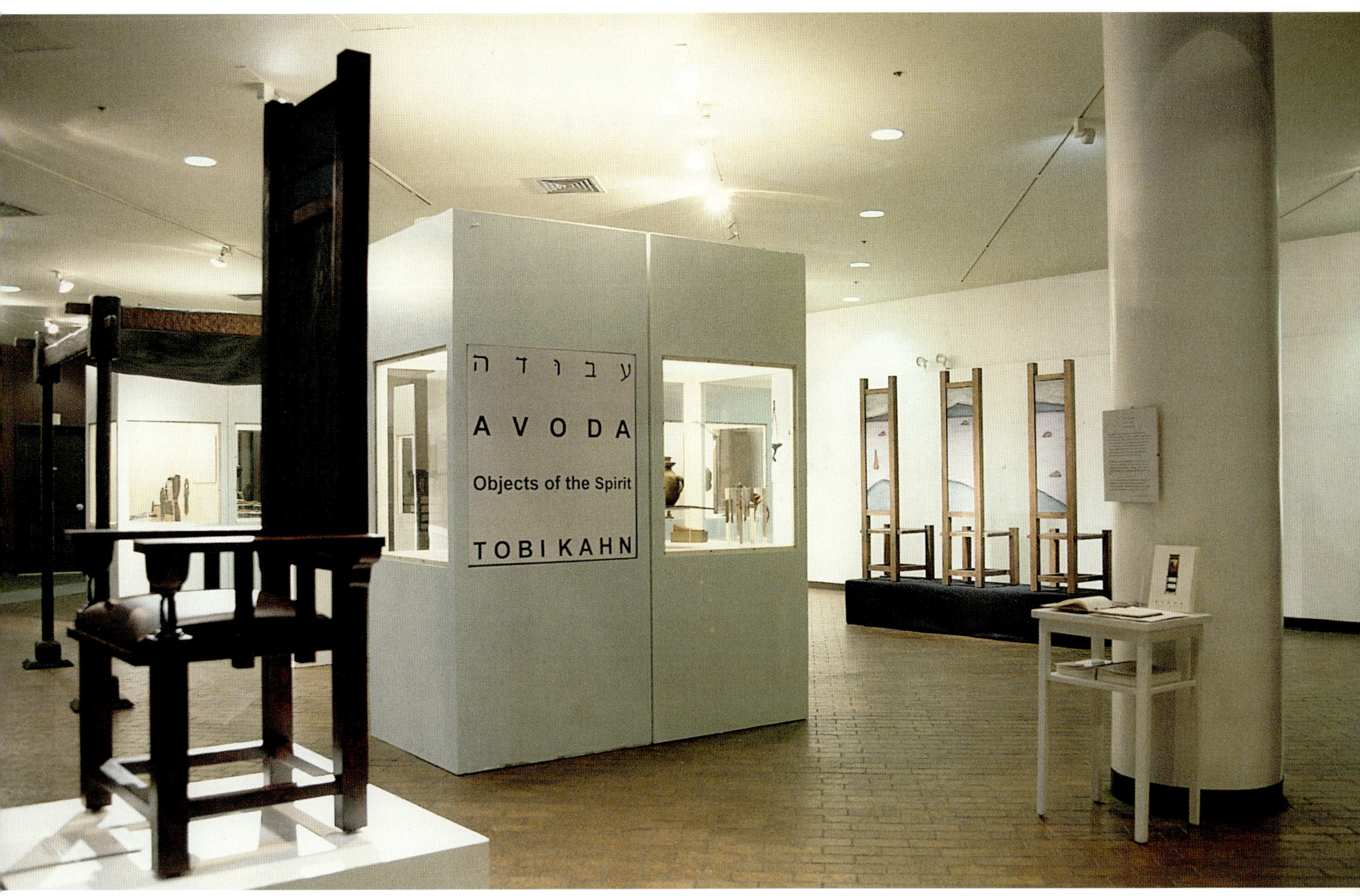

Fig. 94
Installation view of the exhibition "Avoda: Objects of the Spirit," 1999

the candles are kindled, an individual communicates with God and a link is created among Jews present, past, and future, near and far. Jewish tradition, furthermore, insists on the importance both of worship in the synagogue and at home, of special occasions and of the everyday. The blessing over the wine on Friday night in the privacy of the home is as important as annual, public, High Holiday worship in the synagogue. In the merging of art and craft, the former connoting the public and the latter the private, Kahn represents another aspect of the tradition. Finally, not just words but gestures and the engagement of the body—*davening* (praying), eating kosher food, bathing—are essential to traditional Jewish practice.

Displaying forms transformed into art objects through their finishing and decoration, rather than the final casts, puts the emphasis on process and thus suggests that in Kahn's vision, the spiritual practice is as much in the making as in the using of these objects. This is consistent with the origins of the project in Kahn's production of ritual objects for his own use and his subsequent encouragement of others to do the same in workshops. The objects in the "Avoda" project took many hours of concentrated labor, of repeated gestures of the hand—labor and gestures that become automatic just as gestures, words, and melodies become automatic to those in the habit of prayer. Both automatisms can help give the heart the freedom to meditate. Those gestures are also like those of a knitter or an embroiderer. A hand-knit sweater, for example, requires hour after hour of contact between the knitter's fingers and the yarn. Time passes, things happen. Knitted into the stitches of the sweater are the conversations engaged in, the meals cooked (or burned), the fights among children resolved, the calamities reported on the evening news, and the music listened to. Likewise, the body bears witness

Fig. 95
Lahav, 1996

Fig. 96
Hadahr II, 1994

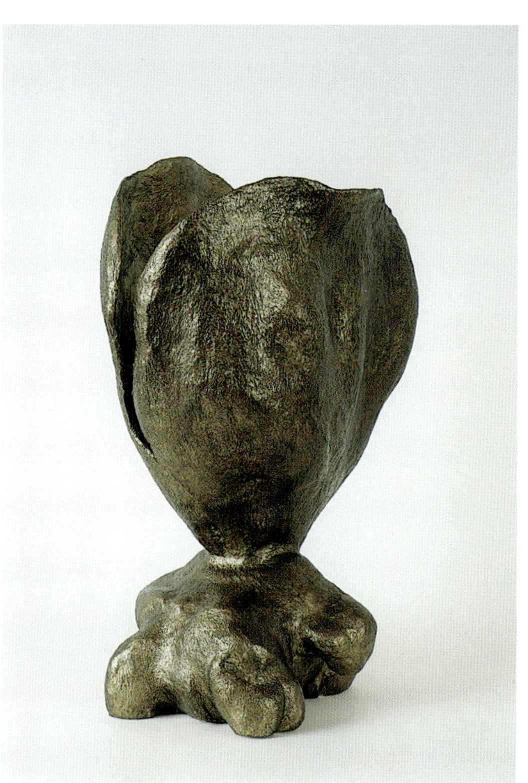

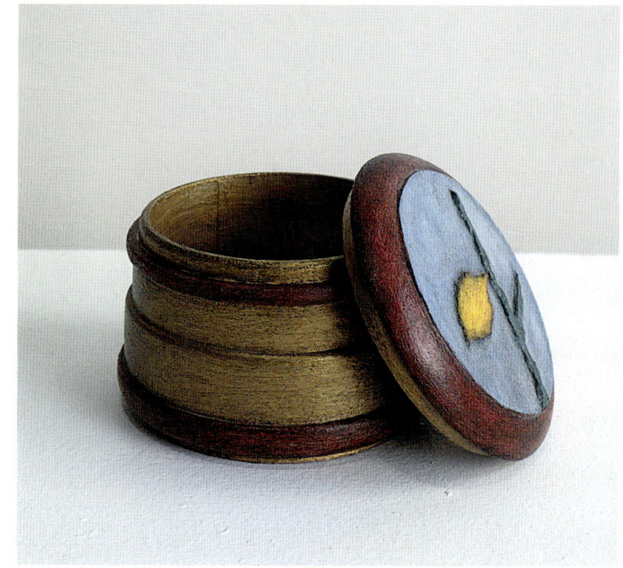

to its labors. Between my left hand's ring finger and its longer neighbor lies a scar inscribed fifteen years ago when I made my living as a furniture maker. The tangible scar reminds me of the bed I was making, of the motion of sanding, of a time in my life now passed. In the "Avoda" installation, Kahn, through the simultaneous display of the finished metal casts (which are infinitely reproducible), beautifully rendered handmade forms for casts lying between the individual and the collective, and unique hand-built objects, displays the different modalities of Jewish observance. The wood that the forms are made of is equally significant. Although many of the objects need to be made out of metal to fulfill their ritual function, wood may better express Kahn's feelings about nature, culture, and time.

Spiritual objects made out of wood incarnate the fundamental human anguish of violence and mortality. Trees have expected life spans and are sometimes cut down to serve the mundane or aesthetic needs of human beings. All the materials from which humans coax beauty, of course, are produced with violence—great shovels carving or boring the earth for metal ore, unspeakable heat in the manufacture of glass and some metals, and harsh blows in the case of stone. But only with wood (and bone) is the material born of death. (It is interesting to note in this context that Kahn often prefers to use found driftwood, i.e., wood that is already "dead.") Wood, moreover, is subject to destruction by the forces of nature; like human life, it is vulnerable and finite. Thus this natural vulnerability and the human violence that transforms trees into wood give an added depth to the meanings of Kahn's spiritual objects. Yet wood's longer life span also enables these objects to embody a belief that the significance of a human life may endure beyond mortal existence.

Kahn's choice of wood exemplifies the critically important place that nature occupies in his vision of the spiritual and the equally, if not more, important place of the human presence, of the hand. This dual emphasis may have influenced Kahn's choice of Art Nouveau as the aesthetic referent for his spiritual pieces. Art Nouveau, practiced at the turn of the last century in Europe, the United States, and Palestine, was a reaction against the mechanization and commercialization of the decorative arts, against literalist historicism, and against the rigid separation of art and craft.[5] Although

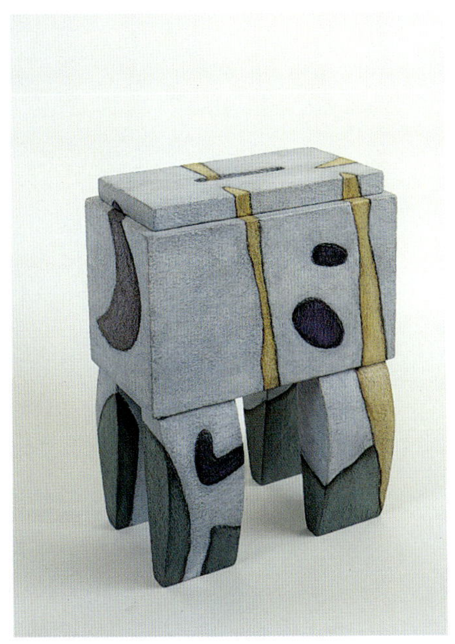

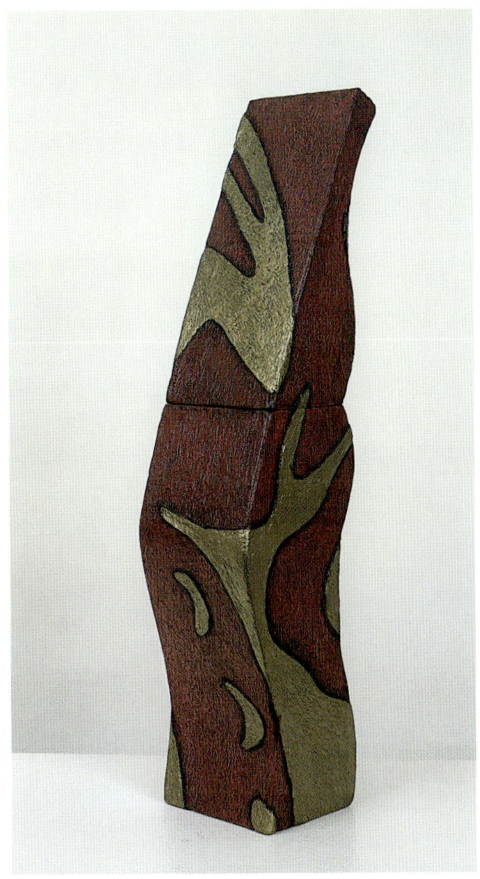

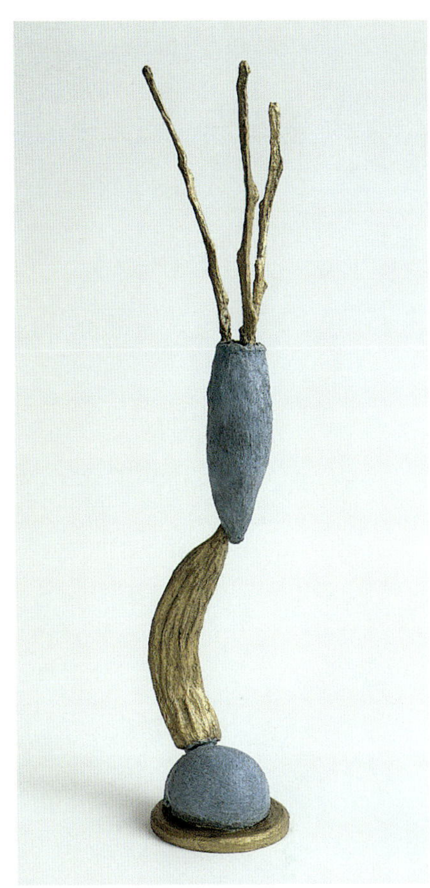

Fig. 97
Zedek X, 2000

Fig. 98
Aruga V, 2000

Fig. 99
Ma'ohr, 1994

Kahn's photography, sculpture, and painting have quite different referents, he turned to the Art Nouveau tradition for his Judaica. In this borrowing, he has followed the tradition of other creators of Jewish ritual objects, who have generally embedded their work within the broader aesthetic traditions of their culture.[6] That reuse of secular forms has connected Jews with their secular worlds even as they practice Judaism and has facilitated the appreciation of ritual objects by non-Jews.

Art Nouveau sought to rehabilitate the place of the individual artisan and artist in the creation and production of the goods of everyday life. Apprenticeship systems were restored and hand labor was valorized. Practitioners of Art Nouveau turned to the natural world for inspiration; much of the work is organic in form, with curves dominating over straight lines and angles. Decorative motifs are often flowers, trees, landscapes, and the human body. The emphasis is on natural materials.

The work of French, Italian, and Austrian Art Nouveau artists seems to have provided ideas for Kahn's smaller pieces, while the furniture-like pieces reflect Art Nouveau in Holland and Scotland. The smaller objects use organic forms, of plants, animals, or humans. They are sensual, substantial, curvilinear pieces, painted with the colors of the desert. The colors of the larger work are in the same range, and the painted surfaces echo Kahn's landscapes, but the form of the pieces, whether chair, *huppah*, or ark, is rigorously linear. The chairs are, in fact, in their lines, angles, and proportions, strongly reminiscent of Charles Rennie Mackintosh's famous Art Nouveau side chairs (Fig. 20). If the organic, sensuous forms of continental Art Nouveau provided Kahn with a repertoire for expressing the spirituality inherent in the movement between the labor of the human hand and the beauty of nature, Scottish Art Nouveau provided him with a way of transferring the spirituality expressed in his "secular" paintings to objects with a Jewish religious referent. Just as he moves between art and craft in his use of casting and his painting on hand-built furniture, he moves between a vision of specifically Jewish spirituality and the universal, the human, the life of the spirit. The arks may hold Torah scrolls, but the landscape paintings that adorn them speak to and from all spiritual traditions that link the natural and the sacred.

On still another level, because no piece of wood can ever be identical to another, the wood objects, whether large or small, allude to the uniqueness of each life. Kahn chose to undermine the uniqueness of wood, however, much as he paradoxically highlighted casting as a technique yet displayed the forms rather than the casts. The wood in "Objects of the Spirit" has become anonymous. Kahn works it against its nature, molding and painting it to look like metal, covering it with layers of acrylic until its natural surface and grain disappear—the very surface and grain that most furniture makers and many sculptors work to emphasize. Kahn might have followed this path, using the color and grain distinctions among woods and, simultaneously, their commonality to make a statement about spirituality and its many different manifestations in collective human life. But one senses that it is not differences that intrigue Kahn, but rather one particularism—Judaism—and its relation to universal human spirituality. He leaves the representation of difference to others.

The move between the particular and the universal in the "Avoda" project is inscribed not only in the materials, techniques, and aesthetic referents of the work, but also in their labeling. The objects in the installation are given single-word titles of no apparent English meaning, although many appear to be transliterated Hebrew, accompanied by a description of the materials used but no hint as to their ritual function. In some cases, the meanings of the Hebrew words are utterly appropriate to the object's apparent religious use.[7] Thus the meaning of *Orah*—the title of a Torah ark (Plate 1)—is light (or happiness); *Hadahr*—the etrog containers for Sukkot (Fig. 96, Plate 14)—means adorn or honor, but could also refer to *pri etz hadar*, or citrus fruit, of which the etrog is an example; *Zedek*, which means righteousness, is the title for a number of *tzedakah* (alms) containers (Fig. 97, Plate 6); *Aruga*, the title of several spice containers to celebrate the end of the Sabbath (Fig. 98, Plate 11), means garden bed, while another possible referent, *arucha*, means healing. *Ahda*, suggesting community or assembly, is used to title *yad*s, or pointers used in reading the Torah (Plate 4). Some of the words or their meanings are more ambiguous. *Ma'ohr*, depending on what Hebrew spelling one uses, can again mean light or luminary, but it can also mean genitals. *Ma'ohr*, a havdalah candleholder, is one of the objects whose ritual function is most difficult to determine from its appearance; its form would make the second meaning not implausible (Fig. 99). *Kayom*, the title given to the eternal lights that one would expect to find in a synagogue (Plate 2), resembles *kiyum*, meaning existence, preservation, or confirmation.

There are enough plausible meanings to make it unlikely that Kahn simply made up these words (as has been suggested for his painting titles, which are similar in type). Here again, Kahn appears to delight in ambiguities. Titling the objects in the manner of artworks could create a distance, transforming them into works to be studied rather than ritual objects to be used. At the same time, the abstractness of the titles makes them accessible to visitors who do not practice Judaism, allowing them to attribute whatever meaning they want to the objects. To use titles that could be Hebrew but are not necessarily—and are, in any case, transliterated—is to place the objects within Jewish tradition and simultaneously take them out of it. In other words, the titles situate the objects between art and craft and between the universal and the particular.

The context of the work is therefore essential to its meanings. When "Avoda" was only a private project, the objects were used and not labeled. Their meaning lay as much in the long moments of their making as in the shorter (but also repeated) moments of their use. These same meanings abide when, in workshops that Kahn has conducted, other people have made their own ritual objects. One imagines those objects being fashioned of many different materials and referring to many aesthetic traditions, according to the needs, skills, and desires of their makers. For Kahn and for those he has guided, the objects serve to externalize aspects of the self. But when an object is commissioned and put on exhibition, its character inevitably changes because production for self-use is not the same as production for use by others. Further, there is a distinction to be made between commission and display for sale to strangers.

Ideally, commissioned work involves intense interaction between the maker and the user: the user declares a need for a Hanukkah menorah, and perhaps suggests a general form; the artist responds with a drawing, which the user in turn modifies. The process can allow artist and purchaser to come to know each other, leaving the artist with the feeling that the object of his or her labor has gone off to a good home. Particularly in an institutional commission, such as one for a synagogue, the artist can even drop in for a visit. Making an object for sale on the market to a stranger is different, in that the alienation is complete, and the maker is left with the fear that when the stitches or the saw marks speak, they will not be heard.[8]

In our current age of mechanical reproduction, a handmade object is generally the product of love or of exploitation. Grandparents pass many hours making toys for their grandchildren, for love; some Indian women spend their lives embroidering dresses for strangers for a pittance. A few artisans and artists make a fair living creating goods by hand for the very rich. "Avoda: Objects of the Spirit," because of its three temporalities and contexts—as production for the self, production on commission, and installation—sits in a complex location. The installation form used (Fig. 94)—stark white walls, bright lights, pedestals, cases—almost maximizes the distance from the original project. Kahn could have chosen to create a domestic setting for the objects, possibly providing a combination of ethnographic labels and titles, and the works could have been available to the touch. Instead, the "Avoda" installation serves to move the objects closer to art than craft, closer to the universal than the particular, and perhaps closer to the secular than the spiritual.

Ultimately, "Avoda: Objects of the Spirit" is an installation of works that refuse to be art or craft, universal or Jewish, public or private. They also, in some sense, resist their placement in a gallery installation at all. Whether intended for ritual practice or for contemplation, their status as spiritual objects, objects designed to inspire the soul, seems unquestionable. But their meanings will change according to their setting. In Kahn's home (Fig. 93), used as part of his own spiritual practice, *Lkah*, *Rkadh*, and *Akahr* (Fig. 58, Plate 20, Fig. 36) represent one individual's handcrafted, personalized devotional objects. Displayed among Kahn's paintings with similar titles in a museum, these same objects become art objects or sculptures. In The Jewish Museum or the Smithsonian's Judaica collection, they would be identified as Shabbat candlesticks, a Miriam's cup, and a havdalah tray, joining a tradition of professionally created Jewish ritual objects.

1. The best text on multiplicity of identities remains Denise Riley, *"Am I That Name?" Feminism and the Category of "Women" in History* (Minneapolis: University of Minnesota Press, 1988).

2. See Kenneth E. Silver and Romy Golan, with contributions by Arthur A. Cohen, Billy Klüver, and Julie Martin, *The Circle of Montparnasse: Jewish Artists in Paris, 1905–1945*, exh. cat. (New York: The Jewish Museum, 1985); Peter Paret, "Modernism and the 'Alien Element' in German Art," and Emily D. Bilski, "Images of Identity and Urban Life: Jewish Artists in Turn-of-the-Century Berlin," in *Berlin Metropolis: Jews and the New Culture 1890-1918*, ed. Emily D. Bilski (Berkeley: University of California Press, 1999), pp. 32–57 and 102–45.

3. *Landscape at the Millennium: Installations by Tobi Kahn and Pat Steir*, exh. cat. (Buffalo: Albright-Knox Art Gallery, 2000).

4. Peter Selz, Michael Brenson, and Dore Ashton, *Tobi Kahn: Metamorphoses*, exh. cat. (Lee, Massachusetts, and New York: Council for Creative Projects, 1997).

5. For a fascinating reading of Art Nouveau, see Debora L. Silverman, *Art Nouveau in Fin-de-Siècle France: Politics, Psychology, and Style* (Berkeley: University of California Press, 1989).

6. See, among many possible examples, the objects represented in the following collections: Violet Gilboa, *Catalogue of the Bernice and Henry Tumen Collection of Jewish Ceremonial Objects in the Harvard College Library and the Harvard Semitic Museum* (Cambridge: Harvard University Press, 1993); Stephen S. Kayser and Guido Schoenberger, eds., *Jewish Ceremonial Art* (Philadelphia: Jewish Publication Society of America, 1955, 1959); Norman L. Kleeblatt and Vivian B. Mann, *Treasures of The Jewish Museum* (New York: Universe Books, 1986); and Grace Cohen Grossman, with Richard Eighme Ahlborn, *Judaica at the Smithsonian: Cultural Politics as Cultural Model* (Washington, D.C.: Smithsonian Institution Press, 1997). For an elaboration of this argument, see Gabrielle Sed-Rajna, *L'Art juif: Orient et occident* (Paris: Arts et métiers graphiques, 1975).

7. I thank Bernice Liberman Auslander for her help with the Hebrew.

8. For an elaboration of this argument, see Leora Auslander, *Taste and Power: Furnishing Modern France* (Berkeley: University of California Press, 1996).

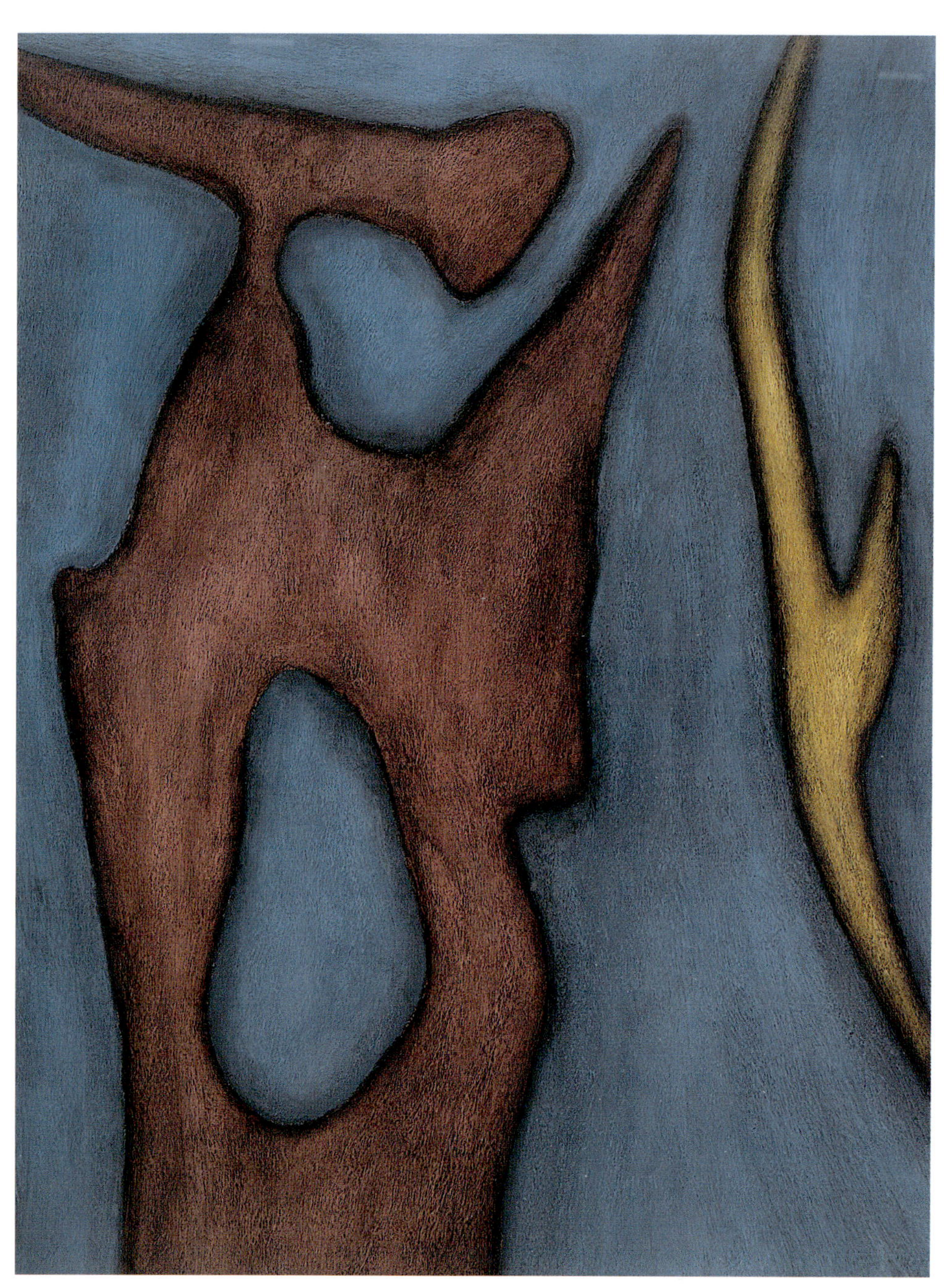

JONATHAN ROSEN

The Birth of Rituals

My daughter counts American flags. She is two years old and does not count very high, but she records each sighting aloud as best she can as she rolls along in her stroller, looking up. "One flag, two flag. 'Nother flag. Big flag. Little flag. Little little flag." Or simply, when she stumbles on a particularly patriotic apartment building, "So many flag!" She has a song she sings whenever she sees one. These days she sings a lot.

Since September 11, flags are everywhere in New York City. They hang like laundry from fire escapes or flap from flagpoles more suited to country porches but artfully anchored in brick facades. There are flags torn out of tabloids and taped into shop windows, tiny flags stuck into flowerpots and flapping from automobile antennas and, most touchingly, flags drawn on paper, pressing their faces against windows like the children who created them.

The American flag was asleep for me before September 11. Calamity and the human response to calamity woke it up. My daughter has made a ritual of counting flags; I have made a ritual of watching my daughter count flags, balancing her innocent pleasure in colorful objects with my darker awareness of what has caused all those flags to sprout up almost overnight.

And something strange has begun happening. Though all American flags are essentially the same, the flags in my neighborhood are somehow acquiring personalities. Some say "God Bless America" in Chinese and English, some in Spanish. The grand swatches of Old Glory suspended from the sides of fancy buildings, crisp-colored and made of heavy cloth, are taking on a homemade quality that makes them, like clothing, oddly personal. The official symbolism of the flag is there, patriotic purpose and civic duty, but filled with individual pathos, recalling for me those frayed original flags that one sees in history textbooks. There is logic to the myth learned in school that the flag was first sewn by Betsy Ross or some other colonial seamstress—a homey, handmade thing, with a circle of stars and stitched stripes, more a quilt for a child than a national standard.

It is remarkable to live through the birth of ritual, to see flags appear or lit candles clustered outside of fire stations, along with heaps of flowers and notes of gratitude written to the living and the dead. I experienced something similar in 1998 when Princess Diana died. I happened to be in London at the time and was engulfed in something peculiarly contemporary, since it was linked to the culture of celebrity, but also ancient, almost primitive. It was like looking into the exposed roots of religion. People poured past Kensington House, where she had lived, and left notes asking for her intercession. They left drawings and photographs, pictures of themselves and their families combined, in collage, with pictures of her. They lit candles and left flowers and brought their children, as if seeking a blessing. It was a collective response to death, amplified by technology but at its core as old as any Druid rite.

A few weeks after September 11, I went to visit Ground Zero. Crowds of people were doing the same thing, but there was no sense of touristic gawking, only a sense of pilgrimage. Vendors who had moved in from Chinatown were holding out red, white, and blue scarves and lapel pins. I bought a little pin and put it on as I moved down Broadway, and the act felt oddly religious, as if I were covering my head in synagogue. It was a sign of respect and solidarity but there was something more primitive in it as well, as if the pin had talismanic power. I felt the childish wish that the little flag would shield me from the anticipated images of horror, the mass grave I was about to see. I still have not taken it off.

Fig. 100
Oule-Zanh, 1995

Children, of course, don't need to be taught about the importance of ritual objects. Everything in my daughter's life, from the plate she eats on to the little pink doll she sleeps with, is invested with an animating power of its own. Eating and sleeping are attended by ceremony, by rituals, and the objects that are still so new in her hands—forks and spoons, for example—still glow with special meaning, as if she understood that eating at all, that being alive, were a sacred mystery requiring special tools. Sleep is a journey that requires companions—stuffed animals, a beloved scarf, a book slid under a velvet pillow shaped like a boat. The texture of this velvet boat soothes her in the night.

My daughter naturally accepts the lighting of candles on Friday night, the covering of bread on the Shabbat table, the ritual hand washing that precedes the blessing over the bread. She accepts, as the most natural thing in the world, the fact that she lives in a world full of flags, though she never ceases marveling at them. I myself still remember being very young and having a deep attachment to certain objects in a way that my daughter has reawakened for me.

When I was in nursery school, I made a menorah out of clay. A less distinguished work of art it would be hard to imagine—an oblong slab, with nine holes stuck in it, imperfectly painted gold. But for years, and perhaps even to this day, it has been my Ur-menorah, bound up with my idea of what Hanukkah is and, beyond that, bound up with my idea of what a ritual object is. Its very imperfection, its personal connection to me, and its simultaneous place in a public world, a grown-up, religious world, gave it its paradoxical power. While my grandmother was alive, it was dutifully employed alongside the fancy, branching Hanukkah menorahs we used on the holiday.

I don't know why it is that children have an instinctive relationship to ritual and ritual objects, the way they seem to have an automatic apprehension of God, but for me all ritual objects reach back toward childhood and its mysteries—the mystery of where we come from and where we go when we are gone, the mystery of sunlight and of darkness, the mystery of the world around us and the unseen elements blowing through it like wind.

My handprints on that menorah bound me to the holiday in a deep and personal way that became harder to maintain the older I got. Gradually, I became a spectator of the mysterious world, not a participant in it. My fingerprints ceased to be on the things that mattered most. I think of my childish menorah now as an artifact from a more complete time, a world that no longer exists, like that menorah carried out of Jerusalem by the Romans who destroyed the Temple, the one pictured on the Arch of Titus.

Thinking about Tobi Kahn's project to create ritual objects of his own, and to encourage others to create ritual objects, I realize how much I have hungered for that humble menorah I once made and for what it represents. The need for such objects, in childhood and in adult life, seems to me to be bound up with the very essence of what it means to be human.

There are, famously, two descriptions of the creation of man in the Bible. The first is abstract and egalitarian: "So God created mankind in His own image, in the image of God He created him; male and female He created them." This is a beautiful description, of course, but there is something disembodied about it. Suddenly, the world has people in it. The second description, which occurs a few verses later, is a far more humbling account of our origins: "There went up a mist from the earth, and watered the whole face of the ground. And the Lord God formed man of the dust of the ground, and breathed into his nostrils the breath of life; and man became a living soul." In this version, human beings themselves turn out to be handmade. We are clay in the potter's hand, a sort of ritual object to be placed in God's garden.

I value the first definition, with its utopian promise that we are divine reflections, but it is the second description that moves me viscerally, the way I suppose the imperfect menorah that I rolled between my hands in nursery school still speaks to me, for all its flawed asymmetry—or perhaps because of it. The breath of life makes us human but so does the earth inside of us. I remember a wonderful passage in Saul Bellow's novel *Herzog*, where the narrator recalls his mother telling him that to know where people come from he need only rub his hands together. The narrator takes her advice and, sure enough, quickly sees tiny black fibers of dirt forming between his palms.

It is hardly surprising that our religious life requires objects that are themselves hybrid, half art and half utensil, half spiritual and half mundane. Tobi Kahn's ritual objects remind me that religious life, however vast, tapers to a human point so that it can be held in the hand—even the small hand of a child. They remind me, as well, that the loftiest creation can come from the basest materials. This is true for art, and it is true for us, too. It may be one of the things that bind us so powerfully to art as a way of exploring what it means to be human.

Long before Kahn's project, I had encountered his paintings and made of one painting in particular a kind of ritual object of my own (Fig. 100). Ten years ago, when I became engaged, my girlfriend was clear that she did not want an engagement ring. The exchanging of simple gold bands under the wedding canopy spoke to her, but the giving of a diamond by the man to the woman did not. Somehow I decided that I would buy her a painting instead. Giving her something that our new shared home would wear on its wall, rather than something she would wear on her finger, made a kind of sense, and she did not object. Art, perhaps, would bridge the gap between tradition and the need for new invention.

It happened that not far from our apartment on the Upper West Side of Manhattan there was a gallery showing the work of Tobi Kahn. (The gallery, owned by Mary Ryan, has since moved to midtown.) I had never seen Kahn's paintings before—they seemed halfway between abstraction and representation, a landscape without people that nevertheless had a human quality that stirred me deeply. The shapes he created seemed familiar but indefinable—they challenged my sense of perspective, the way magnified blood cells, moving like traffic through an artery, confuse the sense of large and small, and lakes seen from an airplane might be amoebas seen through a microscope. In Kahn's work, streams of color ran in long fingers, the way that water, abandoned by the retreating tide, flows over hard sand in its own sensual path. Everything had a kind of analogue in the organic world, though the paintings constituted their own abstract universe of suggestive forms that eluded ultimate definition.

Far-flung elements seemed joined in Kahn's paintings, and I felt that sense of earth and sky coming together that is emblematic to me of the most important things, in art and in life. Seeing his paintings was like reading the second description of Creation, where the modest earth is combined with the divine breath of life. Painting, which may have grown long ago out of magic and ritual, still has that primitive element about it. At least Kahn's paintings do.

I bought a painting with two figures in it—one figure was maroon and looked like it might have been inspired by a piece of driftwood, but it seemed half human to me, too, a kind of robed figure that made me think of a magician. The other figure, facing the robed figure, was gold but far simpler. Erect, solitary, it looked like a stick or a beckoning finger. And these two figures facing each other—the stick floating in the air like something enchanted, the robed figure hidden but alive—seemed like elemental principles, male and female. An ideal wedding gift, I thought. The background of the painting was blue.

I later learned that Kahn had created this painting while his wife was pregnant with their first child, and indeed, now it is impossible for me to look at it without realizing that in the center of the "robed figure" is a womb-shaped hollow, filled with the blue of the background, and that the "robe" itself bulges out to accommodate the hollow within. At the time, my mind was on marriage, not children, and I had room for only the two figures in my imagination, though now that we have a child I can't help feeling that the picture, in some mystical fashion, changed with us.

I was nervous about having bought this painting instead of the more conventional ring, and I gave myself a chance to back out of the deal. The gallery owner agreed to put the painting in the window and leave it there overnight. This way, I could walk past with my girlfriend and gauge her reaction.

That night we took a walk and I directed us along Columbus Avenue to the gallery. We stopped in front of the window, and there, like a mysterious mirror, was Kahn's painting, with its two figures against their background of blue. My wife-to-be loved the painting; I told her it was for her.

In some sense, Tobi's painting functions in my mind less like an alternate engagement ring than like an alternate *ketubah*, the ancient wedding contract with talmudic origins that is read aloud under the wedding canopy. We had a *ketubah*, and it was duly read aloud, but this other document, hanging on our wall like our *ketubah*, seems to preside over our marriage in a similar way, as if our lives were held together not merely by words and by the *ketubah*'s explicit contractual elements, but by art and the deep irrational elements that art is made of. Tobi's painting is like a homemade flag that somehow represents our larger citizenship in the public world, and the private country of our life together.

Tobi Kahn's ritual objects, like the rest of his work, bridge worlds. They bridge the world of childhood, when everything feels homemade, and the world of adulthood, where we find ourselves in a world already furnished by custom and habit and conformity. They bridge the world of art and the world of utility. The world of the *ketubah* and the world of painting. And they bridge those two stories in Genesis—the ideal of divine creation *ex nihilo*, and the more earthbound essence of our origins. Like the ladder in Jacob's dream—a kind of flagpole, in its way—Tobi Kahn's work is anchored among earthly things but pointing endlessly upward.

March 2002

Meditations

NESSA RAPOPORT

ARON KODESH

Open to me, my sister, my bride, so that your law and lore can be the orchard of our lives. Open to me, draw near, not far away but in our mouths and hearts, embodying your words: Choose life, hear, cleave to me, beloved, open to me.

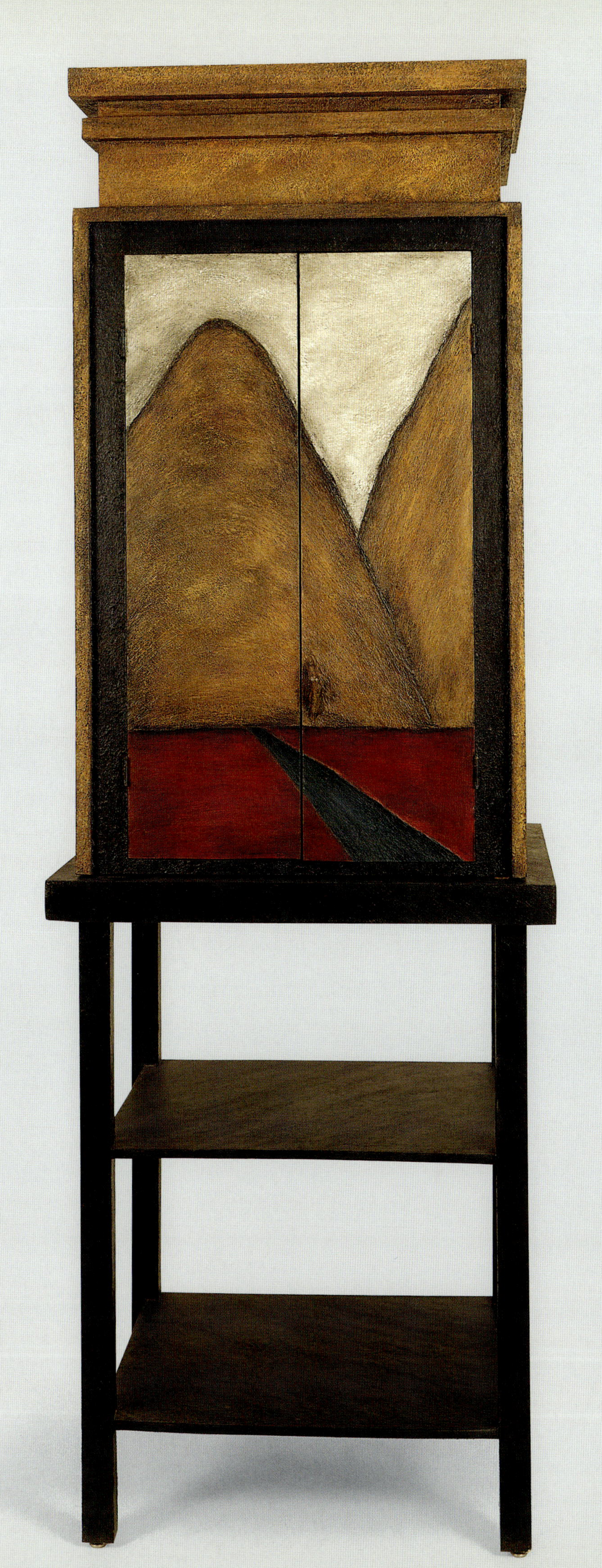

NER TAMID

There is no darkness that your light cannot reproach, no terror that cannot be dispelled by your lucidity. Shine through our despair, turn us from obscurity to bask in your transparent peace, always, endlessly.

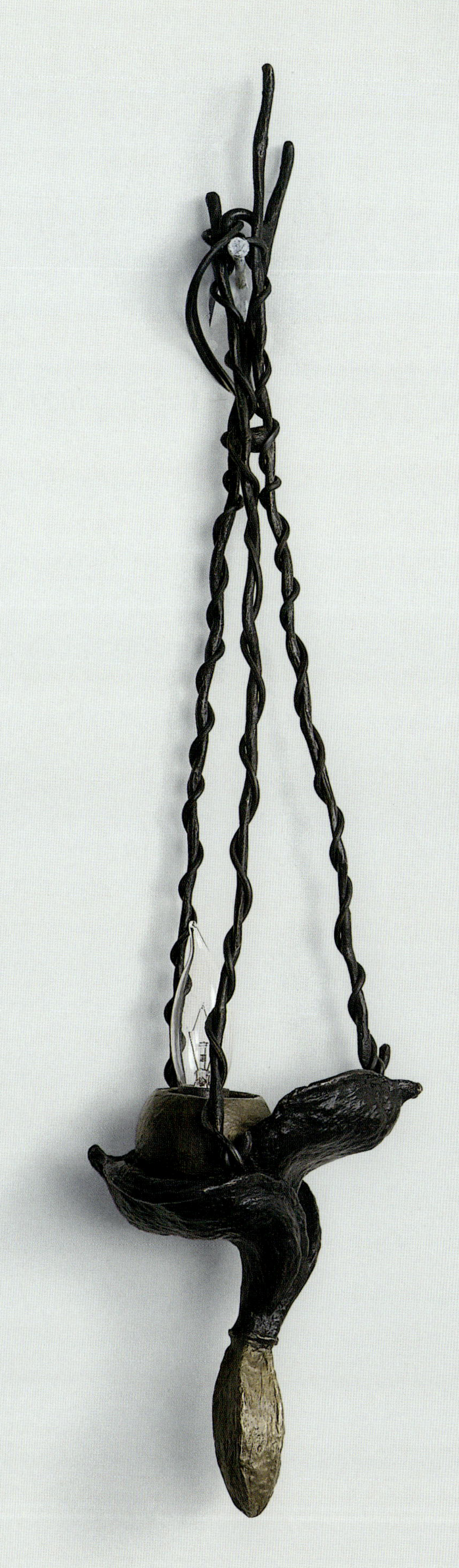

RIMMONIM

Fruit of the ravishing tree to which I cleave,
pomegranate of infinite seed, pairing eternal life with
fertility, unfurling covenant between our betrothal
to You and love's embodiment.

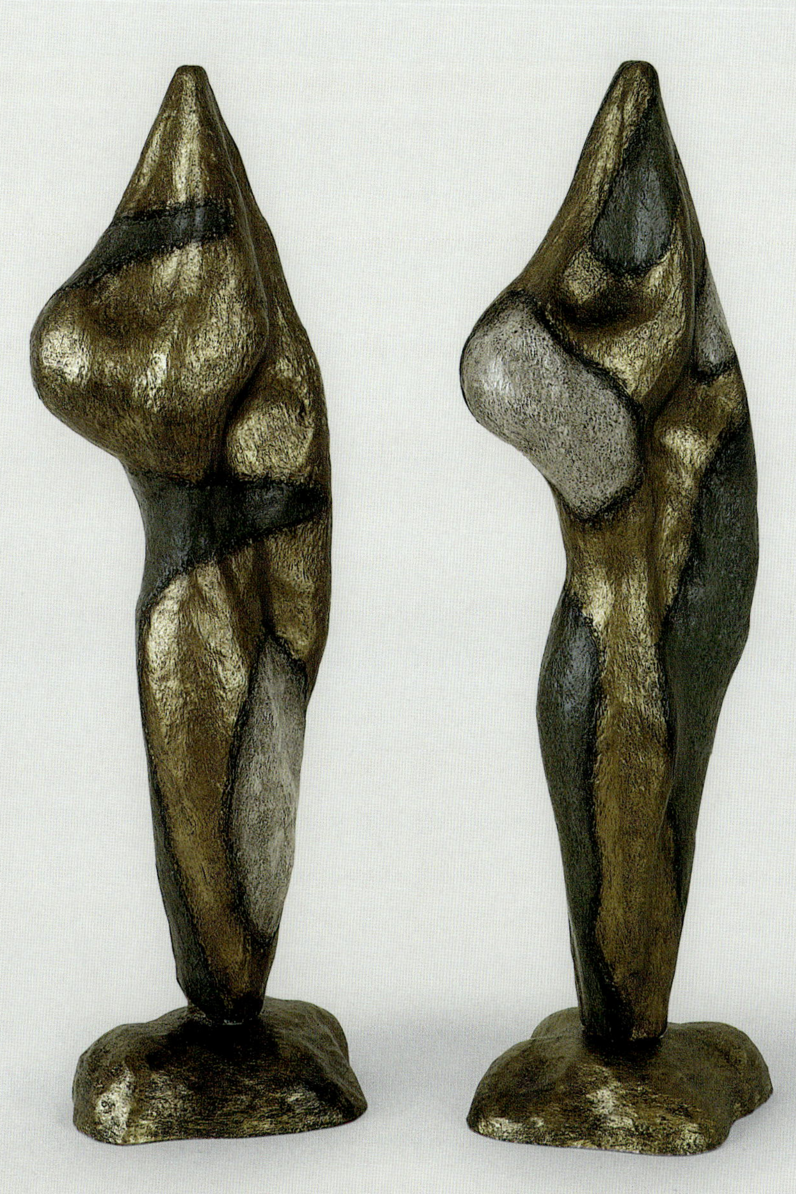

YAD Your outstretched arm, pointing from mortal to miraculous, your healing hand, grasp of infinity, unfaltering, from the letter of arrival to the sign of where we long to be.

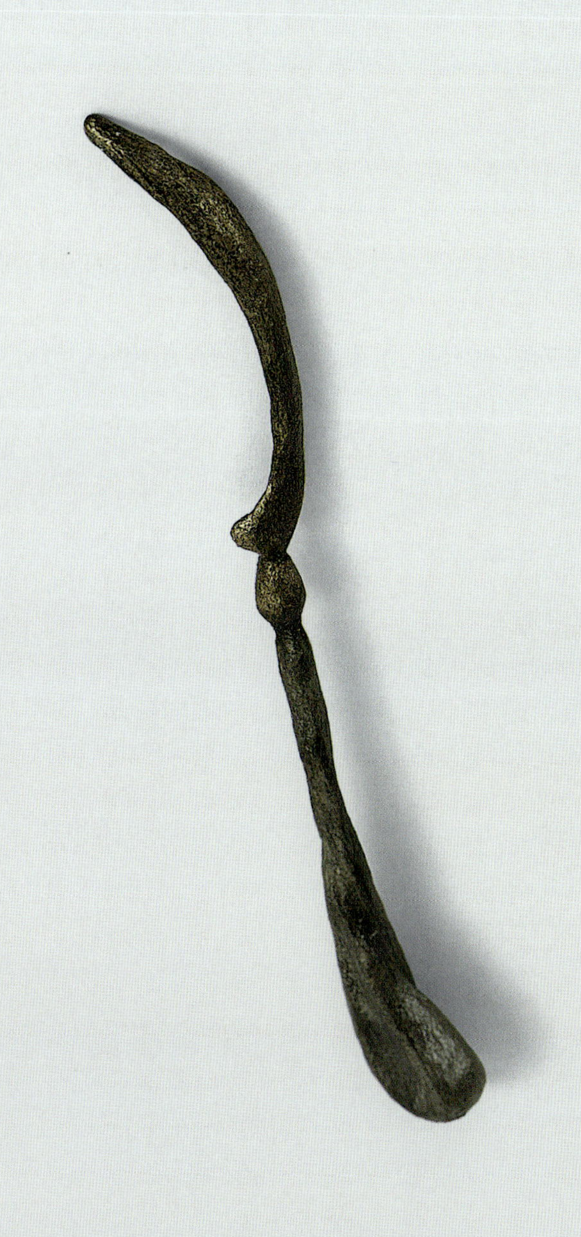

MEZUZAH CONTAINER

Guardian of my soul, protect this house, wrapping
me in language when I sleep and when I wake,
syllables engraved on every doorpost, every gate,
sealed upon our hearts when we enter and embark,
listening for Your voice, a furled banner over us
as we, inscribed, dwell within Your sovereign,
consecrated love.

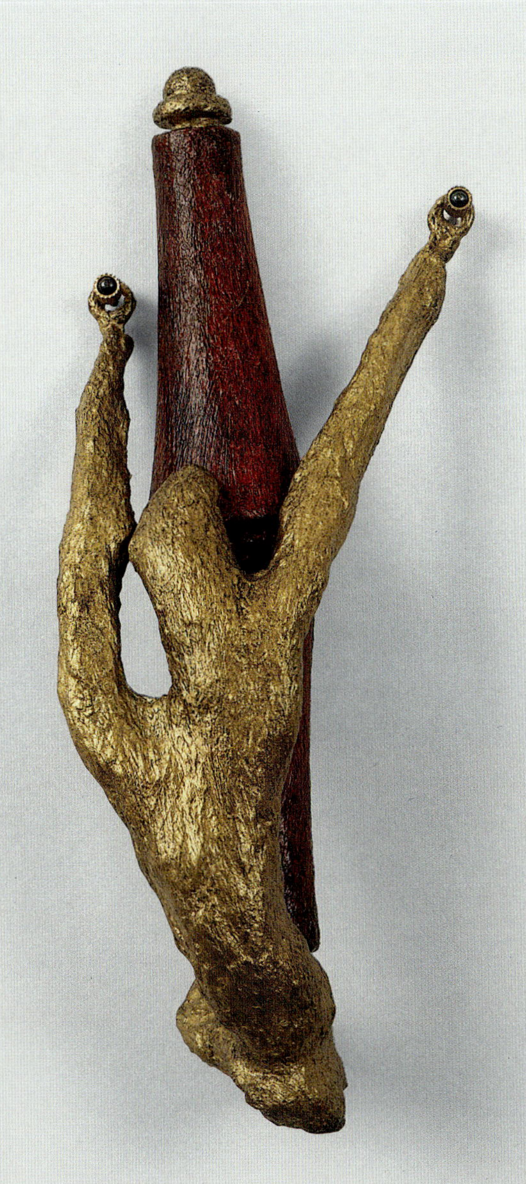

TZEDAKAH CONTAINER

Contain what cannot be contained, as You are
gracious and merciful to us, so we, reflecting the
image in which we are uniquely made, return what
we were given, rooted in our imperfect earth,
aspiring to heaven.

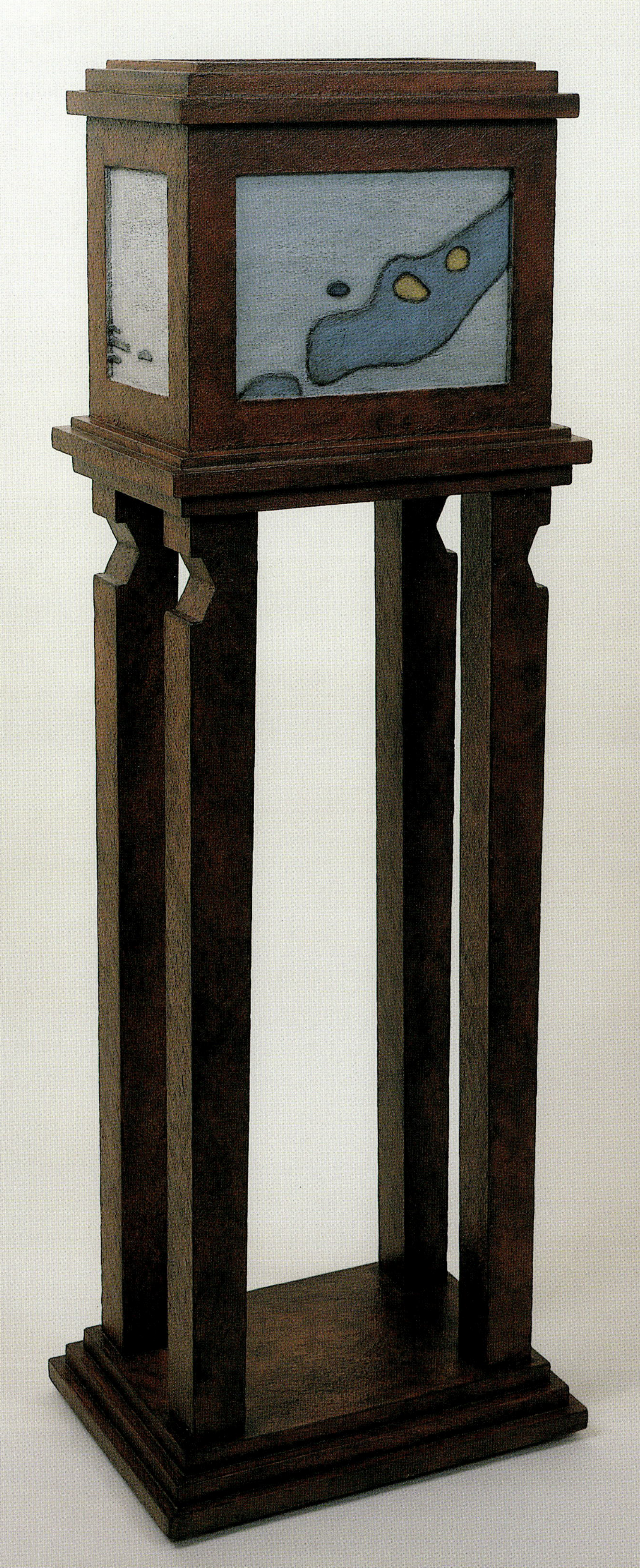

NETILAT YADAYIM

Spirit, hover over water, transparent bounty, hand to
hand, spilling elemental blessing, immerse us in the
silence of thanksgiving, the sustenance of command.

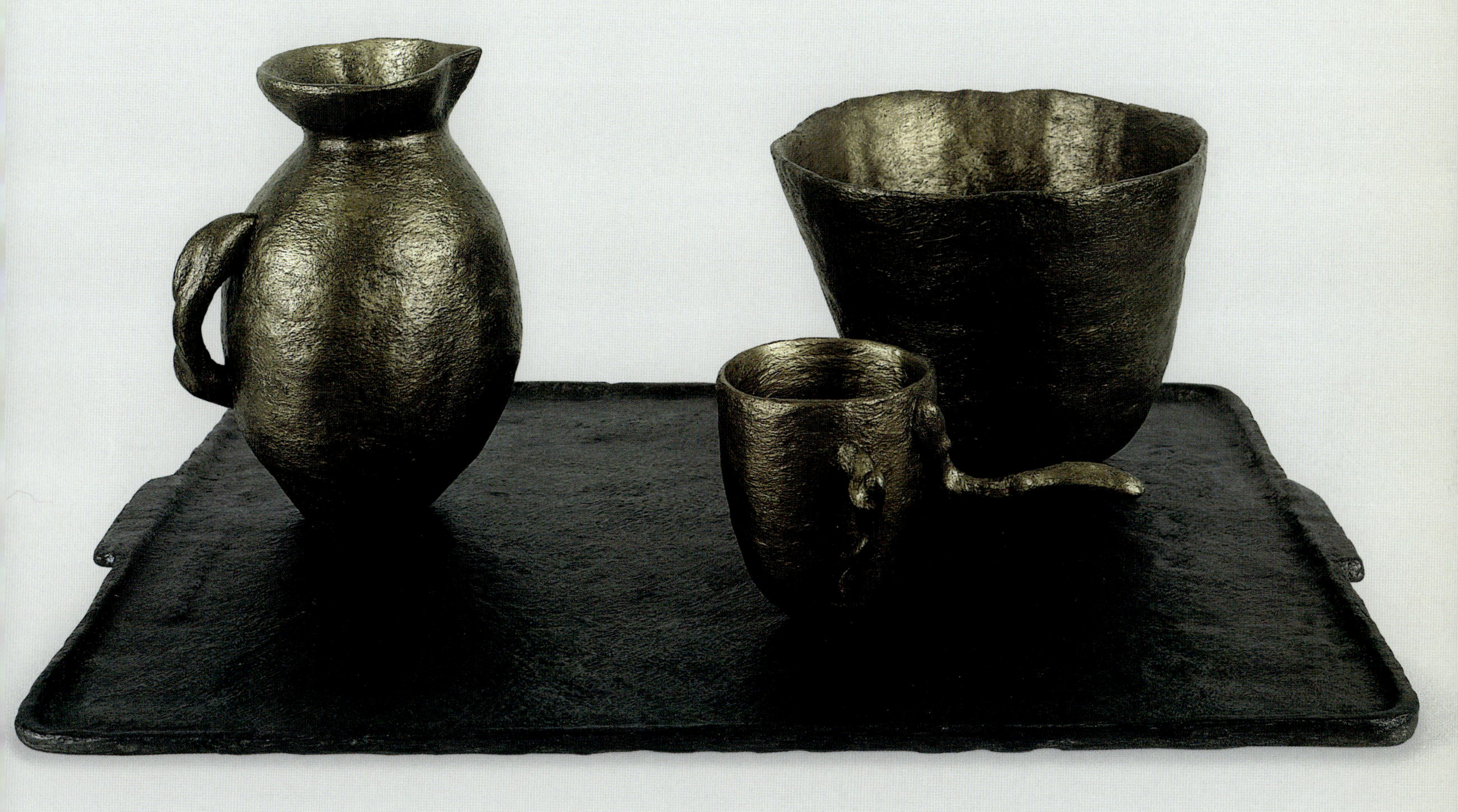

SHABBAT THRONE

On this day, jewel of the week, we are sons and daughters of majesty, the crown of creation, each an heir, anointed to bear the mantle of royalty, resting in You on this day of delight, rejoicing in our aristocracy.

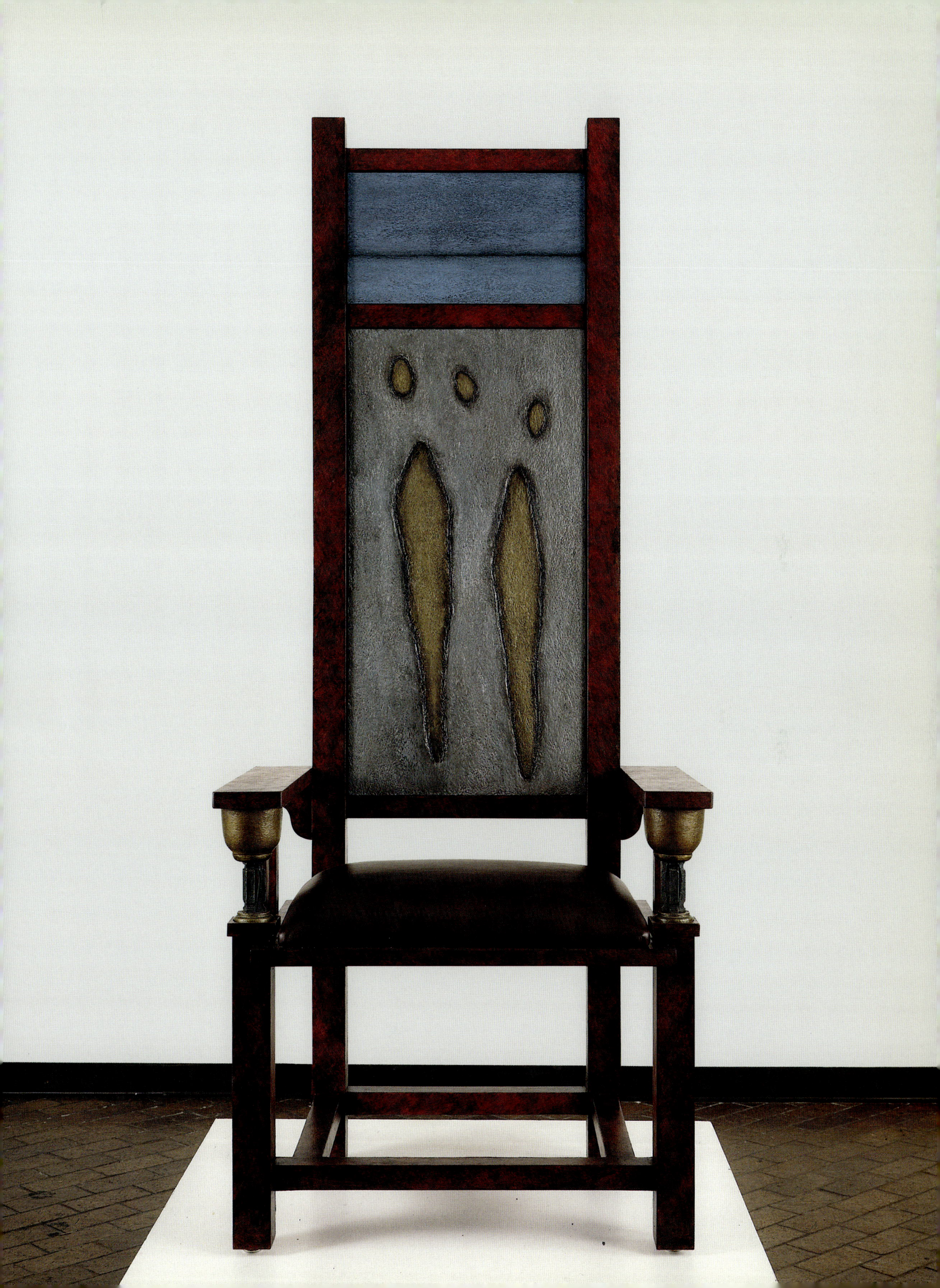

KIDDUSH CUP

Sky, earth and stars: Circle this vessel with love
and rest, with tenderness for every living thing,
sanctifying separateness, slaking our thirst for
dominion, transforming, briefly, doing into being,
what was rent made whole by the lovingkindness
of this evening.

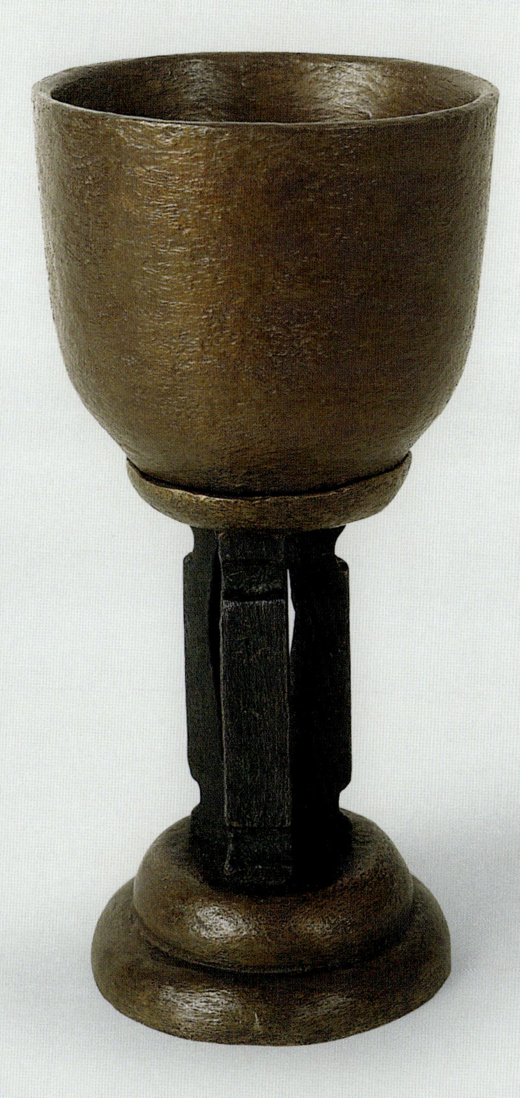

SHABBAT CHALLAH TRAY

Braid my soul, amplified, to You, sustain me with abundance multiplied, the desert leavened, sifting wilderness for providence, releasing from earth the gifts of heaven.

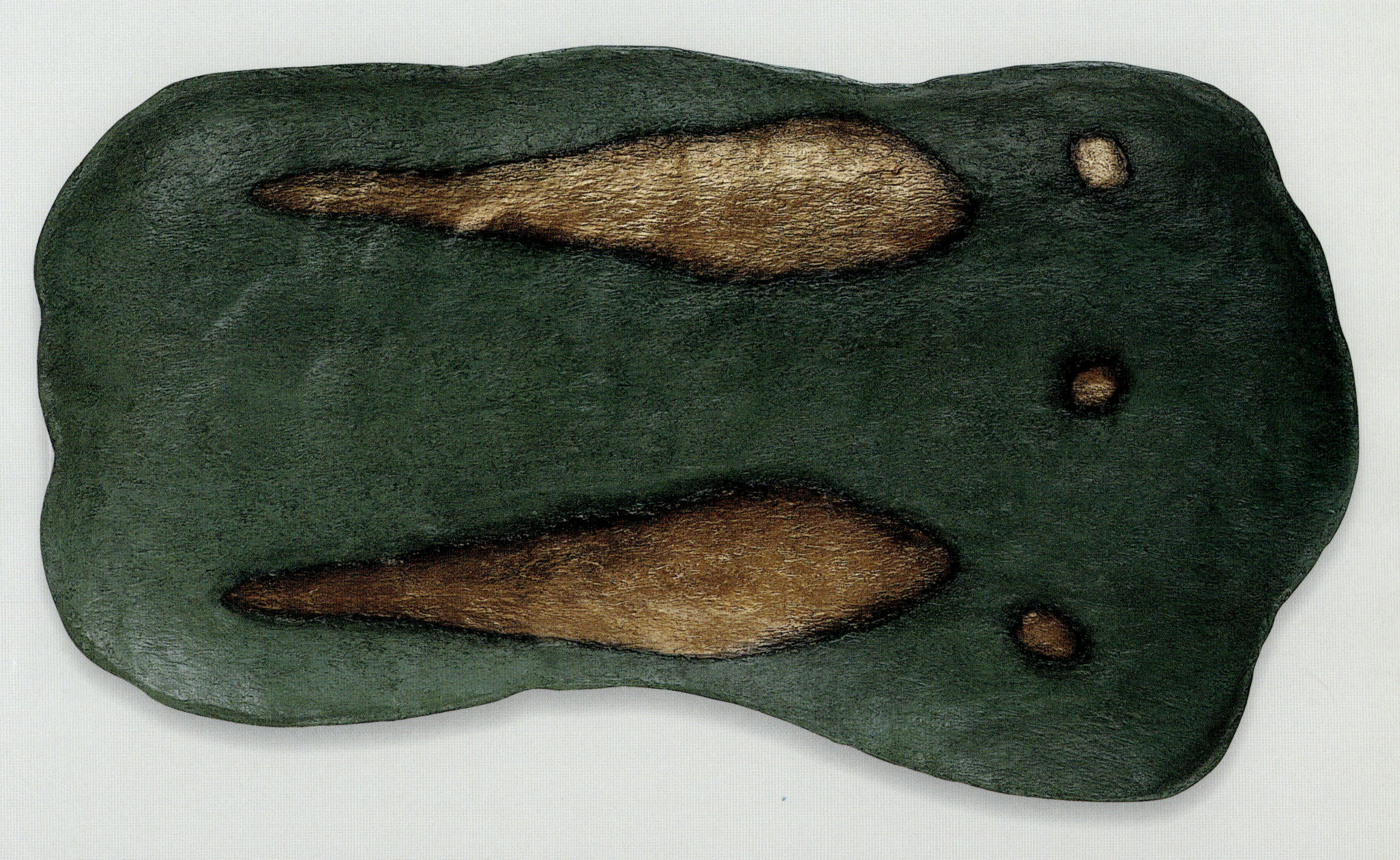

BESAMIM

CONTAINER

The time for rest is ended. May labor be sweet and joyfulness suffuse the week. May we be blessed by fruitfulness and may the perfume of a good name accompany us. Our tongues, our hearts aligned with what is true and the work of our hands honoring You. The light will soon be quenched. I am not afraid. The world redeemed, Creator, day by day.

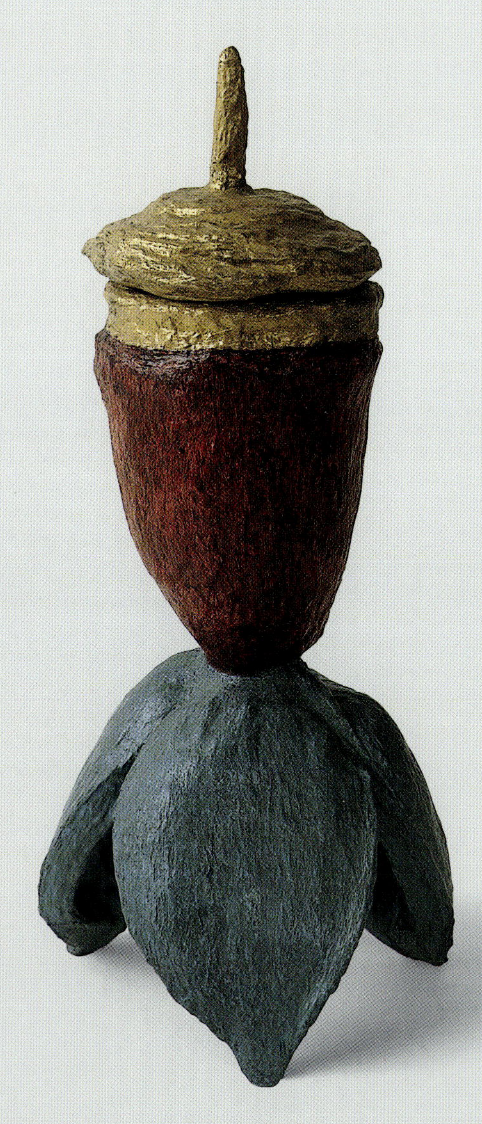

ROSH HODESH OIL HOLDER

Glory to God for the newest moon, composed of night,
the bounty of birth and blessing, peace and well-being,
the requests of our hearts fulfilled for the good, from
eclipse to amity in clement light.

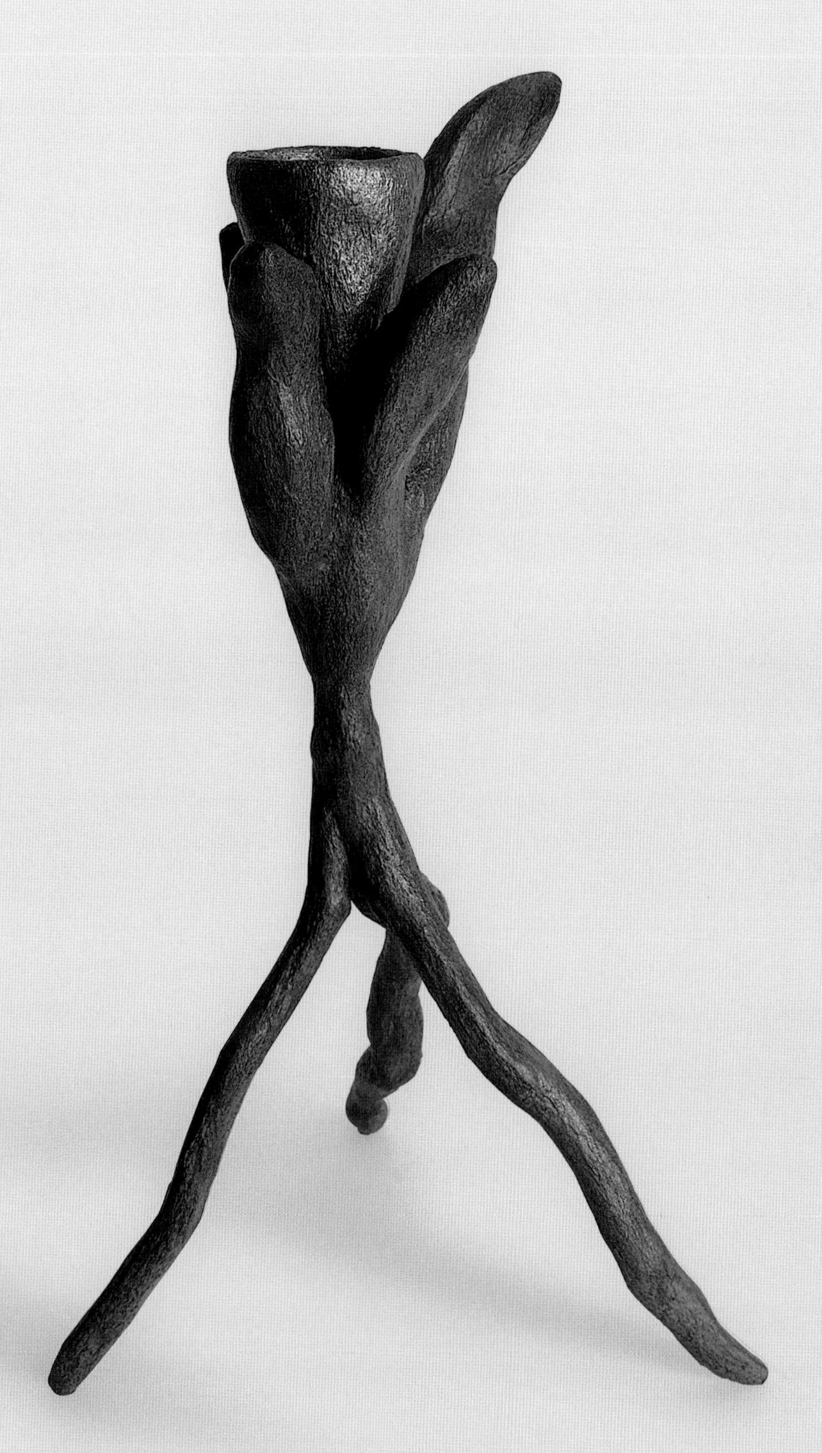

ROSH HASHANAH APPLE-AND-HONEY SET

Awaken to the year as it is born, the aleph bet
beginning, writing our destiny. Sovereign of sweetness,
refute severity, remember us as we return to You,
word by word, assemble us, Scribe, let us hear Your call
as we summon You into our lives.

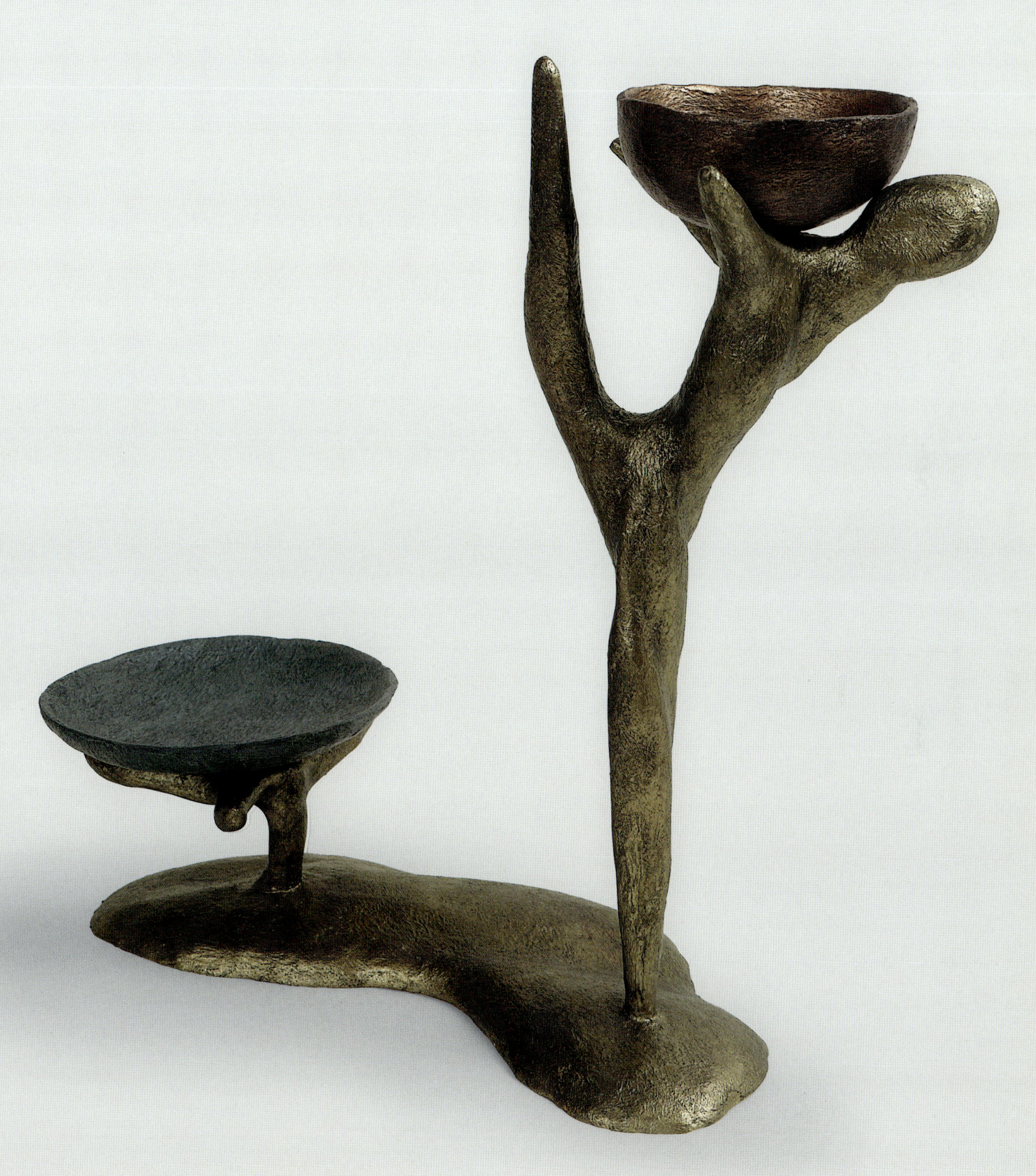

ETROG CONTAINER

Bearing the scent of the east, touch, see, taste a sensual companion to speech, seasoning commandment. This is the feast of joy, contained by the wisdom of old age and prayers for rain. Embrace abundance, be profligate with blessings, immoderate, harvest the king's caution with a surfeit of mercy and compassion.

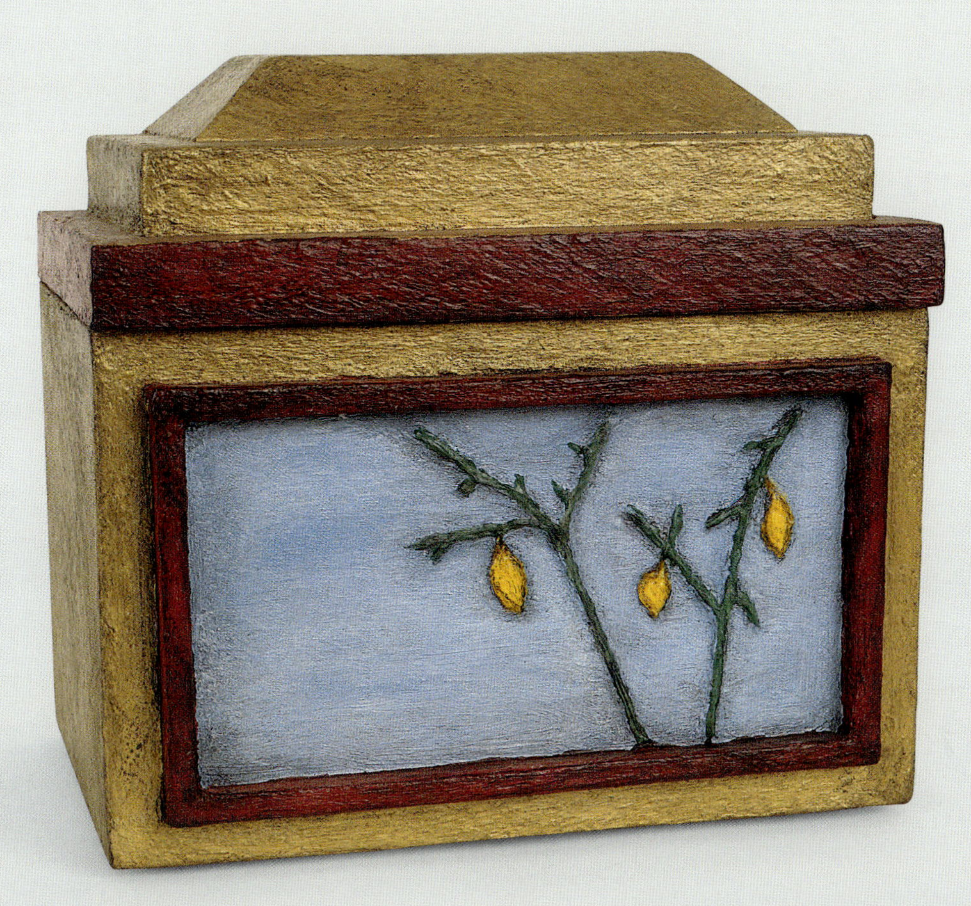

MENORAH

Light my way in the long night and shortened day. Light augmented, ablaze, consigning falseness to shade, shattering the idols of the market until the radiant heart illuminates this season with beacons of courage and of freedom.

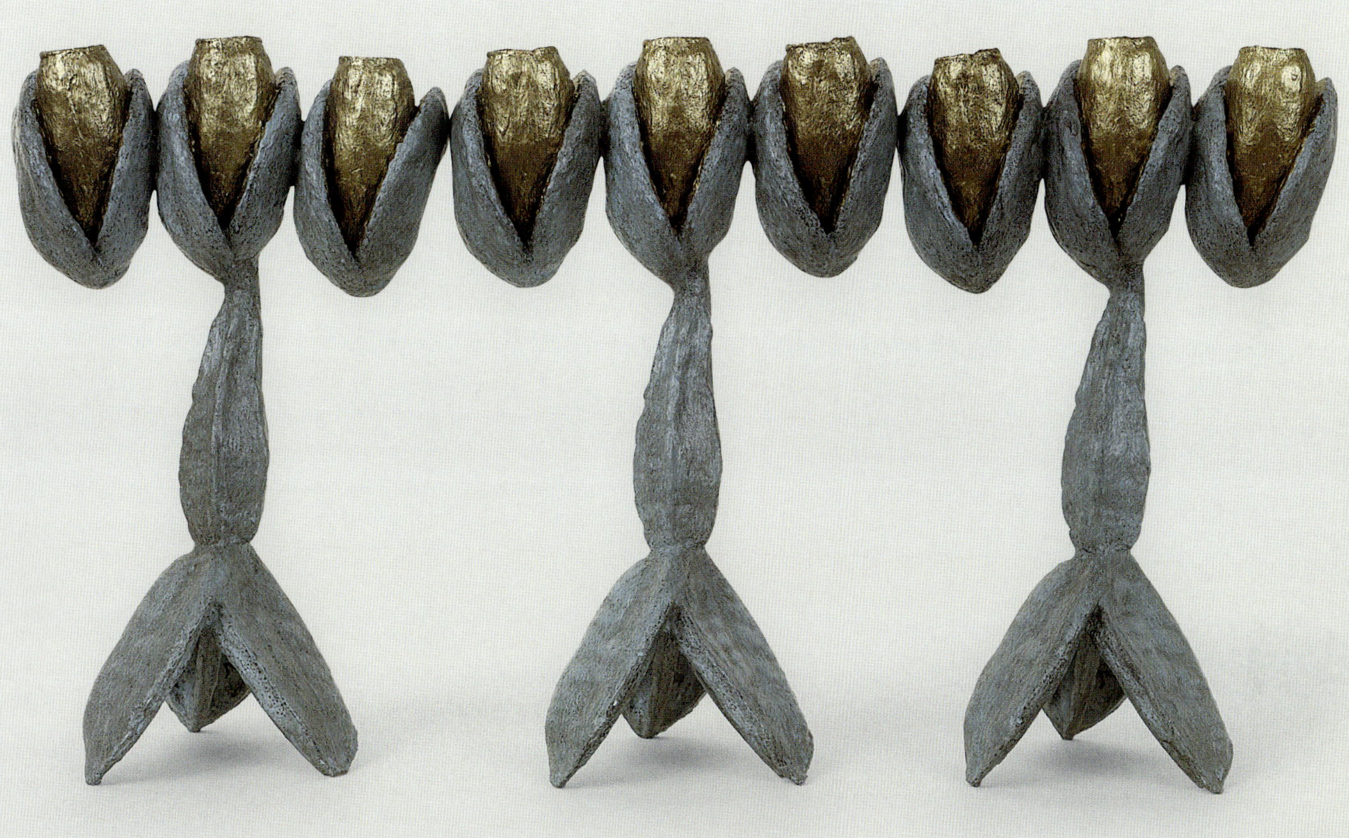

MEGILLAH COVER

Hidden within, heroine, turn our lot from lament to festivity, from silence to deliverance, the darkening chamber lit by a single star, repeal the harsh decree with words of peace and beauty, honor those who pay tribute from afar: Did you not attain royalty for this appointed hour?

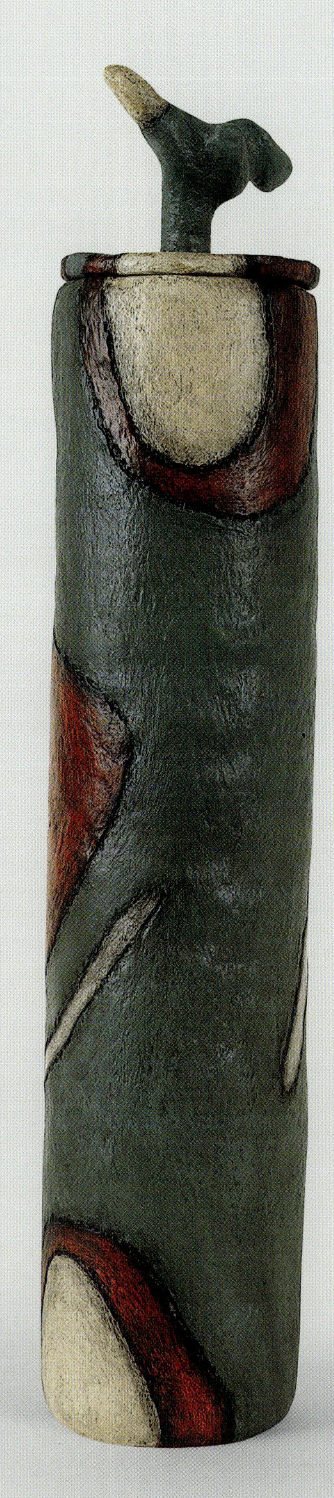

PURIM GROGGER

Blot out the name of the evil one whose deeds we must remember and retell, daze him with din, turn his proclamations into pandemonium, alphabet to babel until his henchmen can no longer tell depraved decree from cacophony.

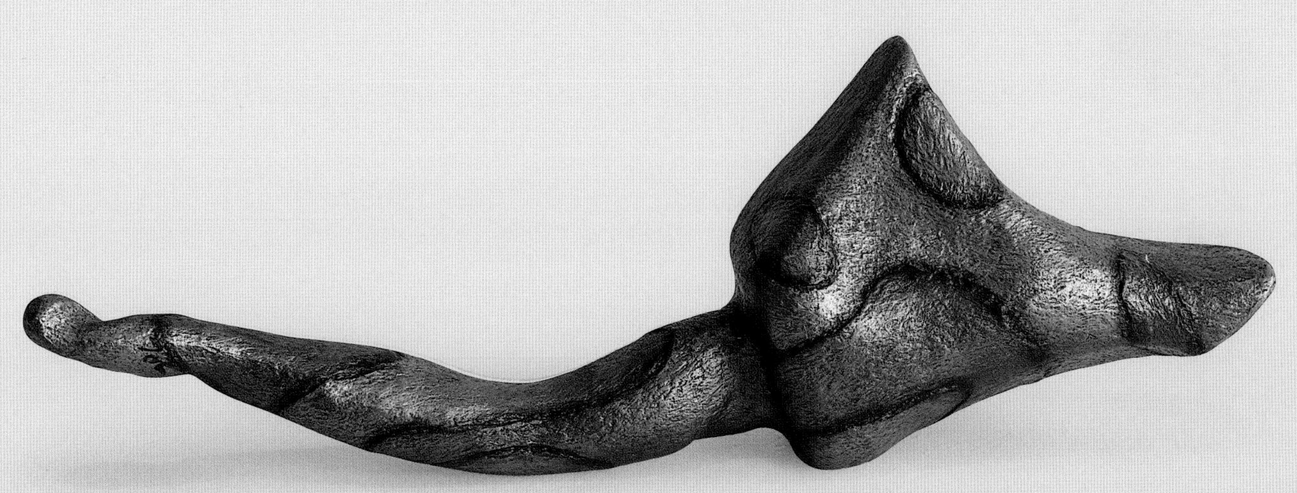

SEDER PLATE

Remember me, remember, the One who leads you
safely through the water, accompanied by mist,
by fire, from enslavement to this splendid hour,
bitter transmuted into sweet, chaos into harmony,
desolation yielding to spring, sacrifice flowering into
songs of paradise.

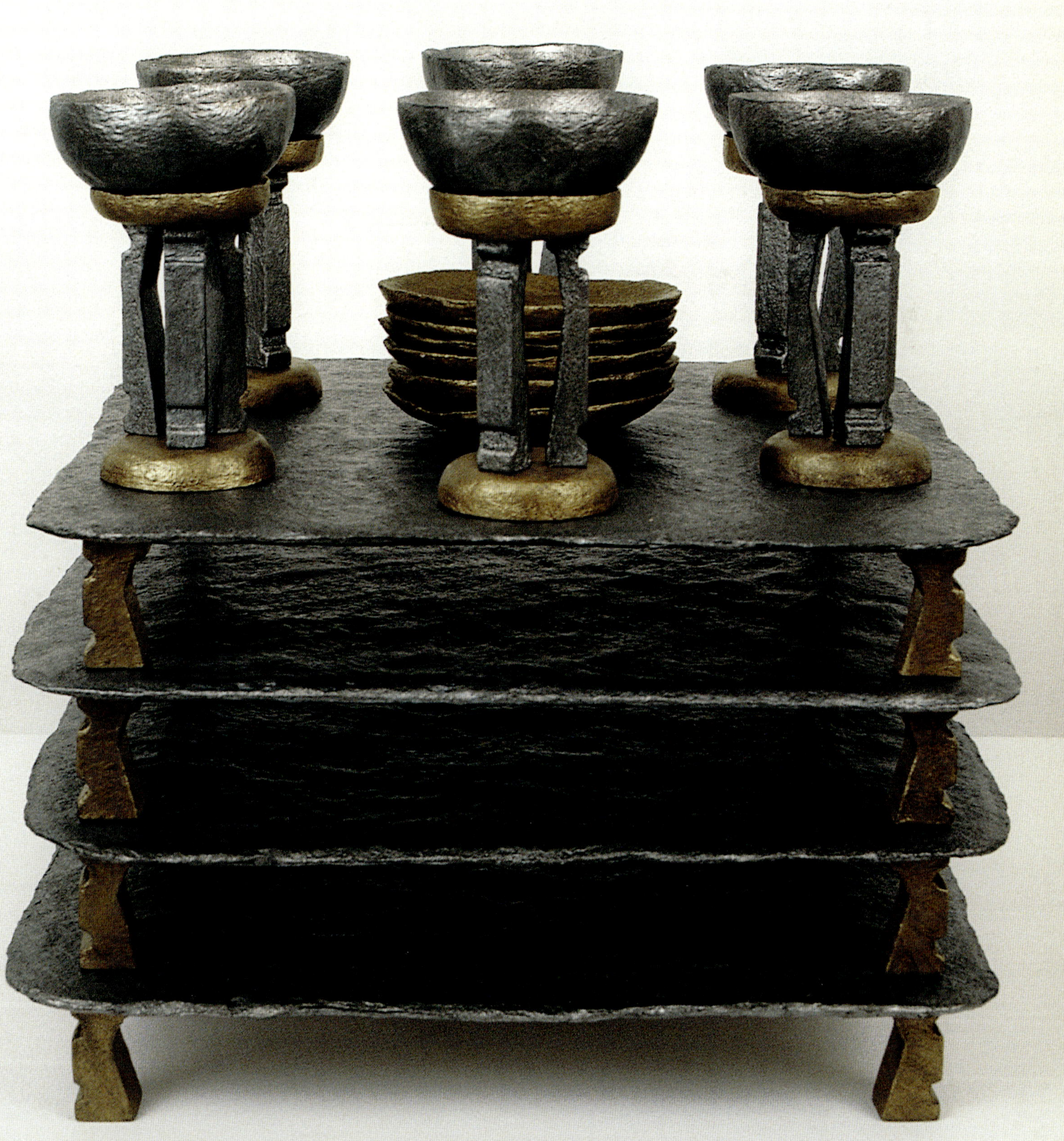

ELIJAH'S CUP

Hurry, reconcile the heart, redeem us from
dissonance, gather us in from the exile of argument,
from earthly fracture to eternity, bring us to the
threshold, speedily, revive our mysteries, witness our
desire, ascending, heavenward, solitary prophet in
a chariot of fire.

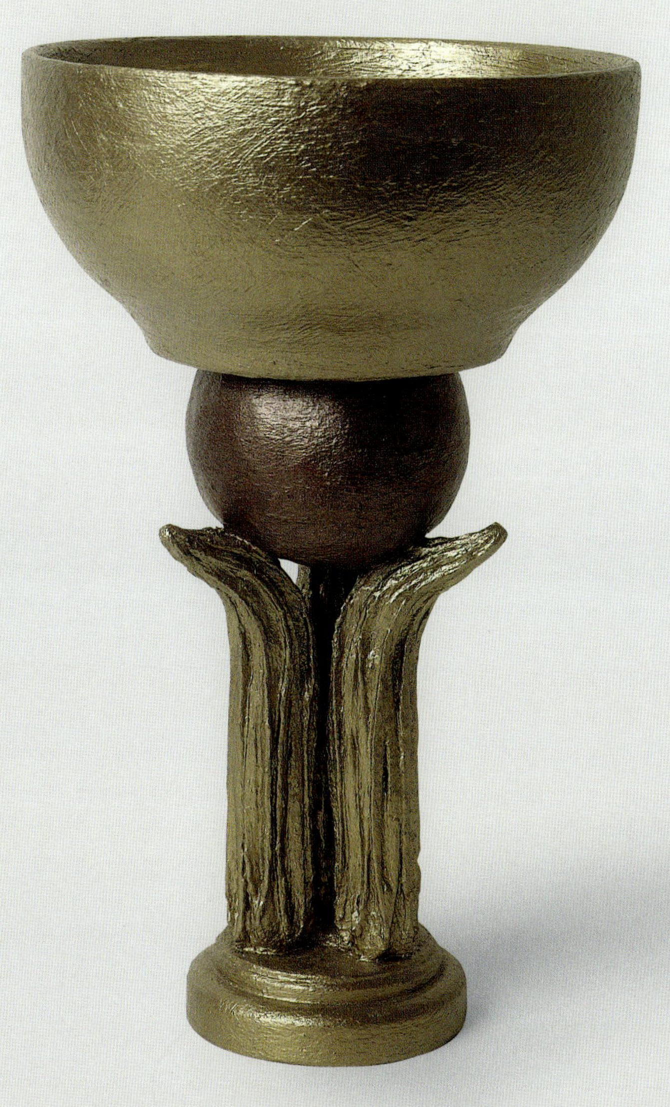

MIRIAM'S CUP

Sing to God of earthly might undone, dance until the body is one with You who have triumphed gloriously, reclaiming us, splitting the sea of invisibility so that we may walk in Your ways, witnesses of bone, limb, spirit, skin: Female and male You created us, drink, exulting, from freedom's cup.

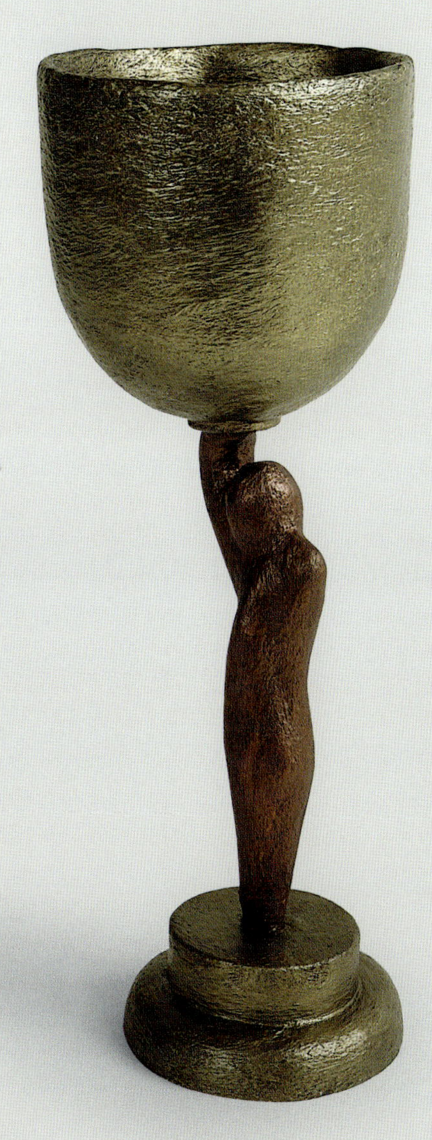

OMER COUNTER

One by one husks fall away, seeds of freedom,
concealed in slavery, lovingkindness in captivity,
Lord of severity, lover of beauty, lead us through the
parting sea, song of exultation, dance of victory, glory
over the unrepentant enemy, the savor of grace and
seal of mercy, from the veiled day in which we began
until the blazing revelation.

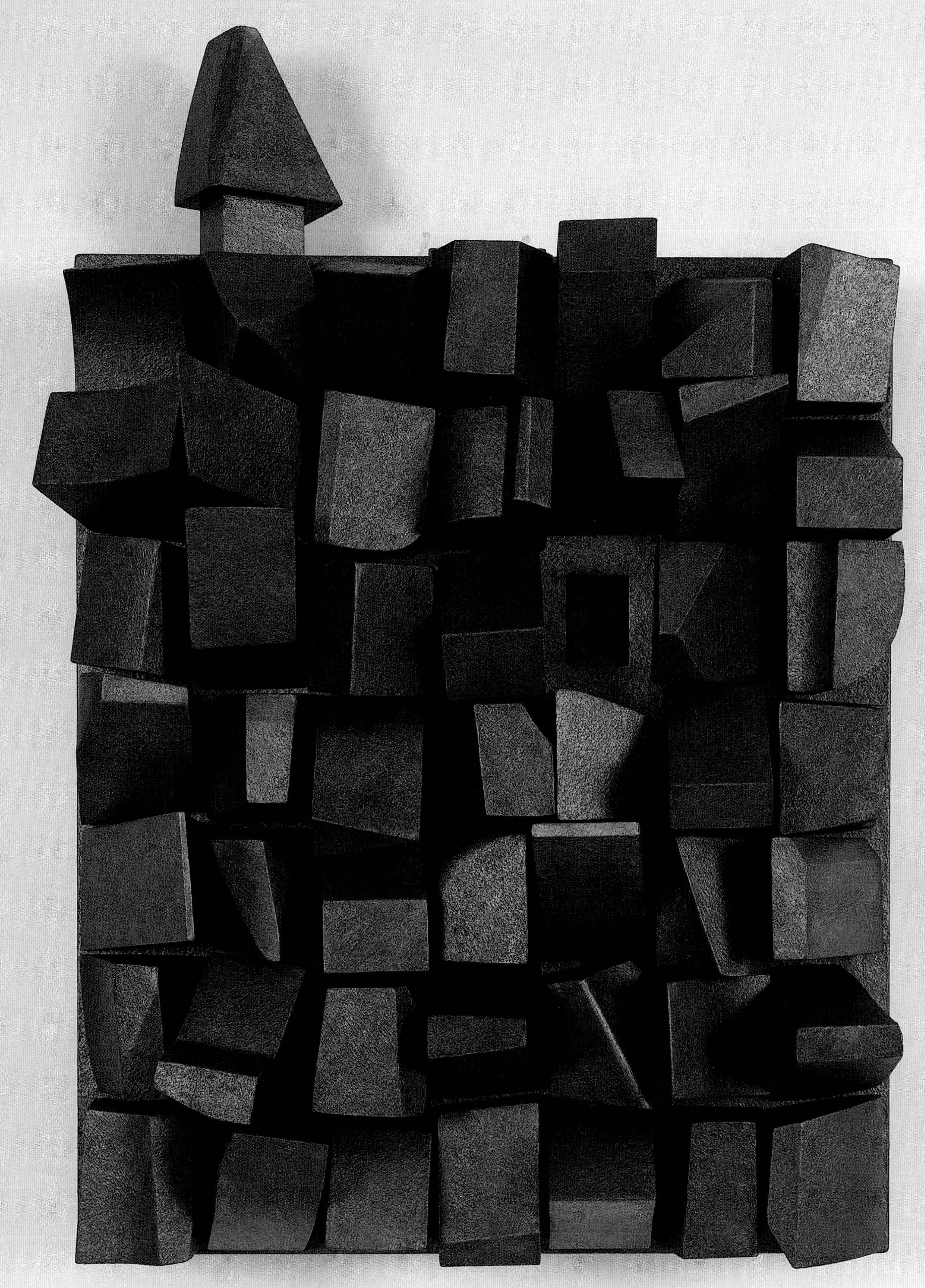

ELIJAH'S CHAIR

Cradled by elders, little one, may this sacrifice redeem
you from all strife and may the cry of covenant
release you into life, resplendent as a multitude of
stars gleaming over sands, welcoming the weary
traveler into his inheritance.

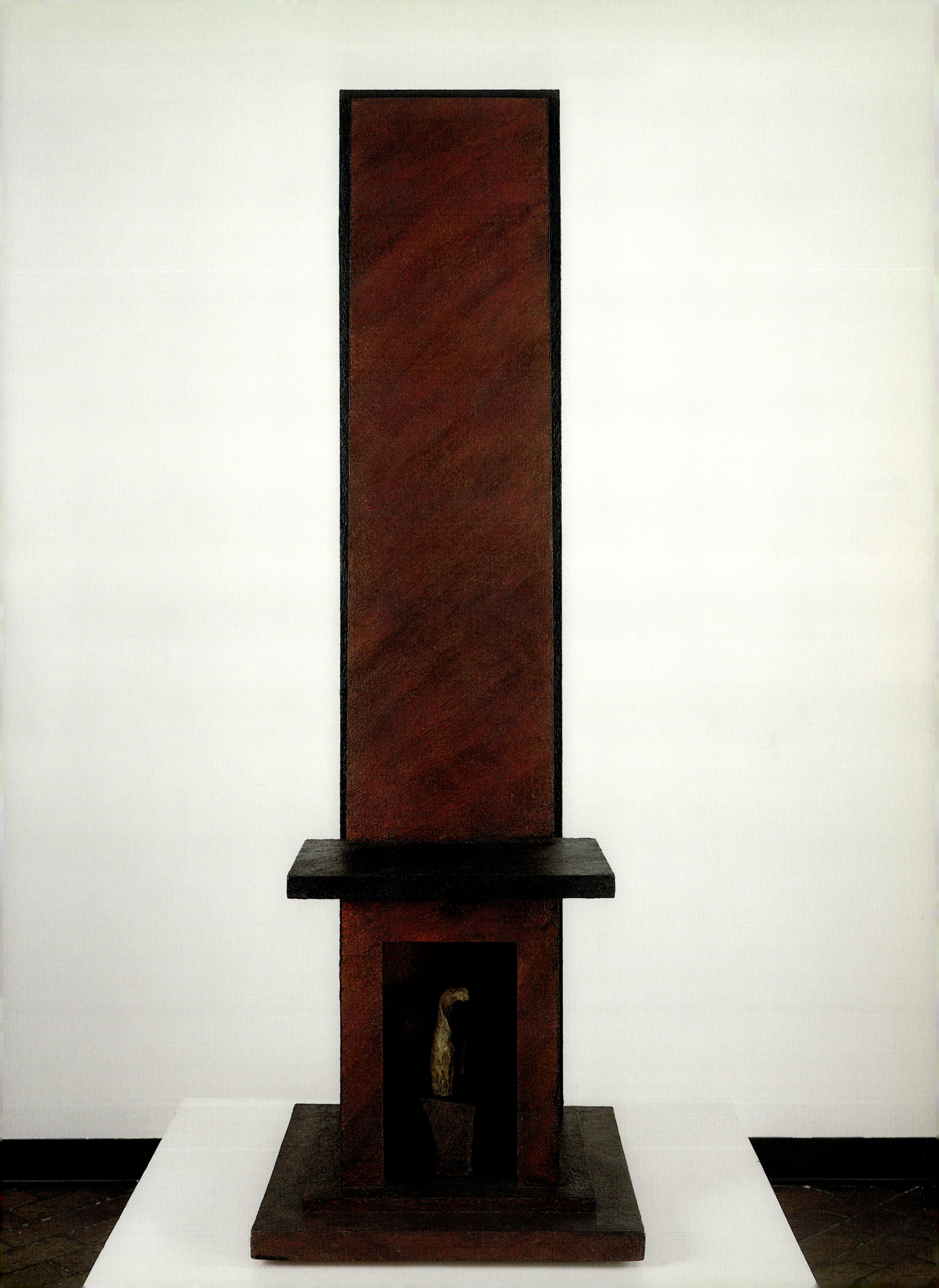

SHALOM BAT CHAIRS

Leap into our lives, from the hidden places to the hills
of spice, garden of pomegranate, apple of paradise,
awakened by the perfume of your name, we sing you
into our mothers' house and listen for your voice.

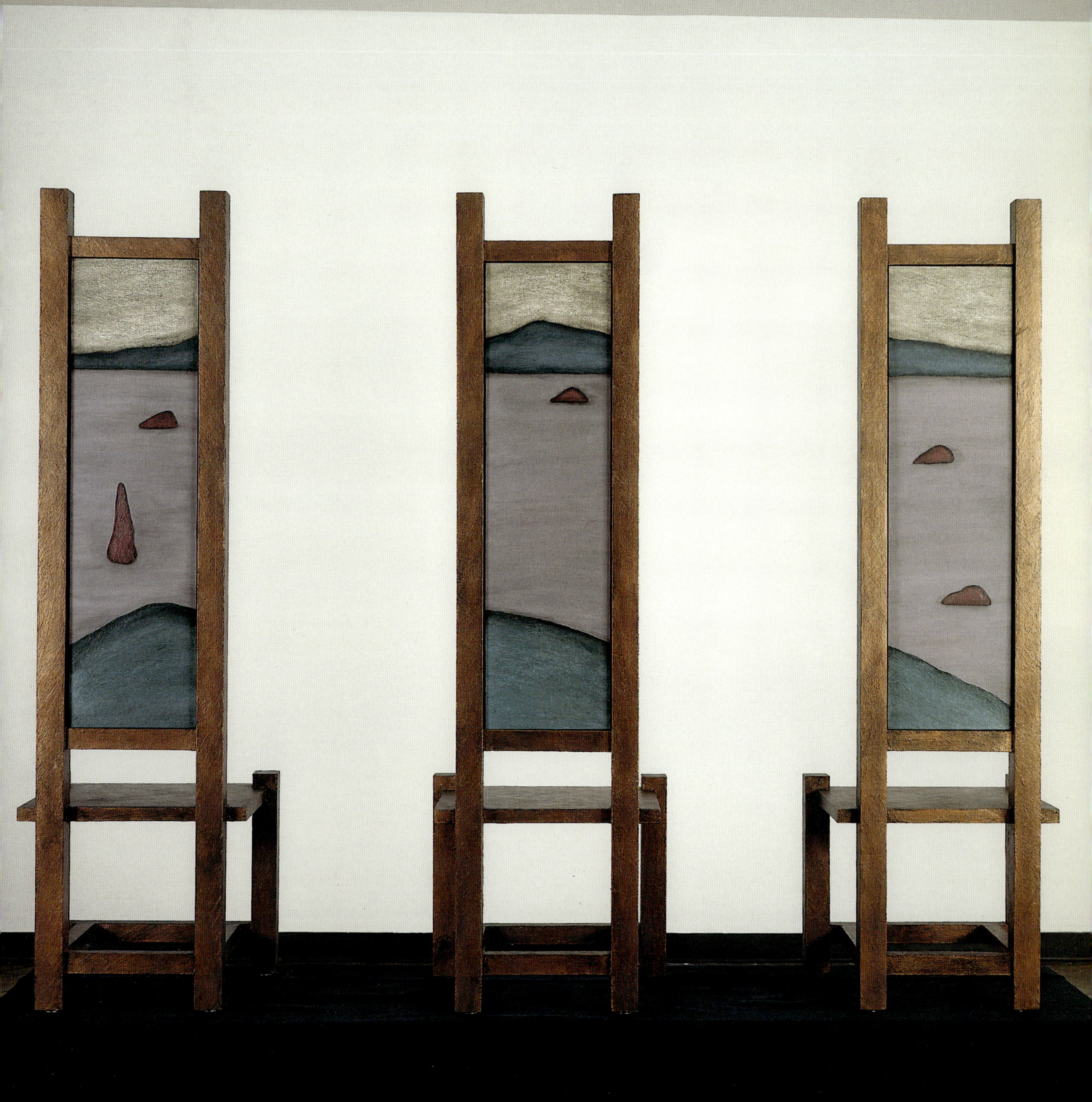

HUPPAH I bind you to me eternally, I bind you to me in justice, tenderly, I bind you to me in faith and faithfulness, so that we shall know You, and You us.

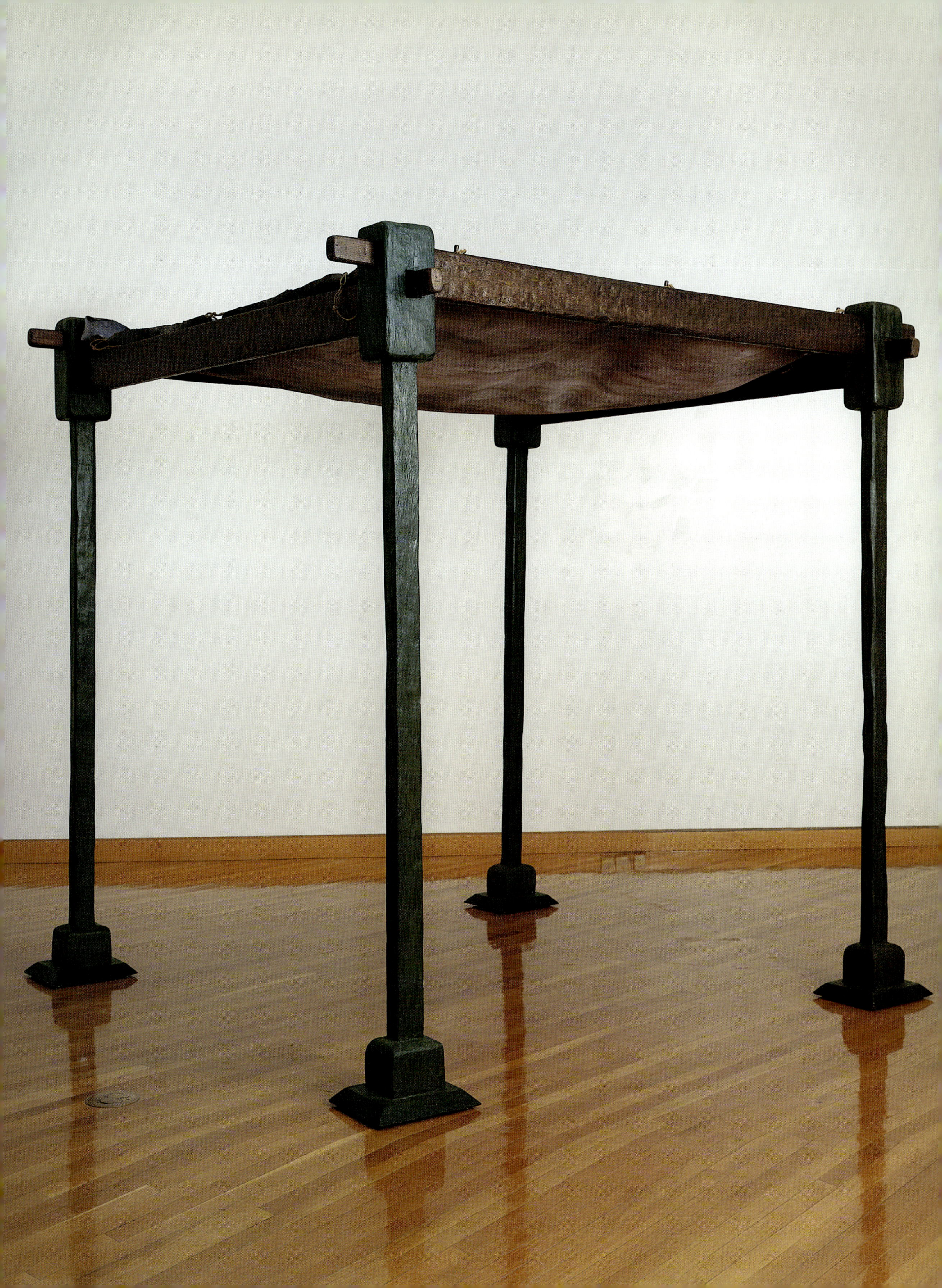

WEDDING CUP

On the threshold, the vessel we will become, the
spilling cup of Your design, felicity unalloyed,
drinking our future in draughts of unquenched joy.

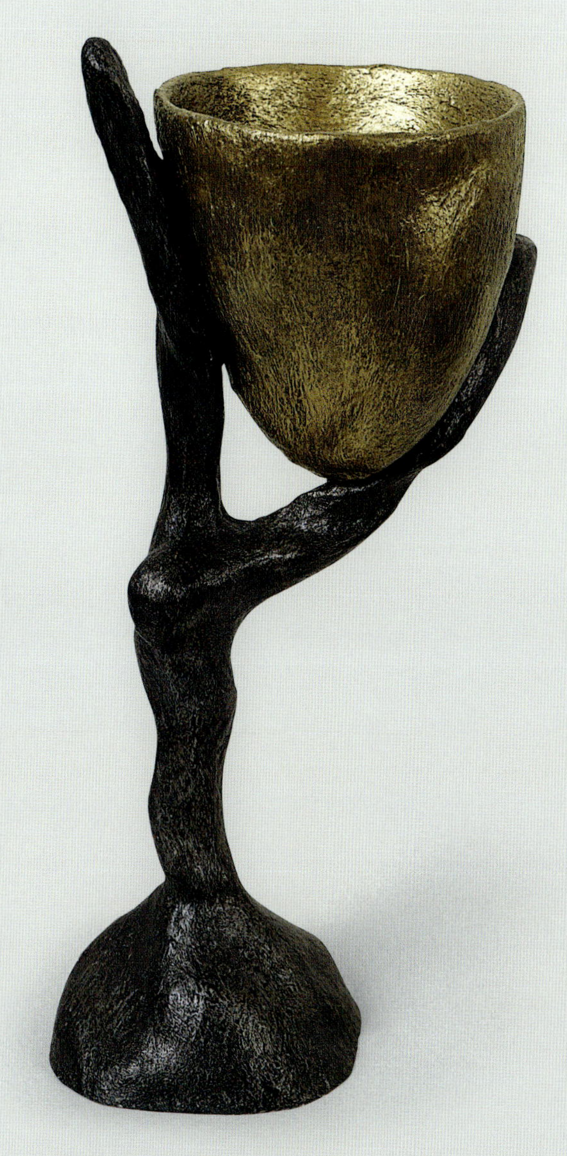

YAHRZEIT CANDLE

Unconsumed through the night like the love you
offered, constant in a darkened house where I, longing
for light, remember you, the walls and ceiling kindled,
your soul, undying before me, incandescent, dazzling.

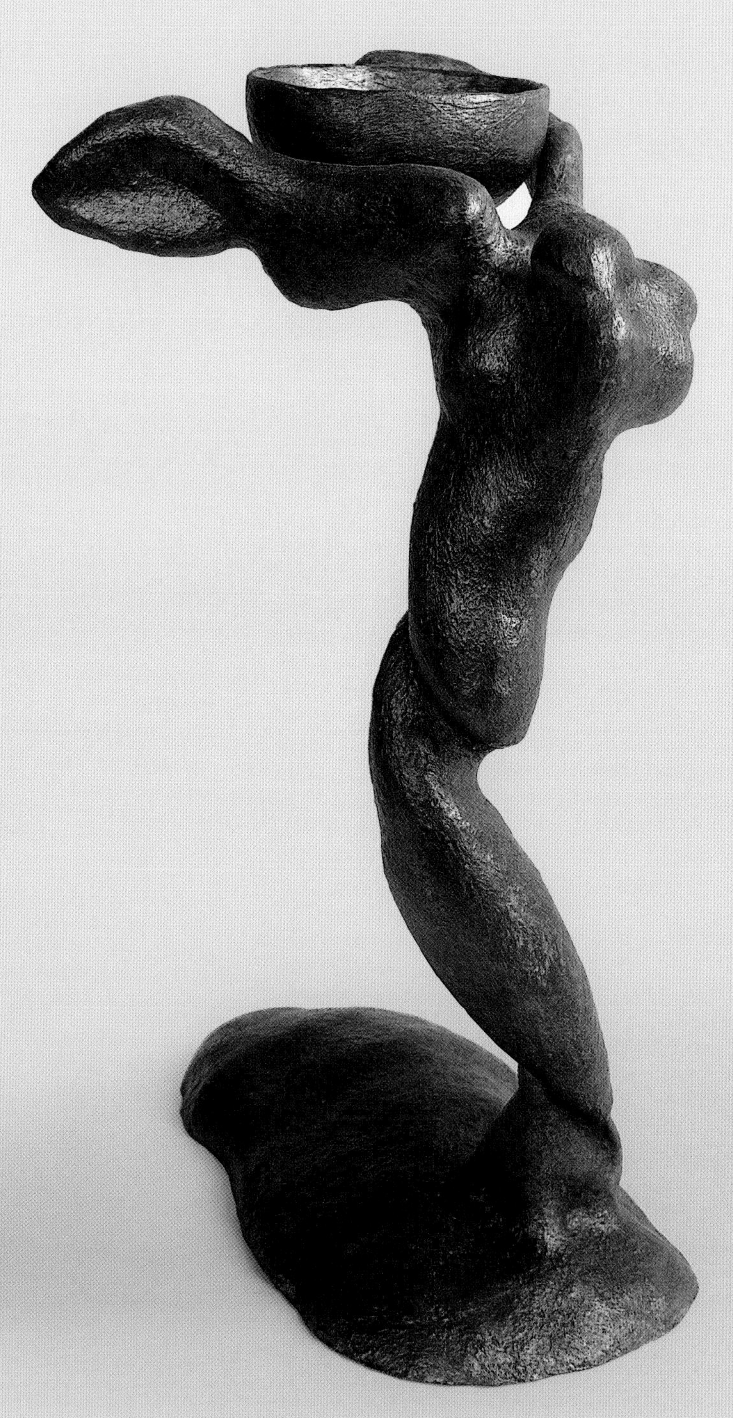

MEDITATIVE ROOM

Breath floating above the water, let there be light, at the birth of evening and the rising day, let there be praise, sanctuary of sky and cradling sea, listening, the gathering dusk radiant with thanksgiving.

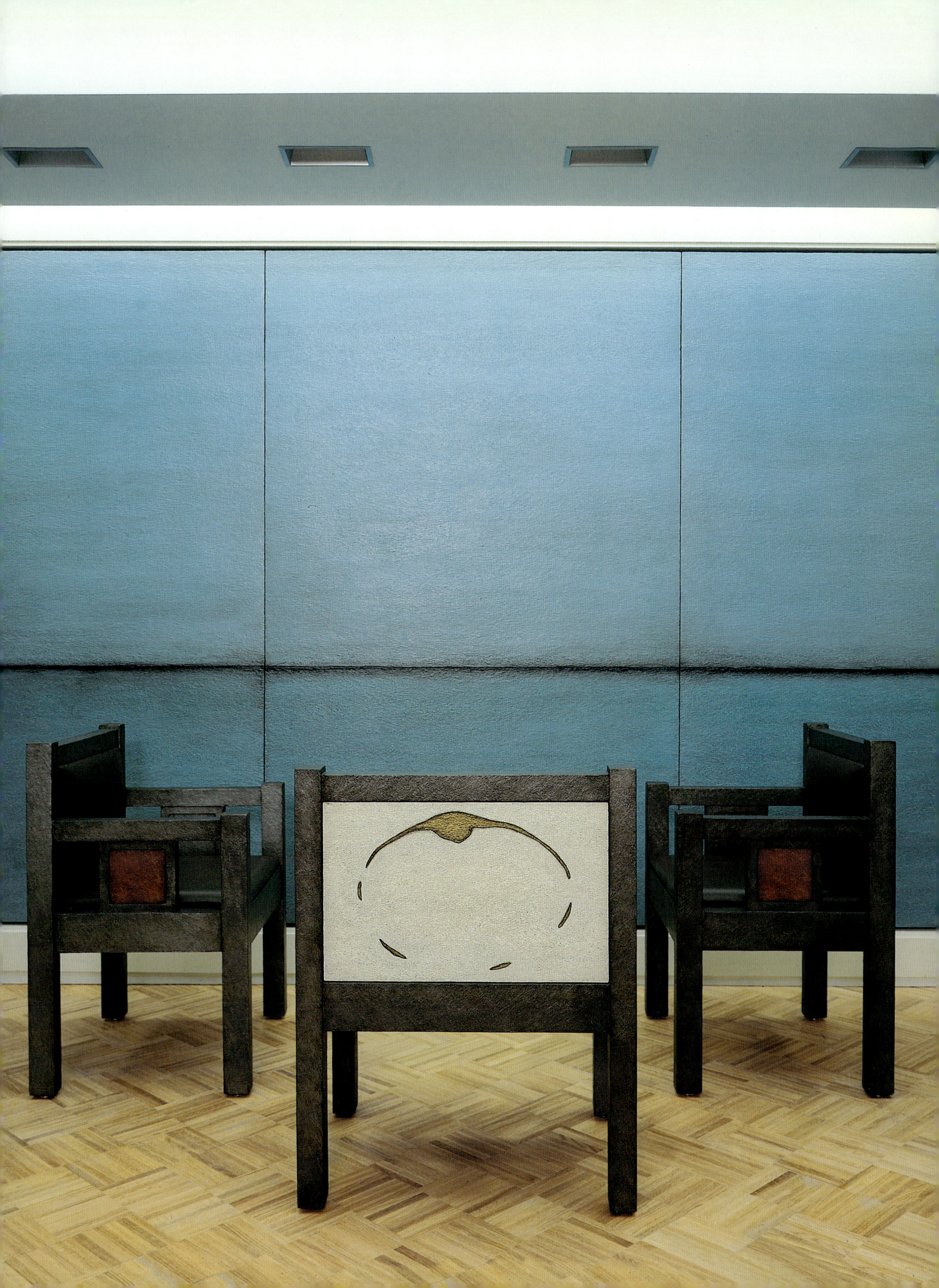

AFTERWORD

Creating Midrash: An Artist's Perspective

RUTH WEISBERG

The origins of Jewish art are quite clearly delineated in the Torah: "The Lord spoke to Moses, saying, 'Tell the Israelite people to bring me gifts, you shall accept gifts for me from every person whose heart so moves him' " (Exodus 1:25). There follows an elaborate description of how to build and decorate the Ark of the Covenant, the cover of gold, the two cherubim in hammered work, and much, much more. Our embroidered Torah mantles, golden crowns, and silver Torah shields are direct descendants of this impulse to decorate. So one of the primary and most enduring principles to affect Jewish art is *hiddur mitzvah*—a mitzvah should be performed in the most aesthetic way possible. Over the millennia, the art of the Jewish people has been overwhelmingly devoted to *hiddur mitzvah*, celebrating and adorning as a gift for God, and always with the sense of being within a like-minded community.

There is, however, another possibility, which I think will be less familiar, but just as generative for those of us whose task it is to produce and activate culture. We are the ones who are called upon to make meaning, to create Jewish culture, be it liturgical, visual, musical, textual, dialogic, institutional, or literary. I propose that art is also a way of knowing, a different kind of intelligence, and an organizing principle. This paradigm of Jewish art as knowing involves a more critical dialogue with its cultural context. Like Jewish study, the most profound experience of art can combine and integrate the ethical, emotional, spiritual, and intellectual aspects of ourselves. It can even provide another avenue for commentary and interpretation. We are the people of the book, we understand the power of the word, but visual art can also create midrash. It, too, can shade, extend, question, and renew the old stories, the timeless insights.

In Judaism, we tend to think of midrash as written or verbal elaborations on the Torah. Indeed, midrash has many roles: sometimes it fills in missing parts of the story, and at other times it answers an implicit question. Midrashic commentary often adds a human dimension or a psychological insight to the narrative. More than anything, it tends to enliven the archetypal stories for successive generations. Visual art can also function in these ways, in its use of specific images, its sensory appeal, and its direct emotive power.

Among artists, Tobi Kahn is exemplary as someone sensitive to the midrashic potential of Jewish liturgical objects. He approaches these objects out of his masterful aesthetic as an artist rather than from a craftsman's point of view. Kahn's art, with its spare evocative forms, which suggest both nature and timeless ancient cultures, tends to offer multiple associations. In *Erhu* (1996; Plate 18), which is loosely based on the German-Jewish stacked form of seder plates, the various feet and spacers that hold up the plates have a subtle reference to Egyptian profiles. In this way, Kahn inserts the lessons of history into his present-day reenactment. It is as if now that we are free, our history can assist us in holding on to our rituals.

Tobi Kahn is also very clear concerning the melding of innovation and tradition. His deep knowledge of Jewish observance allows him to incorporate the new without breaking with the old. The three chairs he designed and built for his daughter's naming ceremony, a relatively new ritual in Judaism, were for his wife, mother, and mother-in-law (Plate 23). Their design forms a commentary on the value of female participation in Jewish life-cycle rituals. Kahn's chairs represent one function of art—as the proof and continuation of a living culture. Art can also shape social and political meaning and belief. For example, in an era of globalization, there is a tendency toward sweeping homogeneity and a certain leveling of experience and identity. The very individuality of an artwork helps preserve uniqueness and difference and, in the process, warns against a utopian view of globalization.

Jewish spirituality has been described as the heightening of our awareness, through blessings and mitzvot, through God and Torah. *Kedushah*—holiness, wholeness, oneness—sometimes comes as a stunning insight into the nature of the universe, a way of knowing that transcends our usual, more everyday understanding. Insight can arrive unexpectedly through a Torah passage, a prayer, the strains of *Kol Nidre*, or even a Yiddish lullaby, but it can also be transmitted by visual artists who add their images to the ongoing conversation. Artists continue to enhance the living, vibrant Jewish culture, which is a gift to ourselves and to our children's children—*le-dor va-dor*, from generation to generation. It adorns God's tabernacle as *hiddur mitzvah* and creates meaning and identity in our twenty-first-century lives.

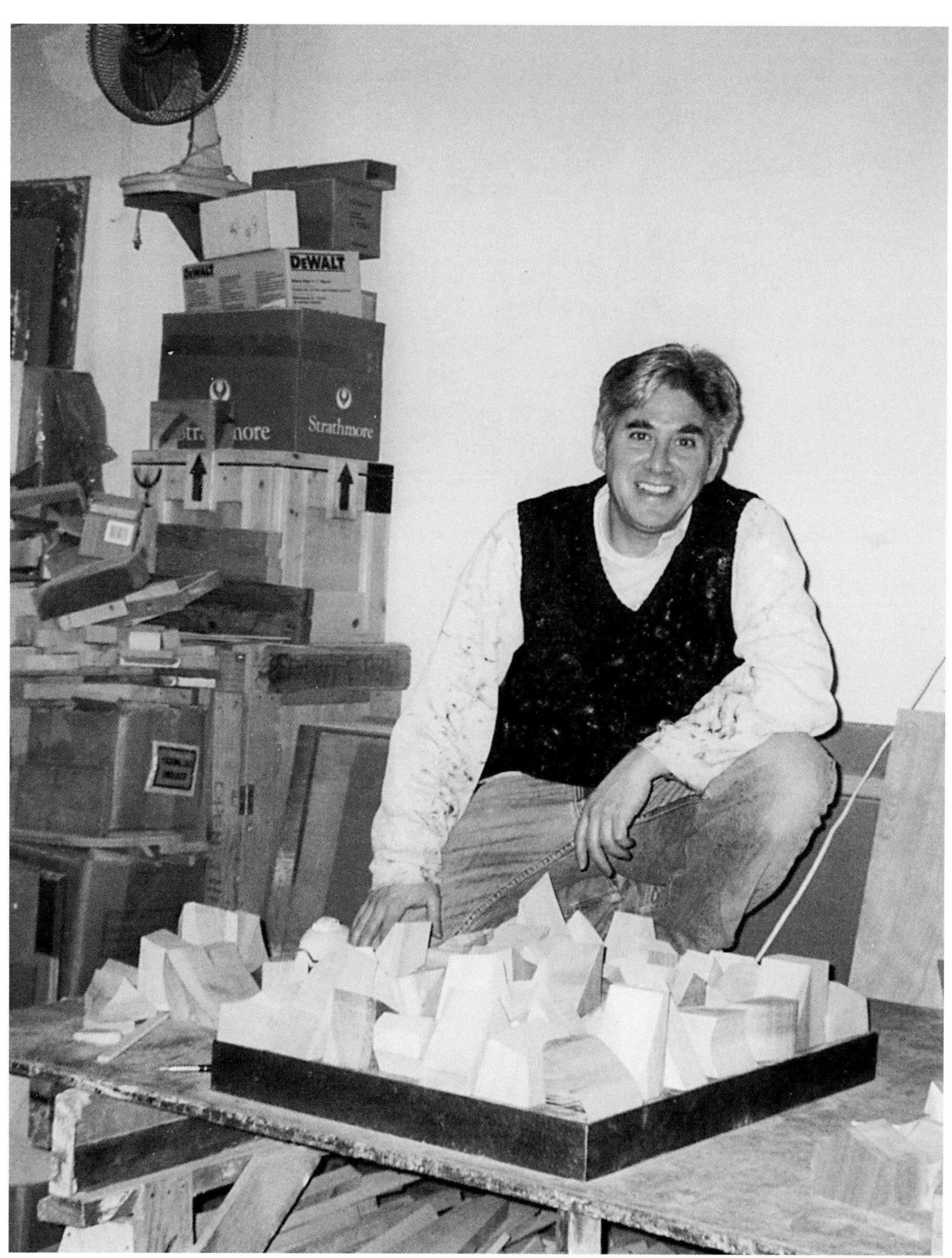
DEWALT
DEWALT
Strathmore

CHRONOLOGY

1952 Born May 8, New York, N.Y. Son of Ellen (née Schapiro) and Herbert Kahn, and younger brother of Felice Kahn (now Felice Kahn Zisken).

1958–1966 Attends Samson Raphael Hirsh Elementary School, New York.

1966–1970 Attends Manhattan Talmudic Academy High School, New York.

1970–1971 Attends Tel Aviv University, Israel.

1971–1974 Travels extensively through the Middle East, Europe, Australia, and Africa. Studies at Yeshivat Har Etzion, Israel.

1974–1976 Graduates from Hunter College with B.A., summa cum laude and kappa pi, where he studies ceramics with Karen Karns and Susan Peterson, photography with Mark Feldstein, and painting with Ralph Humphrey and Doug Olsen, among others. Receives the Estelle Levy Award for Outstanding Merit in Art, and the Herman Muehlstein Foundation Graduate School Award.

1976–1978 Enters Pratt Institute, master's degree program, Brooklyn. Receives internship, art program, Pratt Institute (1977). Studies painting with George McNeill and puppetry with Kermit Love. Receives Pratt Institute Fellowship Award in painting (1978). Graduates from Pratt Institute with M.F.A. in 1978.

Adjunct lecturer, New York Technical College, City University of New York, Brooklyn (through 1985).

Founds art department at Manhattan Hebrew High School, Riverdale, New York. Teaches photography, fine arts workshops, and art history classes (through 1980).

Leases studio in Long Island City, New York, with four other artists, including painter Sharon Florin, with whom he continues to share a studio.

1979 First solo exhibition, Fordham University, New York.

Artist-in-residence, Kaufman Cultural Center, New York (through 1985).

1981 First museum group show, Queens Museum, Flushing, New York.

1983 Solo exhibition, Althea Viafora Gallery, New York (1984, 1986, 1987, and 1989).

Conducts gallery and art museum lecture series for a group of collectors through the Jewish Community Center on the Palisades, New Jersey (until the present).

1984 Solomon R. Guggenheim Museum, New York, is gifted *Iza II* for its permanent collection.

1985 Seventeen paintings and two sculptures included in "New Horizons in American Art: 1985 Exxon National Exhibition," Solomon R. Guggenheim Museum, New York.

Visiting artist, Mishkenot Sha'ananim, Jerusalem.

1986 Marries writer Nessa Rapoport, April 10.

Teaches painting at the School of Visual Arts, New York (until the present).

Hoya, an edition of thirty-six etchings, is commissioned and published by the Jewish Theological Seminary of America.

1988	Solo exhibition, Mary Ryan Gallery, New York (1991, 1993, 1995, and 1997); and Gloria Luria Gallery, Bay Harbor Islands, Florida (1990, 1992).
	Creates sets for Solomons Dance Company, *Aspen Grove* and *Bone Yard*, premiered at the Joyce Theater and Saint Mark's Church, New York.
	Son Joshua is born, May 10.
1989–1990	Creates set for Elizabeth Swados, *Song of Songs*, premiered at Central Synagogue, New York; and for Muna Tseng, *Aluat-El*, premiered at Riverside Park, New York.
	Creates set for Elizabeth Swados, *Jonah*, premiered at the Public Theater, New York; and for Muna Tseng, *Ways, Shrines, Mysteries*, premiered at Florence Gould Hall, New York.
1991–1993	Daughter Mattie is born, March 17, 1992.
	Creates first monumental outdoor sculpture, *Shalev*, bronze and stone, commissioned by Jane Owen and the Robert Lee Blaffer Trust for New Harmony, Indiana. Designs the label for New Amsterdam Beer's Winter Anniversary Limited Edition.
1994–1996	Commissioned by the Nathan Cummings Foundation to create *The Twelve Tribes* and *Creation of the World*, a series of twelve works on paper and one painting for the Jewish Family Congregation, South Salem, New York. Creates *Eyda*, an installation of seven paintings, commissioned by Mitchell & Company, Boston. *Rigu-Saar* appears on the cover of *Collected Writings of Adrienne Rich* (New York: Quality Paperback Book Club, 1994).
	Study for Doekh appears on the cover of *The American Journal of Pathology* (January 1996). Originally commissioned by Dr. Mark Tykocinski for his article "Antigen-Presenting Cell Engineering."
1997	Solo museum exhibition, "Tobi Kahn: Metamorphoses," curated by Peter Selz, with accompanying catalogue including essays by Peter Selz, Dore Ashton, and Michael Brenson, begins traveling to eight museums around the United States.
	Creates *Gan Hazikaron: Garden of Remembrance*, an outdoor installation of six bronzes as a Holocaust memorial for the Jewish Community Center on the Palisades, New Jersey, commissioned by Holocaust survivors and their children.
	Mezuzah commissioned for front door of the Museum of Jewish Heritage, Battery Park City, New York.
1998	Daughter Doria Bella is born, February 3.
1999	Solo museum exhibition, "Avoda: Objects of the Spirit," curated by Laura Kruger, opens at Hebrew Union College–Jewish Institute of Religion, New York, beginning a five-year national tour.
	Creates *Sky and Water*, a nine-painting installation, for the exhibition "Landscape at the Millennium," curated by Douglas Dreishpoon, with accompanying catalogue, at the Albright-Knox Art Gallery, Buffalo.
2000	Receives 2000 Alumni Achievement Award from Pratt Institute, Brooklyn.
	Creates an outdoor installation that includes bronzes and landscaping as a Holocaust memorial for the Lawrence Family Jewish Community Center of San Diego County, La Jolla, California.
	Receives grant from the Charles H. Revson Foundation for "Avoda: Objects of the Spirit" project.
	Receives grant from the Covenant Foundation for "Avoda: Objects of the Spirit" project.

2000 Solo exhibition, "Tobi Kahn: Correspondence," curated by Mark A. White, with accompanying catalogue, begins traveling to five museums in the United States.

2001 Solo exhibition, "Tobi Kahn: Heads," curated by Peter Selz, with accompanying catalogue, Rubelle and Norman Schafler Gallery, Pratt Institute, Brooklyn.

2002 Creates meditative room for the HealthCare Chaplaincy, New York, consisting of nine murals and sculptural furniture.

Solo exhibition, "Tobi Kahn: Microcosmos," curated by Reba Wulkan, with accompanying catalogue, Yeshiva University Museum, New York.

2003 Solo exhibition, "Sky and Water," curated by Dede Young, with accompanying catalogue, Neuberger Museum of Art, Purchase College, Purchase, New York.

SELECTED EXHIBITION HISTORY

SOLO EXHIBITIONS

1979 Fordham University, New York.

1980 Robert Brown, New York.

1981 Blumberg Harris, New York.

1983 Althea Viafora Gallery, New York (1984, 1986, 1987, 1989).

1985 Bernard Jacobson, Los Angeles.

J. Robert Fisher Hall at Mishkenot Sha'ananim, Jerusalem.

1987 Krygier/Landau Contemporary Art, Los Angeles.

John Berggruen Gallery, San Francisco.

Philadelphia Museum of Judaica.

1988 Harcus Gallery, Boston.

Cleveland Center for Contemporary Art, Cleveland (1993), curated by Marjorie Talalay.

Mary Ryan Gallery, New York (1991, 1993, 1995, 1997).

Gloria Luria Gallery, Bay Harbor Islands, Florida (1990, 1992).

1990 Marilyn Butler Fine Art, Scottsdale, Arizona.

1993 Thomson Gallery, Minneapolis.

Litwin Gallery, Wichita.

1994 Allene Lapides Gallery, Santa Fe, New Mexico.

1995 Andrea Marquit Fine Arts, Boston (1998).

1996 The Warehouse Gallery, Lee, Massachusetts.

Harmon-Meek Gallery, Naples, Florida (2000).

1997 The Hyde Collection, Glens Falls, New York, curated by Randall Suffolk.

M. Louise Aughinbaugh Gallery, Grantham, Pennsylvania.

"Tobi Kahn: Metamorphoses," curated by Peter Selz, traveled through 1999 to the Weatherspoon Art Gallery, Greensboro, North Carolina; Trout Gallery, Carlisle, Pennsylvania; Museum of Contemporary Religious Art (MOCRA), St. Louis; Thomas J. Walsh Gallery, Fairfield, Connecticut; Colby College Museum of Art, Waterville, Maine; Museum of Fine Arts, Houston; Judah L. Magnes Museum, Berkeley, California; Skirball Cultural Center, Los Angeles.

1998 Hooks-Epstein Galleries, Houston.

1999 Albright-Knox Art Gallery, Buffalo, curated by Douglas Dreishpoon.

"Avoda: Objects of the Spirit," curated by Laura Kruger, a five-year traveling museum exhibition, opens at Hebrew Union College, New York.

2000 "Tobi Kahn: Correspondence," curated by Mark A. White, travels through 2003 to Edwin A. Ulrich Museum of Art, Wichita; Holtzman Gallery, Towson University, Towson, Maryland; Evansville Museum of Arts and Science, Evansville, Indiana; Sheldon Swope Art Museum, Terre Haute, Indiana.

2001 "Tobi Kahn: Heads," curated by Peter Selz, Pratt Institute, Brooklyn.

2002 "Tobi Kahn: Microcosmos," curated by Reba Wulkan, Yeshiva University Museum, New York.

2003 "Sky and Water," curated by Dede Young, Neuberger Museum of Art, Purchase College, Purchase, New York.

SELECTED GROUP EXHIBITIONS

1980 Zolla/Lieberman, Chicago.

1981 "Annual Juried Exhibition," Queens Museum, New York. Curated by John Perreault (catalogue).

1983 "Saints," Harm Boukaert Gallery, New York.

1984 "From the Abstract to the Image," Oscarsson Hood Gallery, New York.

"2500 Sculptors Across America," Civilian Warfare Gallery, New York.

1985 "Contemporary Sculpture on a Pedestal." Originated at the Sarah Moody Gallery of Art, University of Alabama. Traveled to University Galleries, University of South Florida; and Huntsville Museum of Art, Huntsville, Alabama. Curated by Susan L. Halper (catalogue).

"New Horizons in American Art: 1985 Exxon National Exhibition," Solomon R. Guggenheim Museum, New York. Curated by Lisa Dennison (catalogue).

"The Doll and Figurine Show," Hillwood Art Gallery, Long Island University, New York. Curated by Judy Collischan Van Wagner and Carol Becker Davis (catalogue).

"Between Drawing and Sculpture," Sculpture Center, New York. Curated by Douglas Dreishpoon (catalogue).

"Drawings," Cleveland Center for Contemporary Art.

1986 "Anchorage/New York: Small Sculpture," Visual Arts Center of Anchorage. Curated by David Donihue (catalogue).

"Jewish Themes: Contemporary American Artists Part II," The Jewish Museum, New York. Curated by Susan T. Goodman (catalogue).

"Landscape in the Age of Anxiety," Lehman Art College, Bronx. Curated by Nina Castelli Sundell. Traveled to Cleveland Center for Contemporary Art (catalogue).

"A View of Nature," Aldrich Contemporary Art Museum, Ridgefield, Connecticut. Curated by Ellen O'Donnell (catalogue).

1987 "Emerging Artists 1978–1986: Selections from the Exxon Series," Solomon R. Guggenheim Museum, New York. Curated by Diane Waldman.

"The New Romantic Landscape," Whitney Museum of American Art, Fairfield County Branch, Stamford, Connecticut.

"Sacred Spaces," Everson Museum of Art, Syracuse, New York. Curated by Dominique Nahas (catalogue).

"Contemporary American Landscape: Reflections of Social Change," Summit Art Center, Summit, New Jersey. Curated by Nancy Cohen, Kiku Fukui, and Liz Kelsey.

1988 "Art on Paper," Weatherspoon Art Gallery, University of North Carolina, Greensboro (catalogue).

"Día de los Muertos," Alternative Museum, New York (catalogue).

"Golem! Danger, Deliverance and Art," The Jewish Museum, New York. Curated by Emily D. Bilski (catalogue).

"Annual Juried Show," Queens Museum, New York. Curated by Irving Sandler (catalogue).

1989 "Rugged Terrain: Landscape Painting," Shea & Beker, New York.

"Contemporary Landscape: Five Views," Waterworks Visual Arts Center, Salisbury, Virginia. Curated by J. Moore (catalogue).

"Monotypes," Cleveland Center for Contemporary Art.

1990 "Southeast Bank Collects: A Florida Corporation Views Contemporary Art." Organized by the Norton Gallery of Art, West Palm Beach, Florida. Traveled to the Bass Museum of Art, Miami Beach; Museum of Fine Arts, St. Petersburg, Florida; Polk Museum of Art, Lakeland, Florida; and Samuel P. Harn Museum of Art, Gainesville, Florida (catalogue).

"Horizons," Pfizer, Inc., through the Art Advisors, Museum of Modern Art, New York.

"Insistent Landscapes," Security Pacific Gallery, Los Angeles. Curated by Mark Johnstone (catalogue).

1991 "Retrieving the Elemental Form," Schmidt-Bingham Gallery, New York. Traveled to Lakeview Museum of Arts and Sciences, Peoria, Illinois; and Fresno Art Museum, California (catalogue).

"Playing Around: Toys by Artists," DeCordova Museum and Sculpture Park, Lincoln, Massachusetts.

1992 "Off the Wall," Cleveland Center for Contemporary Art.

"ECO-92," Museum of Modern Art, Rio de Janeiro (catalogue).

"Contemporary American Painting and Sculpture," Art in Embassies, U.S. Department of State, American Embassy, Tel Aviv. Curated by Louise Eliasof and Renne Du Pont Harrison.

1993 "Timely Timeless," Aldrich Contemporary Art Museum, Ridgefield, Connecticut. Curated by Douglas F. Maxwell (catalogue).

"25 Years," Cleveland Center for Contemporary Art. Curated by Marjorie Talalay.

"Aspects of Sculpture," Edwin A. Ulrich Museum of Art, Wichita. Curated by Donald Knaub.

"Sanctuaries: Recovering the Holy in Art," Museum of Contemporary Religious Art (MOCRA), Saint Louis University. Curated by Terrence Dempsey.

1994 "A Bouquet for Juan," Nancy Hoffman Gallery, New York.

"Landscape Not Landscape," Gallery Camino Real, Boca Raton, Florida. Curated by Douglas F. Maxwell (catalogue).

1995 "Art on Paper," Weatherspoon Art Gallery, University of North Carolina, Greensboro (catalogue).

"Never Again," Cathedral of Saint John the Divine, New York. Curated by Noga Garrison.

"Painting North," Art in Embassies, U.S. Department of State, American Embassy, Santiago, Chile (catalogue).

1996 "By the Sea," Fotouhi Cramer Gallery, New York. Curated by Robert G. Edelman and Renee Fotouhi.

"Destiny Manifest: American Landscape Painting in the Nineties," Samuel P. Harn Museum of Art, Gainesville, Florida. Curated by Dede Young (catalogue).

"The Figure in 20th Century Sculpture," Edwin A. Ulrich Museum of Art, Wichita. Traveled to eleven venues in the United States.

1997 "Aerial Perspectives," DC Moore Gallery, New York, and the Kendall Campus Art Gallery, Miami. Curated by Margaret Mathews Berenson.

"Vertical Painting," P.S. 1 Contemporary Art Center, Long Island City, New York. Curated by Alanna Heiss.

1998 "Contemporary Landscape Artists," Elise Goodheart Fine Arts, Sag Harbor, New York.

1999 "Waxing Poetic," Montclair Art Museum, New Jersey, and the Knoxville Museum of Art, Tennessee (catalogue).

2000 "Living in the Moment," Skirball Museum, Cincinnati, and Hebrew Union College–Jewish Institute of Religion, New York. Curated by Laura Kruger.

"Ethereal and Material," Delaware Center for the Contemporary Arts, Wilmington. Curated by Dede Young.

2001 "Jewish Artists on the Edge," Yeshiva University Museum, New York. Curated by Ori Z. Soltes.

"Like a Prayer," Tryon Center for Visual Art, Charlotte, North Carolina. Curated by Theodore L. Prescott.

SELECTED BIBLIOGRAPHY

1981 John Perreault, *Annual Juried Exhibition, 1981*, exh. cat., Queens Museum, Flushing, New York.

1983 Michael Brenson, "Review," *New York Times*, December 16, 1983, p. C30.

1984 Douglas Dreishpoon, "Review," *Arts Magazine*, January 1984, p. 7.

Grace Glueck, "Review," *New York Times*, November 2, 1984, p. C25.

1985 Douglas Dreishpoon, "Essence of Vision: The Art of Tobi Kahn," *Arts Magazine*, January 1985, pp. 81–83.

Susan A. Harris, "Review," *Arts Magazine*, January 1985, p. 40.

Meg Perlman, "Review," *ARTnews*, April 1985, pp. 144–45.

Kristine McKenna, "Review," *Los Angeles Times*, May 3, 1985, sec. 4, p. 15.

Amei Wallach, "New Horizons in Guggenheim Exhibit," *New York Newsday*, September 15, 1985.

Michael Brenson, " 'New Horizons' at the Guggenheim," *New York Times*, September 20, 1985.

Theodore Wolff, "Promising Artists at Guggenheim," *Christian Science Monitor*, October 7, 1985.

Karin Lipson, "By Artists for Artists," *New York Newsday*, October 18, 1985.

Ellen Glassman, "Tobi Kahn Is an Artist Who's Coming into His Own," *Pratt Folio* (Fall 1985), pp. 6–7.

Jane Bell, "New Horizons in American Art," *ARTnews*, November 1985.

Judy Collischan Van Wagner, *The Doll and Figurine Show*, exh. cat., Hillwood Art Gallery, C. W. Post, Long Island University, New York, 1985, p. 37.

Douglas Dreishpoon, *Between Drawing and Sculpture*, exh. cat., Sculpture Center, New York, 1985.

Judd Tully, "New Horizons in Art: Exxon's Best National," *Art World*, October 1985.

Michael Brenson, "Art: 8 Artists in 'Between Drawing and Sculpture,' " *New York Times*, December 20, 1985, p. C29.

1986 Virginia Rembert, "Sculpture on a Pedestal," *Art Papers*, March/April 1986.

Amei Wallach, "Two Theme Shows: At the Guggenheim, At the Jewish," *New York Newsday*, July 25, 1986, p. 16.

Michael Brenson, "Bringing Fresh Approaches to Ages-Old Jewish Themes," *New York Times*, August 3, 1986, p. 27.

Eleanor Heartney, "Review," *ARTnews*, October 1986, p. 148.

Robert G. Edelman, "Review," *Art in America*, October 1986, pp. 165–66.

1987 Douglas Dreishpoon, "Review," *Arts Magazine*, January 1987, p. 127.
Vivien Raynor, "Views of Nature on Exhibit at Ridgefield's Expanded Aldrich," *New York Times* (Connecticut), January 11, 1987, p. 30.

Vivien Raynor, "Center for Visual Arts: Landscape as Reflections of Social Change," *New York Times* (New Jersey), March 15, 1987, p. 30.

1987 Eileen Watkins, "Inventive Landscapes Reflect Inner Visions in Jersey Center for Visual Arts Exhibit," *Newark Star-Ledger*, March 1987, p. 24.

Kenneth Baker, "Review," *San Francisco Chronicle*, March 28, 1987, p. 37.

Colin Gardner, "Review," *Los Angeles Times*, May 22, 1987, part 6, p. 14.

David Bourdon, "For Spacious Skies," *House & Garden*, August 1987, p. 44b.

Michael Brenson, "Review," *New York Times*, November 6, 1987, p. C37.

1988 Susan Kandel, Elizabeth Hayt-Adkins, "Tobi Kahn," *ARTnews*, January 1988, p. 164.

Margaret Moorman, "The Multitude of Styles at the Queens Museum Show," *New York Newsday* (New York Weekend section), January 8, 1988, p. 21.

Leslie Judd Ahlander, "Miami Art Scene," *Miami News*, January 15, 1988, p. C3.

Helen Cullinan, "Our Collective Hang-Ups," *Plain Dealer* (Cleveland), February 22, 1988, p. 32.

Susan Mernit, "Artist Worth Watching: Tobi Kahn," *MD Magazine*, May 1988, pp. 35, 38, 43.

Vivien Raynor, "Tracking the Creative Process," *New York Times* (Westchester), May 22, 1988, p. 26.

Alexandra Enders, "Openings," *Art and Antiques*, October 1988, p. 52.

Michael Brenson, "Ambiguous Golem," *New York Times*, section C, December 16, 1988.

1989 Paul Barringer, "Landscapes of Self vs. Picturesque Conventions," *The Arts Journal*, April 1989, p. 17.

Shaw Smith, "North Carolina, Contemporary Landscape: Five Views," *New Art Examiner*, May 1989, p. 52.

Michael Kimmelman, "Review," *New York Times*, May 19, 1989, p. C33.

Suzanne Davis, "Contemporary Landscape, Five Views," *Atlanta Art Papers*, May/June 1989, pp. 57–58.

Ricardo Pau-Llosa, "A Convergence of Visual Cultures," *Art International*, Spring 1989, pp. 17–23.

Michael Brenson, "Rugged Terrain," *New York Times*, June 23, 1989, p. C26.

1990 Susan Kleinman, "Making Mountains Skip," *Forward*, July 6, 1990, pp. 9–11.

James Magruder, "Call Me Leviathan," *Village Voice*, April 3, 1990, p. 102.

Edith Newhall, "In the Belly of the Beast," *New York Magazine*, February 26, 1990, p. 36.

1991 Edith Newhall, "Review," *New York Magazine*, September 23, 1991, p. 61.

Deborah Solomon, "Introduction," exh. cat., October 16, 1991, Mary Ryan Gallery, New York.

1992 Dionisio D. Martinez, "Tobi Kahn," *Organica Quarterly*, Spring 1992, p. 23.

Nancy Grimes, "Review," *ARTnews*, February 1992, pp. 131–32.

Dionisio D. Martinez, "Review," *Art Papers*, March/April 1992, p. 57.

1993 Judy Arginteanu, "Review," *Minneapolis Star-Tribune*, May 28, 1993.

Diane Lewis, "Abstract Meanings," *Wichita Eagle*, February 27, 1993, pp. C1–4.

Holland Cotter, "Tobi Kahn," *New York Times*, Weekend section, November 26, 1993.

Douglas Dreishpoon, "Introduction," exh. cat., February 1993, Litwin Gallery, Wichita.

1994 Janet Koplos, "Review," *Art in America*, May 1994, pp. 120–21.

Ann Berman, "In Total Harmony," *Town and Country*, June 1994, p. 159.

1995 "Noted Artist Tobi Kahn Unveils Works from South Salem Synagogue Sanctuary," *Lewisboro Ledger*, Lewisboro, New York, January 26, 1995, p. 12.

Robin Cembalest, "Painting His Way to Transcendence," *Forward*, February 3, 1995, p. 10.

"Tobi Kahn Commission Unveiled by JFC," *Antiques and the Arts Weekly*, February 17, 1995, p. 49.

Grace Glueck, "Kahn-Do Spirit," *New York Observer*, October 23, 1995.

Francine Koslow Miller, "Review," *Art Forum*, November 1995, pp. 94–95.

1996 Alison Schneider, "Religion and Modern Art Find Common Ground," *The Chronicle of Higher Education*, April 26, 1996, pp. B4–5.

Kerry Dwyer, "Kahn's Mindscapes Take Over Where Memory Leaves Off," *South Advocate*, May 22, 1996, p. 13.

1997 John Mendelsohn, "Painting as Reverie," *Jewish Week*, October 3, 1997 (illustrations of *Erba*, *Lahav*).

Margaret Moorman, "Tobi Kahn," *Art News*, October, 1997, p. 161 (illustration of *Qinta*).

Tom Patterson, "Transformation," *Winston-Salem Journal*, October 19, 1997 (illustration of *Tzyla*).

Peter Selz, Dore Ashton, Michael Brenson, *Tobi Kahn: Metamorphoses*, exh. cat., Lee, Massachusetts, and New York, Council for Creative Projects, 1997.

Allison Nazarian, "Planting a Garden of Memory," *New Jersey Jewish Standard*, November 21, 1997, cover story, pp. 6, 42 (illustrations of *T'kumah*, *Lahav*, *Hoshana*).

Sandy Cullen, "Artist's Works Plumb Emotional Depths of Reality," *Patriot-News*, Harrisburg, Pennsylvania, November 23, 1997, p. E2.

Barbara Blank, "Memory Transforms Reality in Tobi Kahn's Art," *Sentinel*, Carlisle, Pennsylvania, November 27, 1997, cover story, pp. D1, D8, D9 (illustrations of *Luzzan*, *Otza II*, *Madai*, *Rigu-Saar*; installation photo and photo of the artist).

1998 Karla Browne, "Seeing Abstractly," *Sentinel*, Carlisle, Pennsylvania, January 27, 1998, School Scene section.

Jeff Daniel, "Kahn's Works Reflect the Sea and the Sky, But They're Not Landscapes," *St. Louis Post-Dispatch*, March 29, 1998, p. E3 (illustrations of *Natah*, *Lifanah*).

Linda Feczko, "Metamorphoses Exhibit at Fairfield University," *Connecticut Post*, July 4, 1998, photo.

Jerry Tallmer, "Tobi Kahn Master of Arts," *Lifestyles*, international edition, Summer 1998. Cover story, pp. 6–9 (four illustrations and a photo of the artist on the cover).

Timothy McElreavy, "Distillations: A Conversation with Tobi Kahn," *Art New England*, August/September, 1998, pp. 28–29 (six illustrations).

Pat Davidson Reef, "The Mind's Eye," *Sun Journal*, Lewiston, Maine, September 14, 1998 (illustration of *Rigu-Saar*).

Phyllis A. Braff, "Contemporary Landscape Artists," *New York Times*, November 1, 1998 (illustration of *Ada-Ishon*).

Cate McQuaid, "Friendly Abstracts: Modernist's Retrospective," *Boston Globe*, November 19, 1998, Living/Arts section (illustration of *Azce*).

1998 “Glassell Exhibit Features NY Artist’s Work,” *Houston Chronicle*, November 18, 1998, section 2, p. 17 (illustration of *Rigu-Saar*).

1999 Abby Cohn, “Son of WWII Refugees Reclaims Time, Memory in Art,” *Jewish Journal*, San Francisco, March 19, 1999, Entertainment/ Arts (illustration of *Brun*).

Naomi Pfefferman, “The Art of Memory,” *Jewish Journal*, Los Angeles, July 2, 1999 (illustration of *Ziba II*).

Josef Woodard, “Simplicity in Symbols,” *Los Angeles Times*, July 23, 1999 (illustration of *Iza II*).

2000 Susan Kleinman, “Blending Modern Art with Objects of the Spirit,” *New York Times*, April 26, 2000, p. E2 (illustration of *Natyh*).

2001 Lynda H. Schneekloth, “Breaking Through Boundaries of Landscape/What Is Landscape,” *Intersight #6: Journal of the School of Architecture and Planning*, State University of New York at Buffalo, 2001, p. 136 (illustrations of *Ornat*, *Madai*; and installation view of *Sky and Water* at the Albright-Knox Art Gallery).

Nancy Haught, “Function Follows Faith,” *Oregonian*, Portland, March 1, 2001, Living section, p. 1 (illustrations of *Yasi* and *Kelaf*).

Margaret Moorman, “Spaces for the Spirit,” *Art News*, Summer 2001, pp. 112–18 (illustrations of *Clarussa*, *Sefa*, *Quya*, *Shalev*, and HealthCare Chaplaincy model).

Gabriella Burman, “Power of Art,” *New York Resident*, November 5, 2001, p. 25 (illustration of HealthCare Chaplaincy model).

2002 Anne Morgan, “Beyond Post-Modernism: The Spiritual in Contemporary Art,” *Art Papers*, January/February 2002, pp. 31–36.

Theodore Prescott, *IMAGE: A Journal of the Arts and Religion*, Seattle, Spring 2002, cover story.

Victoria Donohoe, “Landscapes with Glamour,” *Philadelphia Inquirer*, April 9, 2002 (illustration of *Azce*).

Mike Itkoff, “A Place for the Weary to Rest,” *Forward*, New York, September 6, 2002.

Richard D. Dujardin, “Making It Holy,” *Providence Journal*, November 16, 2002.

2003 Benjamin Genocchio, “Nature’s Majesty,” *New York Times*, August 3, 2003, p. 8 (photo of Neuberger Museum installation of eighty paintings).

Stephanie Cash, “Public Art, 2002 in Review,” *Art in America*, *Annual Guide 2003*, p. 56 (photo of *Emet* meditative space).

Julia Goldman, “A Landscape for Contemplation,” *Jewish Week*, July 11, 2003, p. 29 (photos of Neuberger Museum installation, Tobi Kahn in his Long Island City studio).

Georgette Gouveia, “Power In Simplicity,” *The Journal News*, May 25, 2003, p. 3E (photos of Neuberger Museum installation, *Ya-Ir XX*).

Mark Daniel Cohen, “The Visual Chant: The Prayer for the Eye in the Art of Tobi Kahn,” *NY Arts Magazine*, February 2003 (illustration of *Tyla*).

David A. Cleveland, *Art News*, February 2003, p. 128 (illustration of *Vyrsa*).

Mario Naves, “Microcellular Big Bang,” *New York Observer*, January 13, 2003, p. 16.

LIST OF WORKS ILLUSTRATED

All works are by Tobi Kahn unless otherwise indicated. Dimensions are in inches, followed in parentheses by centimeters; height precedes width precedes depth. Unless otherwise indicated, all objects are in the collection of the artist. Unless otherwise indicated, all objects by Tobi Kahn were photographed by Nicholas Walster. Objects only accompanying meditations are listed on page 155.

Frontispiece
Vanah, 2000
Rosh Hodesh (new moon) plaque
Acrylic on wood, 11 x 9 (27.9 x 22.9)

Fig. 1
Aviya II, 1998
Kiddush cup for Passover
Bronze, 7½ x 3¾ x 3¾ (19.1 x 9.5 x 9.5)

Fig. 2
Zedek III, 1989–99
Tzedakah (alms) container
Acrylic on wood, 19 x 7½ x 7½
(48.3 x 19.1 x 19.1)

Fig. 3
Vanessa Bell, cupboard, c. 1917, in the artist's bedroom at Charleston, Sussex, England
Photograph courtesy the Charleston Trust

Fig. 4
Wardrobe, 1985, in the artist's home
Acrylic on wood, 78 x 27½ x 30½
(198.1 x 69.9 x 77.5)

Fig. 5
Lifanah, 1985
Shrine
Acrylic on wood, 16⅝ x 10¾ x 10½
(42.2 x 27.3 x 26.7)

Fig. 6, Plate 24
Odyh, 1986
Huppah (wedding canopy)
Acrylic on wood, canvas, and twine; nine pieces in all
Four pieces, 92 x 7 x 2½
(233.7 x 17.8 x 6.4)
Four pieces, 92 x 12 x 10½
(233.7 x 30.5 x 26.7)
One piece rolled up, 82 x 5 x 5
(208.3 x 12.7 x 12.7)

Fig. 7, Plate 1
Orah, 1987
Aron kodesh (Torah ark)
Acrylic on wood, 80 x 27 x 23
(203.2 x 68.6 x 58.4)

Fig. 8
Torah ark, Modena, Italy, 1472
Carved wood and wood marquetry
Musée du Moyen Age (Cluny), Paris
Photograph by G. Blot/C. Jean © Réunion des Musées Nationaux / Art Resource, New York

Fig. 9
Gustav Stickley, square table, from 1909 Craftsman furniture catalogue
29 x 30 x 30 (73.7 x 76.2 x 76.2)
From *Gustav Stickley after 1909*, ed. Stephen Gray (New York: Turn of the Century Editions, 1990)
Courtesy Turn of the Century Editions

Fig. 10
Leah, wife of Hananiah Ottolenghi, curtain for Torah ark, Italy, 1698/99
Silk embroidery on linen, 72⅜ x 49 7/16
(184 x 125.5)
The Jewish Museum, New York; Gift of Dr. Harry G. Friedman
Photograph by Malcolm Varon © The Jewish Museum / Art Resource, New York

Fig. 11
Isa, 1985
Acrylic on panel, 18¾ x 15 (47.6 x 38.1)
Private collection

Fig. 12
Caspar David Friedrich, *Das Kreuz im Gebirge* [*The Cross in the Mountains*] (*Tetschen Altarpiece*), 1807–8
Oil on canvas, 45¼ x 43⅜ (115 x 110)
Galerie Neue Meister, Staatliche Kunstsammlungen, Gemäldegalerie, Dresden

Fig. 13, Plate 22
Osha, 1987, front view
Elijah's chair (chair for circumcision ceremony)
Acrylic on wood, 64 x 20 x 22
(162.6 x 50.8 x 55.9)

Fig. 14
Osha, 1987, rear view
Elijah's chair (chair for circumcision ceremony)
Acrylic on wood, 64 x 20 x 22
(162.6 x 50.8 x 55.9)

Fig. 15
Ollu, 1985
Shrine
Acrylic on wood, bronze with patina, 15½ x 10½ x 10½ (39.4 x 26.7 x 26.7)

Fig. 16
Azba II, 1984
Acrylic on canvas over wood, 74¾ x 59 (189.9 x 149.9)
Private collection

Fig. 17, Plate 23
Natyh, 1987
Shalom bat chairs (chairs for ceremony welcoming a baby girl)
Part of set design for *Song of Songs* by Elizabeth Swados
Acrylic on wood
Three chairs, 70 x 21½ x 19
(177.8 x 54.6 x 48.3) each

Fig. 18
Gerrit Rietveld, *Berlin Chair*, 1923
Painted mahogany plywood, linden ash, 42 x 28 x 23 (106.7 x 71.1 x 58.4)
The Minneapolis Institute of Arts; Gift of Norwest Bank Minnesota

Fig. 19
Gerrit Rietveld, *Children's Chair*, 1919
Wood, leather seat and back
Collectie Centraal Museum, Utrecht

Fig. 20
Charles Rennie Mackintosh, high-back chair for Ingram Street Teahouse, Glasgow, 1900
Oak, stained dark, with horsehair upholstery, 59⅜ x 18⅝ x 17
(151 x 47.3 x 43.3)
Courtesy Glasgow School of Art Collection

Fig. 21
Robert Wilson's production of *A Dream Play*, by August Strindberg, 2000
Courtesy Sara Krulwich / *New York Times*

Fig. 22
Golg, 1985
Acrylic on panel, 19½ x 16⅜ (49.5 x 41.6)

Fig. 23
Aruga I, 1987
Besamim (spice) container
Acrylic on wood, 13½ x 6 x 6¾ (34.3 x 15.2 x 17.2)

Fig. 24
Synagogue in Szczebrzeszyn, Poland,
From *Jewish Art in European Synagogues (From the Middle Ages to the Eighteenth Century)*, by George Loukomski (London: Hutchinson, [1947]), p. 76

Fig. 25
Synagogue in Nowe-Miasto, Poland, view of south front
From *Jewish Art in European Synagogues (From the Middle Ages to the Eighteenth Century)*, by George Loukomski (London: Hutchinson, [1947]), p. 117

Fig. 26
Arekah, 1987
Acrylic on canvas over panel, 64 x 12 (162.6 x 30.5)
Collection of Howard Eisenberg

Fig. 27
Spice container, Frankfurt, mid-fourteenth century
Silver: cast, engraved, and gilt, 9⁵⁄₁₆ x 2⁵⁄₁₆ (23.7 x 5.9)
The Jewish Museum, New York
© The Jewish Museum / Art Resource, New York

Fig. 28
Aruga II, 1993
Besamim (spice) container
Acrylic on wood, 5½ x 13 x 2 (14 x 33 x 5.1)

Fig. 29
Nagalski and Psyk, spice container, Poland, c. 1900–1921
Silver: cast, repoussé, traced, punched, and gilt, 4½ x 3⅞ x 2³⁄₁₆ (11.4 x 9.8 x 5.6)
The Jewish Museum, New York; Gift of Dr. Harry G. Friedman
© The Jewish Museum / Art Resource, New York

Fig. 30
Richard Riemerschmid, *Chamberstick*, c. 1898
Brass, 7½ x 11 x 7 in. (19.1 x 27.9 x 17.8)
The Minneapolis Institute of Arts; Gift of Norwest Bank Minnesota

Fig. 31
Amhi, 1992
Acrylic on canvas over wood, 50 x 40 x 2 (127 x 101.6 x 5.1)
Collection of the School of Visual Arts, New York

Fig. 32
Leemor, 1992
Iridescent pigment and acrylic on wood, 12 x 11 x 2½ (30.5 x 27.9 x 6.4)
Private collection

Fig. 33
Zedek II, 1989
Tzedakah (alms) container
Acrylic on wood, 18½ x 12 x 9 (47 x 30.5 x 22.9)

Fig. 34
Keba, 1988
Acrylic on wood, 30 x 22½ (76.2 x 57.2)

Fig. 35
Head and neck figurine, Cycladic period, c. 3000–1000 BCE
White marble and light tan encrustation, 9¾ (24.8)
© N. P. Goulandris Foundation—Museum of Cycladic Art, Athens, Greece

Fig. 36
Akahr, 1994
Havdalah tray
Acrylic on wood, 2 x 23½ x 11½ (5.1 x 59.7 x 29.2)

Fig. 37
Seyall, 1992
Acrylic on wood, 18 x 24 (45.7 x 61)
Private collection

Fig. 38
Ilica, 1993
Acrylic on canvas over wood, 24 x 70 x 2 (61 x 177.8 x 5.1)
Collection of the Colby College Museum of Art, Maine

Fig. 39, Plate 8
Ysai, 1998, front view
Shabbat throne
Acrylic on wood with bronze, 70 x 21 x 29 (177.8 x 53.3 x 73.7)
Private collection

Fig. 40
Ysai, 1998, rear view
Shabbat throne
Acrylic on wood with bronze, 70 x 21 x 29 (177.8 x 53.3 x 73.7)
Private collection

Fig. 41
Jhibu (variation), 1996
Acrylic on wood, 48 x 18 x 2 (121.9 x 45.7 x 5.1)
Private collection

Fig. 42, Plate 10
Ysha, 1995/98
Shabbat challah tray (Sabbath bread plate)
Acrylic on wood, 2 x 20½ x 11½ (5.1 x 52.1 x 29.2)

Fig. 43
Luzzan, 1993
Acrylic on canvas over wood, 50 x 40 x 2 (127 x 101.6 x 5.1)

Fig. 44
Albert Pinkham Ryder, *Moonlit Cove*, early to mid-1880s
Oil on canvas, 14⅛ x 17⅛ (35.9 x 43.5)
The Phillips Collection, Washington, D.C.
© The Phillips Collections, Washington, D.C.

Fig. 45
Ara-Ilam, 1987
Acrylic on panel, 33 x 48 (83.8 x 121.9)
Collection of Sunrise Financial Group, New York

Fig. 46
Caspar David Friedrich, *Der Mönch am Meer* (*The Monk by the Sea*), 1808–10
Oil on canvas, 43⅜ x 67½ (110 x 171.5)
Nationalgalerie, Staatliche Museen zu Berlin
Photograph by Joerg P. Anders
© Bildarchiv Preussischer Kulturbesitz / Art Resource, New York

Fig. 47
Mark Rothko, *Untitled (Black on Grey)*, 1970
Acrylic on canvas, 80¼ x 69 (203.3 x 175.5)
The Solomon R. Guggenheim Museum, New York; Gift of the Mark Rothko Foundation, Inc., 1986
Photograph by David Heald © 2003 Kate Rothko Prizel and Christopher Rothko / Artists Rights Society, New York

Fig. 48
Barnett Newman, *The Voice*, 1950
Egg tempera and enamel on canvas, 96½ x 105½ (245.1 x 268)
The Museum of Modern Art
© 2003 Barnett Newman Foundation / Artists Rights Society, New York
Digital image © The Museum of Modern Art / Licensed by SCALA / Art Resource, New York

Fig. 49, Plate 5
Kelaf I, 1993
Mezuzah container
Bronze, 5½ x 2 x¼ (14 x 5.1 x .6)

Fig. 50
Tura II, 1990
Acrylic on canvas over board, 48 x 33 x 2 (121.9 x 83.8 x 5.1)
Private collection

Fig. 51
Illuminated Hebrew Bible, southern France, 1301
Vellum, 12⁹⁄₁₆ x 9¼ (31.9 x 23.5)
The Royal Library, Copenhagen

Fig. 52
Ymah I, II, III, 1993
Mezuzah containers
Acrylic on wood
6½ x 2¾ x 3 (16.5 x 7 x 7.6)
5¼ x 3¼ x 2¼ (13.3 x 8.3 x 5.7)
13 x 4¼ x 2¼ (33 x 10.8 x 5.7)

Fig. 53
Al'akh, 1995
Acrylic on wood, 8 x 11 x 2¾ (20.3 x 27.9 x 7)
Collection of artist, on loan to MOCRA, St. Louis

Fig. 54
Holocaust Memorial Garden, La Jolla, California, 2000
Bronze and landscaping, 99 x 42 x 53 (251.5 x 106.7 x 134.6)
Jewish Community Center of San Diego County, La Jolla, California

Fig. 55, Plate 3
Ymahn, 1998
Rimmonim (set of two finials for Torah)
Acrylic on wood, 13½ x 4 x 3 (34.3 x 10.2 x 7.6) each

Fig. 56
Kayom II, 1997
Ner tamid (eternal light)
Bronze, 30 x 7 x 5 (76.2 x 17.8 x 12.7) + hanging rods
Collection of the Ramaz Middle School, New York

Fig. 57
Kayom III, 1998
Ner tamid (eternal light)
Bronze, 31 x 9 x 5 (78.7 x 22.9 x 12.7) + hanging rods

Fig. 58
Lkah, 1994
Shabbat candlesticks
Bronze, 11½ x 4½ x 4½
(29.2 x 11.4 x 11.4)

Fig. 59
Itsan, 1994
Acrylic on wood, 11 x 7 x 2½
(27.9 x 17.8 x 6.4)

Fig. 60
Lkah II, 2000
Shabbat candlesticks with tray
Bronze
Candlesticks, 6 x 4¼ x 5¼
(15.2 x 10.8 x 13.3) each
Tray, 10 x 12½ x½ (25.4 x 31.8 x 1.3)

Fig. 61, Plate 12
Z'chut, 2000
Rosh Hodesh (new moon) oil holder
Bronze, 16½ x 8 x 7½ (41.9 x 20.3 x 19.1)

Fig. 62, Plate 15
Quya, 1996
Menorah (Hanukkah lamp)
Bronze, 11¼ x 21 x 4½ (28.6 x 53.3 x 11.4)

Fig. 63
Johann Adam Boller, Hanukkah menorah, Frankfurt, 1706–32
Silver: cast, engraved, filigree, hammered, and gilt, with enamel plaques,
17 x 14½ (43.2 x 36.8)
The Jewish Museum, New York;
Gift of Mrs. Felix Warburg
© The Jewish Museum / Art Resource, New York

Fig. 64
Quya II, 1996
Menorah (Hanukkah lamp)
Bronze, 15 x 10½ x 4 (38.1 x 26.7 x 10.2)

Fig. 65
Alyz, 1996
Acrylic on wood, 30 x 24 x 2¼
(76.2 x 61 x 5.7)
Collection of Mitchell & Company, Boston

Fig. 66
Hanukkah lamp, Israel, 1950s
Bronze: cast and patinated,
6½ x 4½ x 2 (16.5 x 11.4 x 5.1)
The Jewish Museum, New York; Gift of Manfred and Judith Anson
© The Jewish Museum / Art Resource, New York

Fig. 67, Plate 25
Rahva, 1998
Wedding cup
Bronze, 8½ x 3 x 4 (21.6 x 7.6 x 10.2)

Fig. 68, Plate 20
Rkadh, 1998
Miriam's cup
Bronze, no. 1 in edition of six,
9 x 3½ x 3½ (22.9 x 8.9 x 8.9)
Collection of the Yeshiva University Museum, New York

Fig. 69, Plate 19
Vayti, 1996
Elijah's cup
Bronze, no. 1 in edition of six,
9 x 5½ x 5½ (22.9 x 14 x 14)
Collection of the Skirball Museum of Art, Los Angeles

Fig. 70, Plate 18
Erhu, 1996
Seder plate
Acrylic on wood, four plates, six cups, six trays, 13¼ x 13 x 13 (33.7 x 33 x 33)

Fig. 71
Three-tiered seder plate, Vienna, 1807
Silver: cast, cut out, and pressed; silk curtain, 18½ x 15 in. (47 x 38.1)
The Jewish Museum, New York; Gift of Edward J. Sovatkin, in memory of his mother, Fanny Sovatkin
© The Jewish Museum / Art Resource, New York

Fig. 72, Plate 7
Tyla I, II, III, IV, 1996
Four-piece hand-washing set
Acrylic on wood
Plate, 23½ x 17½ x¾ (59.7 x 44.5 x 1.9)
Cup, 4½ x 7½ x 4 (11.4 x 19.1 x 10.2)
Basin, 7 x 9 x 9 (17.8 x 22.9 x 22.9)
Pitcher, 9½ x 7 x 6 (24.1 x 17.8 x 15.2)

Fig. 73
Wide-mouth juglet or cup, ancient Israel, Hasmonean or early Roman period, third century BCE–first century CE
Clay: wheel-turned, handle pulled, slipped, fired, 3⁵⁄₁₆ x 3¹³⁄₁₆ (8.4 x 9.7)
The Jewish Museum, New York; Gift of the Betty and Max Ratner Collection
© The Jewish Museum / Art Resource, New York

Fig. 74
Bowl, ancient Israel, Hasmonean or early Roman period, mid-second century BCE–mid-first century CE
Clay: wheel-turned, slipped, fired,
2⅛ x 4⅜ (5.4 x 11.2)
The Jewish Museum, New York; Gift of the Betty and Max Ratner Collection
© The Jewish Museum / Art Resource, New York

Fig. 75
Bird figurine, ancient Israel, Iron II A–C, 1000–700 BCE
Clay: hand-molded and fired, 1¾ (4.5)
The Jewish Museum, New York
© The Jewish Museum / Art Resource, New York

Fig. 76, Plate 16
Dahsa, 1998
Megillah cover (Scroll of Esther cover)
Acrylic on wood, 18½ x 4 x 4
(47 x 10.2 x 10.2)

Fig. 77
Enclosure VII, 1975
Ceramic, 7 x 7 x 6 (17.8 x 17.8 x 15.2)

Fig. 78
Aasha II, 1999
Purim grogger (noisemaker)
Acrylic on wood, 17½ x 7 (44.5 x 17.8)

Fig. 79
Gal-Gal, 1993
Pull-toy
Acrylic on wood, 20 x 20 x 5½
(50.8 x 50.8 x 14)
Private collection

Figs. 80 and 81, Plate 21
Saphyr, 2002
Omer counter
Acrylic on wood, 27½ x 22¼ x 9½
(69.9 x 56.5 x 24.1)

Fig. 82
Joseph Cornell, *Untitled (Caravaggio Boy)*, c. 1953
Mixed media box construction,
15¼ x 10¼ x 2⅜ (38.7 x 26 x 6)
Cordier & Ekstrom, Daniel Varenne, Geneva
Private collection, France, acquired in the early 1970s
Sotheby's Surrealism: Dreams and Imagery, London, February 5, 2002, lot 77
© The Joseph and Robert Cornell Memorial Foundation / Licensed by VAGA, New York

Fig. 83
Omer calendar, Holland, eighteenth century
Wood, oil paint, gold powder,
14 x 14 (35.5 X 35.5)
The Israel Museum, Jerusalem; Gift through the Ministry of Education and Culture, Israel

Figs. 84 and 85, Plate 27
Meditative Space, New York HealthCare Chaplaincy, 2002
Mixed media installation, acrylic on canvas over wood, consisting of:
Six panels, 86 x 39 (218.4 x 99.1);
Three panels, 86 x 53 (218.4 x 134.6)
Three chairs, 26½ x 26 x 21
(67.3 x 66 x 53.3) each
Four benches, 18 x 48 x 18
(45.7 x 121.9 x 45.7) each
One bookcase, 49 x 17 x 15
(124.5 x 43.2 x 38.1)
The HealthCare Chaplaincy, New York

Fig. 86
Sky and Water, for "Landscape at the Millennium" exhibition, Albright-Knox Art Gallery, Buffalo, 1999
Nine paintings
Photograph by Biff Henrich / Keystone Productions, courtesy the Albright-Knox Art Gallery, Buffalo, New York

Fig. 87
Dan Flavin, Santa Maria in Chiesa Rossa, Milan, 1997
© 2003 Estate of Dan Flavin / Artists Rights Society, New York
Photograph by Paola Bobba, courtesy Fondazione Prada

Fig. 88
Hans and Torry Butzer and Sven Berg of Butzer Design Partnership, Cambridge, Massachusetts
Field of chairs at the Oklahoma City National Memorial, 1999
Photograph by G. Jill Evans © 2002 Oklahoma City National Memorial Trust

Fig. 89
Shirin Neshat, *Speechless*, 1996
RC Print, 46¾ x 33⅞ (118.7 x 86)
Photograph by Larry Barns, courtesy Barbara Gladstone Gallery, New York

Fig. 90
Michael Tracy, Emmanuel Chapel for the Corpus Christi Cathedral, Texas, 1985
Photograph by Hickey and Robertson, courtesy the artist

Fig. 91
Louise Nevelson, Errol Becker Chapel of the Good Shepherd in Saint Peter's Lutheran Church, Citicorp Center, New York, 1977

Fig. 92
Meditative Space, New York HealthCare Chaplaincy, 2002
Mixed media installation, acrylic on canvas over wood, consisting of:
Six panels, 86 x 39 (218.4 x 99.1);
three panels, 86 x 53 (218.4 x 134.6)
Three chairs, 26½ x 26 x 21 (67.3 x 66 x 53.3) each
Four benches, 18 x 48 x 18 (45.7 x 121.9 x 45.7) each
One bookcase, 49 x 17 x 15 (124.5 x 43.2 x 38.1)
The HealthCare Chaplaincy, New York

Fig. 93
The artist's home, with *Kinamon* (spice containers) on the cabinet top, 2003

Fig. 94
Installation view of the exhibition "Avoda: Objects of the Spirit," 1999
Traveling exhibition, 1999–present

Fig. 95
Lahav, 1996
Yahrzeit (memorial) light
Acrylic on wood, 19 x 10½ x 8 (48.3 x 26.7 x 20.3)

Fig. 96
Hadahr II, 1994
Etrog container
Acrylic on wood, 4 x 5¼ x 5¼ (10.2 x 13.3 x 13.3)

Fig. 97
Zedek X, 2000
Tzedakah (alms) container
Acrylic on wood, 17¾ x 18 x 5¾ (45.1 x 45.7 x 14.6)

Fig. 98
Aruga V, 2000
Besamim (spice) container
Acrylic on wood, 14 x 3¾ x 2¾ (35.6 x 9.5 x 7)

Fig. 99
Ma'ohr, 1994
Havdalah candleholder
Acrylic on wood, 14 x 2¾ x 2¾ (35.6 x 7 x 7)

Fig. 100
Oule-Zanh, 1995
Acrylic on wood, 12 x 9 (30.5 x 22.9)
Private collection

Plate 2
Kayom I, 1994
Ner tamid (eternal light)
Bronze, 23 x 5½ x 4 (58.4 x 14 x 10.2) + hanging rods

Plate 4
Ahda I, 1984
Yad (pointer for Torah)
Acrylic on wood, 14½ x 1 x 1 (36.8 x 2.5 x 2.5)

Plate 6
Zedek V, 2000
Tzedakah (alms) container
Acrylic on wood, 47¼ x 15⅞ x 11⅛ (120 x 40.3 x 28.3)

Plate 9
Aviya I, 1991
Kiddush cup for havdalah
Bronze, 4¾ x 2 x 2 (12.1 x 5.1 x 5.1)

Plate 11
Aruga III, 1994
Besamim (spice) container
Acrylic on wood, 9½ x 4 x 4 (24.1 x 10.2 x 10.2)

Plate 13
Tokah, 1998
Rosh Hashanah apple-and-honey set
Bronze; four pieces, 13½ x 14 x 6 (34.3 x 35.6 x 15.2) each

Plate 14
Hadahr, 1992
Etrog container
Acrylic on wood, 7 x 7½ x 5¼ (17.8 x 19.1 x 13.3)

Plate 17
Aasha III, 1999
Purim grogger (noisemaker)
Acrylic on wood, 14½ x 5¼ (36.8 x 13.3)

Plate 26
Ahran, 1997
Yahrzeit (memorial) light
Bronze, 14 x 11 x 7 (35.6 x 27.9 x 17.8)

GLOSSARY

COMPILED BY JENNIFER SYLVOR

Akedah — lit., "binding"; the biblical story of Abraham's near sacrifice of his son Isaac (Genesis 22).

Aleph bet — alphabet; *aleph* and *bet* are the two first letters of the Hebrew alphabet.

Ark of the Covenant — the ark built to hold the tablets on which the Ten Commandments were inscribed.

Aron kodesh — cabinet used to house the Torah scrolls.

Avodah — Hebrew word for "worship," "work," or "service." The title for the body of Tobi Kahn's work consisting of Jewish ceremonial objects—"Avoda"—derives from this term. Kahn's decision to drop the final *h* is in keeping with his general approach to titling his works. Here, he liked the symmetry of the letter *a* at the beginning and end of the title.

Bar/Bat mitzvah — a young man or woman who has attained the age of Jewish legal maturity; the ceremony marking his or her coming of age.

Besamim container — container of fragrant spices used during the havdalah ceremony to suggest the sweetness and pleasure of the Sabbath day.

Brit milah — ritual circumcision, traditionally performed on the eighth day following an infant boy's birth.

Challah (pl., challot) — traditional braided bread, eaten on Sabbath and festivals.

Elijah's chair — seat reserved for the prophet Elijah at the circumcision ceremony.

Elijah's cup — goblet of wine left on the seder table for the prophet Elijah, an expected guest at the Passover service.

Etrog — citron, a fragrant fruit, used during the observance of Sukkot, often kept in a decorative box reserved for that purpose.

Golem — mythical figure formed of clay and animated by means of mystical incantations.

Grogger — noisemaker, used during the reading of the Purim megillah to drown out the name of Haman, the story's villain.

Halakhah — Jewish law.

Halakhic — pertaining to *halakhah*.

Hamsa — from the Arabic word for "five"; this hand-shaped amulet, suggestive of the protective hand of the Creator, is used to protect against evil spirits.

Hanukkah — lit., "dedication"; Festival of Lights, commemorating the victory of the Maccabees over Syrian oppression in 165 BCE, the rededication of the Temple, and the establishment of religious freedom in ancient Israel.

Hanukkah lamp — lamp consisting of eight lights for each of the eight days of the festival, plus a *shamash*, or servitor light, used to light the other eight.

Havdalah — lit., "separation"; the ceremony marking the conclusion of the Sabbath and the beginning of the workweek.

Hiddur mitzvah — lit., "the beautification of a mitzvah"; the tradition of enhancing ritual acts through the use of beautiful implements.

Holy of Holies — the innermost chamber of the Temple, containing the Ark of the Covenant and the Ten Commandments.

Huppah — wedding canopy.

Ketubah — Jewish marriage contract stipulating the legal, financial, and conjugal obligations between husband and wife.

Kiddush	lit., "sanctification"; the blessing over the ritual wine, recited on the Sabbath and holidays, generally using a kiddush cup reserved for this purpose.
Kol Nidre	lit., "all vows"; this solemn and dramatic prayer, written in Aramaic, begins the evening service of Yom Kippur, the Day of Atonement. The *Kol Nidre* prayer, recited three times by the service leader, declares null and void all vows and promises that Jews make and fail to fulfill in the coming year.
Kosher	ritually fit.
Lulav	a single palm branch bound together with willow and myrtle and used, together with the etrog, during the festival of Sukkot.
Matzah (pl., matzot)	unleavened bread eaten during the eight days of Passover.
Megillah	lit., "scroll"; often used to refer specifically to Megillat Esther, the Scroll of Esther, which recounts the Purim story.
Menorah	lit., "lamp"; a seven-branched menorah is believed to have stood in the Temple in Jerusalem. An eight-branched menorah, or *hanukkiah*, is used in the celebration of Hanukkah.
Mezuzah (pl., mezuzot)	parchment with Deuteronomy 6:4–9 and 11:13–21 written on it, traditionally contained in a decorative case and affixed to the right-hand side of the doorpost.
Midrash	interpretive tradition of the ancient Rabbis, using parables, imaginative stories, and poetic readings to illuminate biblical texts.
Miriam's cup	a goblet of water used in a feminist-inspired contemporary Passover ritual to remember and celebrate Miriam's role in sustaining the Israelites during their desert wanderings.
Mitzvah (pl., mitzvot)	lit., "commandment"; one of the 613 commandments described in the Torah; used colloquially to refer to any good deed or kindness.
Ner tamid	eternal light; a continuously burning lamp that hangs before the Torah ark in most synagogues.
Netilat yadayim	lit., "lifting of the hands"; ritual washing of the hands before a meal.
Omer	lit., "a measure" or "sheaf"; the first sheaf of grain cut during the barley harvest and offered in the Temple on the second day of Passover.
Omer counter	calendar used to mark the counting of the omer, the 49-day period between the second day of Passover and Shavuot.
Passover (Pesach)	the spring pilgrimage festival, commemorating the Israelites' Exodus from slavery in Egypt.
Purim	lit., "lots"; the Feast of Lots, marking the triumph of the Jews of Persia over Haman, the king's wicked adviser, who sought their death.
Rimmonim	lit., "pomegranates"; decorative finials used to adorn the staves of the Torah scroll.
Rosh Hodesh	new moon; the reappearance of the moon and the beginning of a new month are celebrated by the recitation of a special blessing and other ritual observances.
Sandak	godfather; serves a ritual function during the circumcision ceremony.
Seder	lit., "order"; the fourteen-part home service of the Passover holiday, at which the retelling of the story of the Exodus is punctuated by ritual eating and drinking.
Seder plate	a plate of symbolic foods used as part of the Passover celebration.
Shabbat	the Jewish Sabbath, extending from sundown on Friday to dark on Saturday.
Shalom bat	See *simhat bat.*
Shamash	the servitor, or helper candle, used to light the eight lights of the Hanukkah lamp.
Shavuot	lit., "weeks"; Feast of Weeks, commemorating the giving of the Torah on Mount Sinai and the bringing of sacrificial offerings to the Temple in Jerusalem.

Shema — lit., "Listen!"; a centerpiece of Jewish liturgy, this prayer affirms the belief in one God.

Shivah — Hebrew word for "seven"; a seven-day period of ritually prescribed mourning during which the family of the deceased remains at home and receives visitors.

Shofar — ram's horn, sounded in synagogues as part of the High Holiday service.

Shtetl — traditional small town or village of Eastern Europe or Russia.

Simhat bat — lit., "rejoicing in a daughter"; a ritual of modern origins designed to celebrate the birth of a baby girl, bestow a name upon her, and mark her entrance into the Covenant. This ceremony is sometimes known as *shalom bat* (welcoming a daughter) or a baby naming.

Spice container — See *besamim* container.

Star of David — six-pointed star said to have adorned the shield of King David.

Sukkah — lit., "booth"; a temporary shelter erected as part of the observance of Sukkot.

Sukkot — the fall harvest holiday.

Tallit — fringed prayer shawl.

Talmud — lit., "learning" or "teaching"; a compendium of commentary and discussion on the Mishnah (code of Jewish law written c. 200 CE) by Rabbis of the academies of Palestine and Babylon c. 300–500 CE.

Tikkun olam — lit., "the repairing of the world," the ongoing work of improving one's world or community.

Torah — the Five Books of Moses. The Torah is traditionally inscribed on parchment and rolled on wooden staves.

Torah ark — See *aron kodesh.*

Tzitzit — the specially knotted fringes on the four corners of the tallit.

Tzedakah — from the Hebrew for "righteousness" or "justice"; alms.

Yad — lit., "hand"; pointer used when reading from the Torah scroll, frequently shaped in the form of a hand.

Yahrzeit — lit., "year's time" (Yiddish); anniversary of the death of a loved one, marked by the recitation of the mourner's Kaddish and the lighting of a Yahrzeit candle.

NOTES ON THE CONTRIBUTORS

LEORA AUSLANDER teaches modern European history, material culture, and gender studies at the University of Chicago. She is the author of *Taste and Power: Furnishing Modern France* and of numerous essays on identity and material culture, including "Sambo in Paris and Racism in the Iconography of Everyday Life," coauthored with Tom Holt, forthcoming in *The Color of Liberty: Histories of Race in France*; "Bavarian Crucifixes and French Headscarves: Religious Practices and the Postmodern European State," in *Cultural Dynamics*; and "Jewish Taste: Jews and the Aesthetics of Everyday Life in Paris and Berlin, 1933–1942," in *Histories of Leisure*.

EMILY D. BILSKI is an independent scholar and curator specializing in nineteenth- and twentieth-century European art and cultural history, contemporary art, and the interface between Jews and Western culture. Her publications include *Art and Exile: Felix Nussbaum (1904–1944)*; *Golem! Danger, Deliverance and Art*; and *Berlin Metropolis: Jews and the New Culture 1890–1918*, which won the National Jewish Book Award in history for 1999.

TERRENCE E. DEMPSEY, S.J. is a Jesuit priest and a professor of art history and theology at Saint Louis University, where he is the founding director of the Museum of Contemporary Religious Art (MOCRA), the first interfaith museum of contemporary art in the world. He has authored numerous articles and has developed and organized more than thirty exhibitions, including eighteen for the Museum of Contemporary Religious Art. He lectures on art and religion nationally and internationally.

TOM L. FREUDENHEIM began his museum career at The Jewish Museum in New York and subsequently has served as director of the Gilbert Collection, London, the Worcester Art Museum, and the Baltimore Museum of Art, as well as deputy director of the Jüdisches Museum, Berlin, and assistant director of the University Art Museum, Berkeley, California. He directed the museum program at the National Endowment for the Arts during the Carter administration and for a number of years had oversight responsibility for all national museums as assistant secretary for museums at the Smithsonian Institution. He has lectured and written extensively on contemporary art, Judaica, crafts, museum ethics, and museum management.

NESSA RAPOPORT is the author of a novel, *Preparing for Sabbath*, and a collection of prose poems, *A Woman's Book of Grieving*. With Ted Solotaroff, she edited *The Schocken Book of Contemporary Jewish Fiction*. Her most recent book is *House on the River: A Summer Journey*.

JONATHAN ROSEN is the author of the novel *Eve's Apple*. His latest book, *The Talmud and the Internet: A Journey Between Worlds*, was a *New York Times* Notable Book of the Year and is being translated into German, Hebrew, Italian, Dutch, and Korean. In 1990, he created the Arts & Letters section of the *Forward*, which he oversaw for ten years. His essays have appeared in the *New York Times Magazine*, the *New York Times Book Review*, *The New Yorker*, *The American Scholar*, and several anthologies.

RUTH WEISBERG is dean of the School of Fine Arts, University of Southern California, and a widely exhibited artist and critic. She has received National Endowment for the Humanities and Senior Fulbright fellowships. Her work is in major collections, including The Metropolitan Museum of Art and the Whitney Museum of American Art, New York, and the National Gallery of Art, Washington, D.C.

AVODA ARTS

STAFF

Carol Brennglass Spinner, Executive Director and Founder
Judith C. Siegel, Associate Executive Director
Tobi Kahn, Artistic Director
Debbie Krivoy, Managing Director
Laura Kruger, Curator
Margaret Mathews Berenson, Exhibition Manager
Jill Vexler, Exhibition Consultant
Mirele Goldsmith, Evaluator
Ben Hesse, Program Coordinator
Shira Stein, Program Associate
Hyim Brandes, Technology Coordinator

ADVISORY COMMITTEE

Dr. Ruth Weisberg, Chair
Tom L. Freudenheim
Stanley E. Pantowich
Adina Savin, Esq.
Victoria E. Schonfeld, Esq.
Professor Abraham Seidman
Adele Silver

PUBLICATION

This book was produced by Offsite: Publications, Planning, Projects.
Publication Director: Mary DelMonico
Editor: Sheila Schwartz

Project Director: Judith C. Siegel
General Editor: Emily D. Bilski
Designer: Katy Homans
Copy Editor: Janice Meyerson
Proofreader: Richard G. Gallin
Publication Assistant: Shira Stein
Printing and Binding: Graphicom